Teaching Music in Higher Education

Teaching Music in Higher Education

Colleen M. Conway
University of Michigan

Thomas M. Hodgman
Adrian College

New York   Oxford
OXFORD UNIVERSITY PRESS
2009

Oxford University Press, Inc., publishes works that further
Oxford University's objective of excellence
in research, scholarship, and education.

Oxford New York
Auckland Cape Town Dar es Salaam Hong Kong Karachi
Kuala Lumpur Madrid Melbourne Mexico City Nairobi
New Delhi Shanghai Taipei Toronto

With offices in
Argentina Austria Brazil Chile Czech Republic France Greece
Guatemala Hungary Italy Japan Poland Portugal Singapore
South Korea Switzerland Thailand Turkey Ukraine Vietnam

Published by Oxford University Press, Inc.
198 Madison Avenue, New York, New York 10016
http://www.oup.com

Oxford is a registered trademark of Oxford University Press.

Library of Congress Cataloging-in-Publication Data
Conway, Colleen Marie.
Teaching music in higher education / Colleen M. Conway,
Thomas M. Hodgman.
p. cm.
Includes bibliographical references and index.
ISBN 978-0-19-536935-9 (pbk.)
1. Music—Instruction and study. 2. Music in universities and
colleges. I. Hodgman, Thomas M. II. Title.
MT18.C66 2008
780.71'1—dc22
2008029447

Printed in the United States of America
on acid-free paper

Contents

Preface

Teaching Music in Higher Education is designed for faculty and graduate assistants working with undergraduate music majors as well as nonmajors in colleges and universities in the United States. It includes suggestions for designing and organizing music courses (applied music as well as academic classes) and strategies for meeting the developmental needs of the undergraduate student. It addresses concerns about undergraduate curricula that meet National Association of School of Music requirements as well as teacher education requirements for music education majors in most states.

A common theme throughout the book is a focus on "learner-centered pedagogy" (Weimer, 2000) or trying to meet students where they are and base instruction on their individual needs. The text also maintains a constant focus on the relationship between teaching and learning and encourages innovative ways for instructors to assess student learning in music courses. Teaching is connected throughout the book to student learning and the lecture model of "teaching as transmission of information" (Bain, 2004) is discouraged. Activities throughout the book ask instructors to focus on what it means to be an effective teacher for music courses. As there is little to no research on teaching music in higher education we have relied on comprehensive texts from the general education field to help provide the research base for our definition of effective teaching (Davis, 2001; McKeachie and Svinicki, 2006). In Davis's (2001) presentation of effective teaching she states:

> For hundreds of years, college teaching was typified by a professor reading a lecture to an audience of note-taking students. The professor's duties were to compose and present authoritative lectures, to test students on their knowledge, and to assign grades. Over the last thirty years, however, this model has given way to a new understanding of what constitutes effective college-level instruction. Research on students' academic success and intellectual development and on theories of learning and cognitive development has demonstrated the effectiveness of modes of instruction that emphasize active learning and collaborative activities and engage students in intellectual discovery. (p. xix)

It is our sense that in the past 30 years music instruction in many schools and departments of music reflects this newer understanding regarding teaching and learning. However, very little has been written or studied within music regarding teaching and learning in higher education. Davis goes on in her definition of effective teaching to suggest that research on teaching in higher education has led to the identification of what she calls four "clusters of instructional skills, strategies, and attitudes that promote students' academic achievement" (p. xix). These include

1. Organizing and explaining materials in ways appropriate to students' abilities.
2. Creating an environment for learning.
3. Helping students become autonomous self-regulated learners.
4. Reflecting on and evaluating one's teaching.

This book is organized into three parts. Part One includes a focus on course preparation and planning and includes chapters dedicated to teaching an undergraduate music course and curriculum design within policy and local curriculum restraints; assessment and grading in music courses; and understanding the learners and syllabus design. This section includes a focus on undergraduate student development and a discussion of the characteristics of undergraduates at various stages including freshman, sophomore, junior, and senior. Vignettes written by undergraduate music majors are used to highlight the content in this section.

Part Two is a focus on teaching and learning and includes chapters on creating a culture for learning, instructional strategies to facilitate active learning, instructional technology, and applied studio teaching. Short quotes from undergraduate students are used to support suggestions throughout this section. Biographical stories written by graduate student instructors and new professors frame a discussion of "identity" as a college professor. The applied music chapter includes reflections from successful applied music faculty in schools and departments of music.

Part Three addresses growth in teaching practice for the college music professor and includes a focus on the job search in higher education; feedback from students and reflection on teaching; documentation of teaching including action research; tenure and promotion for music professors, and professional development for the college instructor.

The book includes an outline of a typical course sequence for a music major; sample performance assessment tools; sample music course syllabi; sample forms for student midterm and final evaluation; a sample Faculty Activities Report for music professors; and a sample tenure and promotion materials packet. Each of the three sections of the book makes reference to relevant research from the higher education or learning sciences literature, as well as suggestions for further reading in the various topic areas.

SUGGESTIONS FOR USE

The text has been designed to fit within a typical 14-week semester. Below are some additional ideas that we used with our graduate students to help them interact with this content in authentic ways. Some of these ideas also appear in questions for discussion and suggested activities at the end of the chapters.

We experienced success in creating panels of undergraduate students to visit classes when working through the chapters regarding undergraduate student development. Our graduate students reported that they found this activity to be one of the most helpful components of this course. We had graduate students develop sample syllabi while working through Part One of the book and then had undergraduate students provide feedback on the syllabi when they came to class.

We also experienced success for midterm and/or final projects by having students complete a mock job interview for a position in higher education. The mock interview often included a master class (for applied areas and conducting) as well as a short teaching demonstration (required for all) in an academic area (music theory, music history, music education) and a 20-minute job interview. Graduate students choose a committee including the course instructor and others and then are responsible to recruit undergraduate students for their master class and teaching demonstration. We usually videorecord the interview so students can view it at a later date.

This activity required the graduate students to model the teaching techniques and ways of interacting with students that have been discussed in class and also requires them to talk about pedagogical content knowledge in the context of the interview. Although the logistics of this activity are challenging with a large class, it has been highly useful for our students.

ACKNOWLEDGMENTS

We wish to thank all of the students over the years who have provided us with the experience by which to write a text on college teaching. In particular, we wish to acknowledge the undergraduate students who provided the vignettes throughout the book including Zerrin Agabigum, Dana Amann, Katrina Deady, John Leahy, Joel Schut, Ryan Shaw, and Rachel Witte. Graduate student contributors included Jeff Barudin, Alana Chown, John Eros, Nicholas Finch, Kristen Pellegrino, and Chad West.

Thanks to Ryan Hourigan from Ball State University and Ann Marie Stanley from the Eastman School of Music for their new professor vignette contributions. We wish to acknowledge Dr. Herbert Marshall from Baldwin-Wallace Conservatory of Music for the percussion syllabus in Chapter 4 and a reflection form in Chapter 11. Dr. Louis Bergonzi from The University of Illinois contributed two of the reflection and observation forms in Chapter 11.

Special thanks to the applied music faculty who responded to our inquires for Chapter 8 including Fritz Kaenzig (tuba professor, University of Michigan), Nancy Ambrose King (oboe professor, University of Michigan), Jeff Lyman (bassoon professor, University of Michigan), and Elizabeth Major (voice professor, Adrian College). We would also like to thank Ann Konz, administrative assistant at Adrian College, for her assistance in assembling sample figures.

A very special thank you to University of Michigan musicology professor Dr. Mark Clague who authored Chapter 9: *Toys or Tools: Instructional Technology.*

Thank you to the reviewers Harold F. Abeles, Teachers College, Columbia University; Don Coffman, University of Iowa; Glenda Cosenza, Northern Illinois University; Bernard J. Dobroski, Northwestern University; Nicholas DeCarbo, University of Miami; Don P. Ester, Ball State University; Roger R. Rideout, University of Massachusetts; and, Margaret Schmidt, Arizona State University.

Finally, we wish to thank Jan Beatty, Cory Schneider, and all the folks at Oxford University Press.

PART ONE

Course Planning and Preparation

CHAPTER 1

Designing an Undergraduate Music Course

One of the first tasks for new music professors or graduate instructors is to reflect on their own undergraduate experiences in the effort to understand their "autobiography as a learner." Remembering what it was like to be an undergraduate music student and thinking about powerful learning experiences (both positive and negative) will help new instructors to form their identities as professors. Think back on the music professors or instructors who had the biggest impact on your learning and begin to consider what it was that these professors did to facilitate your growth. You might also think back on difficult learning experiences in your undergraduate career so that you can avoid some of the teacher behaviors that may have led to your difficulty.

It is also important to become familiar with the culture of the school or department where you will be working. The college or university where you will be teaching may or may not be like the program you attended as an undergraduate. Differences in college size, musical environment, entrance requirements, and student culture can greatly affect classroom instruction, curriculum, and assessment. Although it is not possible to generalize student characteristics across colleges and universities you will often find different kinds of students in different settings. There are excellent students and weaker students in every setting. However, getting a sense of the "typical" student in a setting is important for course planning and preparation. Is this setting a school where they accept most students and help them achieve? Or is this an elite conservatory where they turn away the majority of applicants? These are two very different environments and there is a continuum of types of programs between these extremes. In a setting where many students are the first to attend college, you may find that these students are working 20–40 hours a week outside of school and still trying to maintain full-time status as students. The amount of practicing and out-of-class studying as well as the quality of homework that is accomplished by the student in this setting is quite different from that in an elite four-year institution. Students who are attending community college as part-time students come with other characteristics that must be considered in course planning and curriculum design. Try to talk with other faculty or department members about the students and their expectations and experiences.

CHECKLIST FOR GETTING TO KNOW THE CULTURE OF THE SCHOOL

1. Examine the school or department web site to get a sense of program offerings, concerts, and general department descriptions.
2. Collect concert programs and other written materials (i.e., program notes, college newspaper articles) to get a sense of past music presentations.
3. Talk with other faculty (could be music or other) about student writing and academic skill.
4. Set up individual meetings with students early on in the semester to get to know them.

New instructors need to consider characteristics of the learners in the new setting, including theories of adolescent growth, individual learning styles, and theories of motivation. Chapter 3 of this text addresses these issues in depth and the reader is encouraged to consider these issues in advance of planning and preparing a course, if possible. However, due to issues of timing (sometimes being hired at the last minute!) often a new professor must quickly gather course materials and repertoire for the course or courses to be taught. When teaching a course for the first time, this can be a daunting task. This chapter outlines some of the "big picture" issues in course planning and design. More detailed discussions of planning for individual class meetings and interacting with students in the classroom will be addressed later in the text.

AVOIDING THE "TRANSMISSION MODEL" OF TEACHING

Choosing materials and repertoire for teaching often leads to a linear model of teaching where the instructor articulates outcomes (goals and objectives), creates a sequence of how to achieve the goals (based on textbook and detailed course calendar); designs lectures and class activities with the sequence (interaction with content), and then creates an evaluation (test). This curriculum design model focuses primarily on the content of a course and what the teacher will do to deliver the content. It is important to note that good music teaching does not usually follow this linear model. A good instructor cannot simply transmit knowledge and expect the students to learn it. In *What the Best College Teachers Do* Ken Bain (2004) suggests that

> At the core of most professors' ideas about teaching is a focus on what the teacher does rather than on what the students are supposed to learn. In that standard conception, teaching is something that instructors do to the students, usually by delivering truths about the discipline. It is what some writers call a "transmission model." In contrast, the best educators thought of teaching as anything they might do to help and encourage students to learn. Teaching is engaging students, engineering an environment in which they learn. Equally

important, they thought of the creation of that successful learning environment as an important and serious intellectual (or artistic) act, perhaps even as a kind of scholarship, that required the best minds in academia. For our subjects, that scholarship centered around four fundamental inquiries: (1) What should my students be able to do intellectually, physically, or emotionally as a result of their learning?; (2) How can I best help and encourage them to develop those abilities and the habits of heart and mind to use them?; (3) How can my students and I best understand the nature, quality, and progress of their learning?; and (4) How can I evaluate my efforts to foster that learning? (pp. 48–49)

Fink (2003) suggests that higher education is in the midst of a change in teaching paradigm (and has been for several decades). He states: "This change is a paradigm shift in which institutions are thinking less about providing instruction (the teaching paradigm) and more about producing learning (the learning paradigm)" (p. 17). Fink cites research by Barr and Tagg (1995) and outlines the following implications of this shift for undergraduate education:

- Mission and purpose: from improving the quality of instruction to improving the quality of learning
- Criteria for success: from "quality of entering students" to quality of "exiting students"
- Teaching and learning structures: from "covering material" to "specific learning results"
- Learning theory: from "learning is cumulative and linear" to "learning is a nesting and interaction of frameworks"
- Productivity and funding: from defining productivity in terms of "cost per hour of instruction per student" to "cost per unit of learning per student"
- Nature of roles: from "faculty being primarily lecturers" to "faculty being primarily designers of learning methods and environments" (Fink, 2003, p. 18)

Good teaching involves an interaction between teaching and learning. It requires awareness that students must construct their own understanding of the content and that merely "telling" students does not constitute teaching. In the effort to avoid the linear "transmission" model, music professors must consider the following questions: Who are these students? Where are they in their development as thinkers and musicians? How will I help them learn? What kinds of musical activities and interactions will help these students to internalize the content in this course? What does it mean to "learn" in this context? It is important to create space in your course outline for interactive learning (fewer lectures and more student engagement). Later chapters provide more information about teaching through interactive learning. However, for now, consider the issues represented in Table 1–1 and note that designing a course with more of the "new paradigm" characteristics may cause a shift in your view of teaching and learning.

PEDAGOGICAL CONTENT KNOWLEDGE FOR THE COURSE

Educational researchers discuss the importance of content knowledge in successful teaching as well as what is referred to as "pedagogical content knowledge" (PCK) (Shulman, 1986). Content knowledge is the knowledge of the subject you are teaching. For example, you may know how to play the clarinet or how to write in two-part counterpoint. Pedagogical content knowledge is knowledge of how to *teach* the content. In

Table 1–1 Old and New Paradigms for College Teaching

	Old Paradigm	**New Paradigm**
Knowledge	Transferred from faculty to students	Jointly constructed by students and faculty
Student	Passive vessel to be filled by faculty's knowledge	Active constructor, discoverer, transformer of knowledge
Mode of learning	Memorizing	Relating
Faculty purpose	Classify and sort students	Develop students' competencies and talents
Student growth, goals	Students strive to complete requirements, achieve certification within a discipline	Students strive to focus on continual lifelong learning within a broader system
Relationships	Impersonal relationship among students and between faculty and students	Personal relationship among students and between faculty and students
Context	Competitive, individualistic	Cooperative learning in classroom and cooperative teams among faculty
Climate	Conformity, cultural uniformity	Diversity and personal esteem; cultural diversity and commonality
Power	Faculty holds and exercises power, authority, and control	Students are empowered; power is shared among students and between students and faculty
Assessment	Norm-referenced (i.e., grading on the curve); typically use multiple-choice items; student rating of instruction at the end of course	Criterion-referenced (i.e., grading to predefined standards); typically use performances and portfolios; continual assessment of instruction
Ways of knowing	Logical–scientific	Narrative
Epistemology	Reductionist; facts; and invention	Constructivist; inquiry; and memorization
Technology use	Drill and practice; textbook substitute; chalk-and-talk substitute	Problem solving; communication; collaboration; information access; expression
Teaching assumption	Any expert can teach	Teaching is complex and requires considerable training

Source: Campbell and Smith (1997, pp. 275–276). Reprinted with permission from Interaction Book Co.

other words, it is the knowledge of how to teach someone else to play the clarinet or write in two-part counterpoint. Most young professors and graduate instructors have solid content knowledge but little understanding of how to teach that content. Pedagogical content knowledge is learned through study and experience. Some materials describing the process of teaching a particular subject or skills are available. For music theory and musicology see:

Mary Natvig (2002). *Teaching music history*. Burlington, VT: Ashgate.

Michael R. Rogers (2004). *Teaching approaches in music theory: An overview of pedagogical philosophies*. Southern Illinois University Press.

John D. White (1981). *Guidelines for college teaching of music theory*.
    Metuchen, NJ: Scarecrow Press.

The new professor is encouraged to read any "how to teach the content" materials that may be available.

In some music content areas there are few resources for how to teach. As a result, some new professors may have to learn on the job. The story below from an undergraduate music student presents the problems created for this student when a graduate instructor in aural skills has strong content knowledge but little pedagogical content knowledge. Awareness of the difference is an important first step in attaining the pedagogical content knowledge needed to be a successful college professor.

UNDERGRADUATE STUDENT VIGNETTE

"I can't help you hear the notes...you have to actually practice so you get better at what you do...," his voice trailed off. I was close to tears; I hated not being able to hear the notes. I am a very hard worker, and I always immerse myself into my work to accomplish my goals. In general, I practiced over an hour each day to become better at "hearing the notes." I never lacked the initiative to do the work, but I lacked the proper guidance as to how to go about "hearing the notes."

"I've been practicing a lot." I replied calmly after a moment, and I looked my aural theory GSI (graduate student instructor) straight in the eyes. He stared back with the familiar "so...?" look; a look every struggling student in his class had become familiar with when they had asked for his help. My suppressed tears finally ebbed, and in their place, anger welled up inside me. "I've been having difficulty hearing the notes because I don't know how to go about hearing them. What do you suggest I do? What notes should I listen for in a V7 chord? When I'm writing my dictation down, where do I start with writing what I hear?" I forced a smile. He looked at me once more, and looked at his watch. "You have to practice V7 chords in order to hear them better. I have to go. I have a class in a minute." He smiled back at me, picked up his backpack, and brushed past me. As I turned around to watch him exit the room, I kept my silly grin plastered to my face. People for the next class began to stream into the room, and I smiled calmly at each person as I walked to the door. An hour later, I was in a practice room; this time grimacing, practicing a $I_{6/4}$ V_7 I progression over and over in different keys. Once in a while, a lonely tear would course down my face and land on the piano keys.

My GSI was a great musician and great theorist; however, he had no clue as to how to teach a subject that came so easily to him. He could not comprehend how or why a simple subject for him was so challenging for others. He was condescending, and unfortunately, unwilling to help those in need. Aural theory as a subject came very naturally to some of my classmates. Other people in class were born with perfect pitch, which enabled them to quickly write the music on a first hearing with good accuracy and understanding. However, there were the students, myself included, who did not know how to go about listening to dictation and process the information to write the music correctly. What I lacked was not musical understanding, but rather a method to use when I was practicing dictation. I asked a few of my friends for advice and what they thought of when they listened to dictation. A few would tell me that they just "heard the notes, and wrote them down." The rest would tell me that "You know, you should talk to your GSI, he can help you out, I think."

By the end of the semester, I had found an aural theory tutor who was a great teacher—supportive, patient, and willing to help. My tutor began our first lesson by asking me what my GSI had taught me during class, and if he had brought up any methods or ways to listen

> to dictations. My tutor was surprised to learn that we had never discussed any methods, and began immediately to teach me how to listen to music. My tutor offered different methods, and I tried each of them out, when one worked for me, we discussed how to modify that method to my exact needs. My tutor never spoke with condescension and never shamed me when I made a mistake. By the end of the semester, I went from failing grades to a passing grade. I was never so proud in my life to earn a B minus.

This story highlights the need for instructors to focus on student individual differences and the necessity of attaining two types of knowledge for the subject: (1) knowledge of the subject content and (2) knowledge of *how to teach* the subject content. Although much of the pedagogical content knowledge will be learned as the professor gains experience, new professors are encouraged to consider this special kind of teaching knowledge as they prepare for class.

COURSE GOALS AND DESCRIPTIONS

It is recommended that the new professor or instructor gather as many course details as possible from the department chair or coordinator in the early stages of planning. Try to obtain a syllabus from the last time the course was taught. Find out what texts and other materials have been used in the past. Be sure to find out if the department or college has a syllabus template (discussed in Chapter 4) or if there are required components for the course design. Some departments require the listing of specific department or state outcomes on every course outline.

At the core of the planning and preparation phase is the answer to the question "What do you want your students to know and be able to do by the end of the semester in your course?" Reflect on this question as you speak with others who have taught the course and review past materials. It is difficult to answer this question when you do not know the students, the culture, or the context. However, sometimes it helps to think about the end goals and then "back up" week-by-week in the term to sequence your instruction from back to front.

As you prepare your syllabi, be sure to consider what it is you want your students to do outside of class in preparation for what will take place in class. McKeachie and Svinicki (2006) suggest that instructors should try to plan early on in the syllabus design for "out-of-class learning" for the students (p. 18):

> It is easy for teachers to imagine that what happens in class is overwhelmingly important to students' learning and that they and their classes are at the center of students' learning universe.... However in studies of what students believe most influenced change during the college years, and of what students believe were their most important experiences at college, ideas presented by instructors in courses, and instructors themselves, rank far behind a range of other influences (Feldman & Newcomb, 1969). In most courses students spend at least as much time studying out of class as they do in class. Thus you need to focus as much on what you expect student to do outside class as on what goes on in class. (p. 18)

Although there is no research within music on this issue, we would imagine that music students often cite applied lessons and ensembles as some of the most influential experiences in their undergraduate years. However, much of the preparation even for these courses takes place in the practice room. For academic courses within music (theory, history, music education) the quote above seems quite relevant. All professors need to consider what they expect students to do outside of class, and then they need to teach students how to do these things. We encourage professors to work to facilitate out-of-class learning by creating study groups, e-mail lists, and group projects. These strategies are discussed in Part Two of the text.

YOUR COURSE IN RELATION TO OTHERS

Try to get a sense of your course in the larger sequence of the department's curriculum. Find out if other instructors have certain expectations for students who complete your course and then come in to theirs. The short vignette below highlights the issues for students when instructors are not aware of their course in relation to others:

> I took an upper level tonal analysis theory class in my junior year. The teacher of this course spent the entire first hour and a half class reviewing cadences. We had learned about all the different types of cadences, reviewed and used them in all four semesters of introductory theory that were a pre-requisite for the course. As a result we were very bored. A calculus teacher doesn't spend time reviewing multiplication tables. This teacher did not need to spend so much time reviewing cadences. She asked questions that were so below us that none of us wanted to answer. As we left the class we were all questioning how on earth we would make it through such a boring class. In hindsight, I understand why she wanted to review cadences on the first day and how it applied to the rest of the course. The problem with the presentation was she focused too much on what we already knew and not enough on what she wanted us to learn. She started way below our level instead of at our level. Had she known a little more about what was being taught in the pre-requisites courses and been a little more familiar with our knowledge on the subject, she could have cut the review down to a few minutes and focused on the areas we needed work in.

Early in the planning process you may be asked for a course description and/or course content paragraph. These are usually three to five broad statements that capture the essence of what students will experience in the course. Start by checking the course description given in the college catalog. Some institutions require that the description on your syllabus match the description in the course catalog.

Examples of course descriptions or course content statements are provided below. More variety in language for descriptions can be seen in the sample syllabi in Chapter 4. Many sample syllabi for various courses can be found online. It is recommended that the new professor begin with the work of others (past syllabi from the institution or syllabi found online) and then adjust that language to meet the specific goals you intend for your course. In some settings instructors are asked to align course content with specific measurable outcomes for assessment purposes. Suggestions for identifying outcomes for assessment are found in Chapter 2.

SAMPLE COURSE DESCRIPTIONS AND CONTENT STATEMENTS

Example 1: Woodwind and Brass Techniques Class for Music Education (Sophomore Level)
Course Description

This course is designed to provide music education students with the skills to model and work effectively with students on other woodwind and brass instruments in the groups beginning instrumental music classes. In addition, students will gain knowledge and skills of instruments for rehearsing with large groups of instrumentalists in secondary ensemble settings.

Course Content

Topics covered will include basics of group music instruction; instrument assembly; instrument care, maintenance, and repair; basic instrument playing positions; breathing; tone production; articulation; common problems of beginners; techniques for more advanced students (multiple tonguing; muting, vibrato); resources for purchasing of instruments and materials (mouthpieces, reeds, etc.); overview of common methods' books and solo literature; basic characteristics of instruments in the secondary ensemble settings.

Example 2: Ear Training I (Freshman Level)
Course Description

This is the first of four courses designed to develop the music student's ability to perceive rhythm, melody, harmony, and form. Through a series of sight reading, listening and aural dictation exercises, the student will enhance his/her ability to hear and understand musical structure.

Course Content

The course will begin with an introduction to rhythm syllables and solfege. We will then proceed with diatonic intervals, triads, simple melodies, and rhythm exercises. Solfege drills in major and minor keys and rhythmic exercises in simple and compound meters will be a focus for the course.

Example 3: Elementary Band Methods for Music Education (Junior Level)
Course Description

This course is designed to engage students in study and discussion of the role of the elementary and middle school band educator. It will assist the student in developing the necessary skills for a position as an elementary or middle school band director.

Course Content

Topics covered will include recruitment of beginning students, program organization and scheduling, building musicianship in beginning band, materials for beginning ensembles, national standards and state frameworks in instrumental music, and classroom management.

Example 4: Survey of Music for Non-Majors

Course Description

Music 101 is an introductory class for non-music majors about "classical music," or art music of the Western European tradition, in its broadest view. The primary goal of the course is to expose students to a variety of music and musical experiences, both in and outside of class.

Course Content

Basic course work will include listening, journal entries, and short reading assignments each week. Students will also attend at least three concerts (including a class field trip to the opera) and write reports about each. Assessments will include three short listening quizzes and two exams. As we progress throughout the semester, you will acquire a general knowledge of musical elements and forms; learn to distinguish among the broad historical styles; and develop a vocabulary with which to discuss music in an informed and intelligent manner. But most importantly, my hope is that you will leave this course as an active, appreciative listener with the skill and the will to keep seeking out new musical experiences on your own!

CHOOSING A TEXT

A new professor is encouraged to adopt a text because it can serve as a template for organizing instruction for a new course. Do not feel as if you must use all parts of the text. It is OK to skip around and combine readings from several textbooks. In some settings there may be a text dictated by the department (especially in settings with multiple sections of core courses taught by a variety of instructors). Most publishers allow instructors to order a "desk copy" of a text that is being considered for use. You may be asked to list the course number and your name may need to appear on a web site with that course in order for the publisher to send the text. Contact the college bookstore to find out how to order texts for your course. The bookstore usually requires at least six-weeks' notice to order texts for a particular course. They may already have a text on order from last year or may have "used" texts from the last time the course was offered. Remember that if you decide to change texts, the bookstore will most likely not buy back the texts from students who have taken the course before. Changing texts too often can get expensive for students and for the bookstore. Once you decide on a text and require students to purchase it, be sure to use it in the course. If there is another text you feel is an important secondary source for students, you may ask the bookstore to offer it as a "recommended text" in addition to the "required text."

McKeachie and Svinicki (2006) state that "Research on teaching suggests that the major influence on what students learn is not the teaching method but the textbook" (p. 14). They suggest the following strategies for textbook review:

1. Winnow the possibilities down to two to five. You may be able to do some winnowing on the basis of the table of contents and preface, by checking with colleagues who have taught the course, or by reading reviews.

2. Read a couple of chapters. It is tempting to simply leaf through each book, reading snatches here and there. But reading a couple of complete chapters will give you a better idea of the difficulty and interest level of each book. Try picking one chapter on a topic you know well and one that is not in your area of expertise.

3. Pick three of four key concepts. See how each text explains them. Will the explanations be clear to students? Interesting?

4. Beware of seductive details or pictures that were included to make the book more attractive but may distract from the basic concepts. (pp. 14–15)

We suggest the following additional criteria in reviewing a textbook for a music course (based in part on suggestions provided in *Tools for teaching* by Barbara Davis, 2001, Jossey-Bass).

1. Is the content accurate and current? Does it reflect the latest research and thinking on the topic?

2. Does it follow the outline for course content you have in mind for class?

3. What previous knowledge of music would students need to understand the text?

4. Do you agree with the "point of view" represented in the book? McKeachie and Svinciki (2006) suggest that students often get discouraged if the text is philosophically different from the instructor views. This does not mean that you must agree with every viewpoint in the text but that you are encouraged to highlight and discuss discrepancies between the text and your presentations.

5. What is the quality of the music and musical performance represented on accompanying audio and/or video recordings?

6. Is the number of musical examples provided on the recordings appropriate? We have found that sometimes there are far too many musical examples for use in class and longer CDs make materials more expensive.

7. Are the musical examples provided interesting for students who are unfamiliar with the content? Are the works representative of the genres?

8. Does the author(s) recognize issues of context in relation to suggestions or does the text read as if the authors approach is the only approach?

Common music textbook publishers include Cambridge University Press, GIA, McGraw-Hill, McMillan, Norton, Oxford, and Prentice-Hall. The web sites for these publishers provide up-to-date titles and descriptions for texts on music.

COURSE CALENDAR

Obtain a copy of the college calendar before outlining your course. There are often unexpected holidays or strange starting/ending dates in college calendars. Students appreciate careful organization regarding class meeting days, times, and places. Include all of the relevant college calendar information in your course syllabus. If you know a class will be rescheduled or canceled, work those details out on the first day of class so students can mark their calendars. Do not add extra days and times beyond the ones stated on the syllabus at the beginning of the term. The course syllabus represents a sort of "contract" between student and professor and if the professor honors the contract, so will the students.

We suggest outlining as much of the content and all assignments, exams, and due dates right on the syllabus. However, for some courses it is impossible to assign specific readings or assignments beyond the first few class meetings since instruction may be dictated by the pace of the class. It is suggested that some system be devised to make it clear there will be an assignment or exam even if the details are not included on the calendar.

Choosing course materials and repertoire for applied music settings is unique as compared to academic course preparation. Chapter 8 of this text is devoted exclusively to the teaching of applied music. In most settings, applied instructors are required to submit course descriptions, expected outcomes, teaching materials, assessment tools, and syllabi in the same manner as academic area teachers. Of course, until an instructor hears a student for the first time in an applied lesson it is nearly impossible to choose specific études and repertoire. Examples of applied music course descriptions and outcomes may be found in the sample syllabi in Chapter 4.

CURRICULUM DESIGN ISSUES IN MUSIC COURSES

Once the calendar is in place, you will need to begin to make difficult decisions about what to include in the course. With regard to the relationship between content and learning, Weimer (2002) suggests that our "strong allegiance to content blocks the road to more learner-centered teaching" (p. 46). It is always difficult in course design to figure out how to "fit in" all the content that we think is important for a particular course. Weimer states:

> At the end of a course, most of us readily admit that we have way too much jammed into the ten or fifteen weeks, but when the time comes to get the syllabus ready for the next semester, it is only after great agony that we decide to leave anything out. (p. 46)

To consider this in a musical context, let us use the "Survey of Music for Non-Majors" course as an example. Professors often state the goals for a non-majors course to be ones of "increased appreciation for music" or "further interest in new musical styles" and yet this course often is presented chronologically in a lecture format from the earliest Medieval chants, into the Renaissance, through Classical and Romantic eras, into the twentieth century. The course often concludes with a focus on Jazz and/or World Music. Most common textbooks for this course follow this format. We have to ask ourselves, can this content "work" to engage students in a 14-week period of time? If we decide it is too much content, then what gets "cut"?

Weimer (2002) suggests that we must let go of our notion of "content coverage" and begin to consider content as a vehicle to establish a knowledge base and then promote lifelong learning in the content. She suggests that this is accomplished through "active learning strategies that allow students firsthand experience with the content" (p. 52). For music courses, "active" strategies involve singing, moving, playing instruments, creating sound, composing, improvising, listening to, and evaluating music.

As music professors consider how to design instruction so that students are involved musically, we must also consider some of what Fink (2003) calls the "situational factors" (p. 68) associated with the course. Table 1–2, reprinted with permission from Fink, provides a checklist of potentially important issues that need to be considered.

As we look at the Fink checklist in relation to music, we begin to see the connections between content/curriculum, characteristics of the learner, and assessment

Table 1–2 Important Situational Factors

Specific Context of the Teaching and Learning Situation

- How many students are in the class?
- Is the course lower division, upper division, or graduate level?
- How long and frequent are the class meetings?
- How will the course be delivered: via live classroom instruction, interactive TV, as an online course, or some combination?

Expectations of External Groups

- What does society at large need and expect in terms of the education of these students, in general, or with regard to this particular subject?
- Do the state or related professional societies have professional accreditation requirements that affect the goals of this learning experience?
- What curricular goals does the institution or department have that affect this course or program?

Nature of the Subject

- Is this subject matter convergent (working toward a single right answer) or divergent (working toward multiple, equally valid interpretations)?
- Is this subject primarily cognitive, or does it include the learning of significant physical skills as well?
- Is this field of study relatively stable, in a period of rapid change, or in a situation where competing paradigms are challenging each other?

Characteristics of the Learners

- What is the life situation of the students at the moment: full-time student, part-time working student, family responsibilities, work responsibilities, and the like?
- What life or professional goals do they have that relate to this learning experience?
- What are their reasons for enrolling?
- What prior experiences, knowledge, skills, and attitudes do the students have regarding the *subject*?
- What are the students' learning styles?

Characteristics of the Teacher

- What prior experiences, knowledge, skills, and attitudes does this teacher have in terms of the *subject* of this course?
- Has the teacher taught this subject before, or is this the first time?
- Will this teacher teach this course again in the future, or is this the last time?
- Does the teacher have a high level of competence and confidence in this subject, or is this on the margins of the teacher's zone of competence?
- What prior experiences, knowledge, skills, and attitudes does this teacher have in terms of the *process of teaching?* (That is, how much does this teacher know about effective teaching?)

Special Pedagogical Challenge

- What is the special situation in this course that challenges the students and the teacher in the desire to make this a meaningful and important learning experience?

Source: Fink (2003, p. 69). Reprinted with permission from Wiley & Sons.

strategies that form the backbone to the "learner-centered" teaching philosophy we are encouraging. However, one of the greatest difficulties for many professors writing a music curriculum or syllabus is deciding where to start. If you are new to a setting it may be difficult to answer many of the questions posed by Fink in Table 1–2. The types of approaches listed in this section represent a variety of starting places for music curricula. There is not one magic formula for combining elements from each of the approaches here. Decisions regarding approaches must be made within a specific context. We provide a brief description of each approach.

OBJECTIVES-BASED APPROACH

The objectives-based approach to course design is common in all streams of education (Tyler, 1949). This is a four-phase process that begins with the development of objectives for the learner, objectives are then sequenced (often referred to as "scope and sequence"), activities are designed to meet the objectives (lesson plans), and evaluation tools are designed to assure that learning takes place (tests). Although this model has been pervasive in curriculum design, many scholars have criticized this approach, suggesting that it is too linear and that real teaching does not occur in such a clear-cut line. Good teachers often mix up the phases of this design. For example, meaningful assessment of student learning does not occur at the end of a linear process, but it must occur throughout the teaching and learning interaction. Good teachers do not follow a restrictive sequence, but adjust their teaching to the needs of a specific context. Real classrooms are multidimensional, and to force curriculum into such a linear model is a compromise. However, many college and university guidelines for courses will require an objectives-based model. As discussed earlier, professors are often asked to submit course descriptions and course objectives before meeting students and they are often asked to align these objectives with departmental or institutional goals. Although this approach to curriculum may be the most common, professors are encouraged to focus on the other approaches listed here as well as the objectives-based approach, so that syllabi and course outlines reflect the "messiness" of good teaching in music classes and not just the jargon of the institution.

LITERATURE-BASED APPROACH

Some musicians have suggested that the music literature chosen for a course is the curriculum (Conway, 2002; Reynolds, 2000). In general curriculum theory, there are scholars who suggest a curriculum based on the project method (Kilpatrick, 1918), which we believe is similar to designing instruction around musical interaction with particular musical literature. In their 2004 overview of Kilpatrick's work, Decker Walker and Jonas Soltis (2004) suggest the following about the "Project Method":

> He characterized the project method as one that combined three elements: wholehearted activity, laws of learning, and ethical conduct with his basic idea that "education is life." He sought a way to replace traditional teaching methods, which forced learning, with a

method in which learning was achieved without compulsion. In daily life, he argued, we learn from the activities we engage in, from our experiences, not from memorizing or studying, but from doing things with a purpose. He believed that this form of "learning-by-living" and "acting with a purpose" should be brought into the school, thus making school and its curriculum not a preparation for life but an actual part of living and life itself. The means for doing this was the "project method." (p. 47)

In considering this idea for music, we think about the repertoire and the musical engagement with the repertoire as "doing things with a purpose" as stated by Kilpatrick. This literature-based approach works very well for music courses. Reflect on the specific musical repertoire to be studied and then address the other approaches (objectives, skills, and knowledge) through the lens of the repertoire. These approaches are meant to be starting places for thinking. A solid curriculum will have elements of all (objectives, repertoire, skill, and knowledge).

SKILLS-BASED APPROACH

A skills-based approach in music courses refers to what students will do musically. These skills should not be confused with what they might be expected to know about music (knowledge-based curriculum). Skills include musical behaviors (singing, moving, playing on instruments, creating sounds, improvising, composing, and listening) as well as aural recognition of musical concepts (tonality, meter, form, musical sensitivity, etc.). The skills-based approach does not include attitudes or preferences toward music, but rather abilities of the student to interact (sing, move, create, listen, or play) within a specific musical context. This is the curriculum approach that instructors are encouraged to focus much thought on, so that active strategies for interacting with music form the core of the approach in music courses. Assessment tools may be designed to measure the skills-based approach and will be discussed in Chapter 2.

KNOWLEDGE-BASED APPROACH

Some music courses focus heavily on the knowledge base of curriculum (musical terms, knowledge of music theory and history, etc.). Since music is an active, aural art, professors are encouraged to include elements of skills-based and repertoire-based approaches even for courses that seem to be primarily "knowledge-based." Again, it is desirable for a music syllabus to reflect all elements of these approaches (objectives, repertoire, skills, and knowledge). The knowledge base is the easiest content to assess, and so many professors fall into the trap of including more knowledge than skill due to ease in course design.

This list of design approaches is by no means exhaustive. However, this list is provided to get the instructor to think about the many important conceptual issues that enter into the course design process. You must start somewhere. We would recommend you choose an approach from this section and begin to formulate ideas. Continue by including concepts from the other approaches in the chapter, focus on the characteristics of the learner, consider ideas for assessment, and you have a good start on a learner-centered curriculum or course outline.

POLICY STAKEHOLDERS

When designing curriculum and planning for instruction, most professors must answer to a variety of policy stakeholders at the national, regional, and/or local (college/university, unit, and department) level. Some institutions require individual instructors to address these policy requirements at the syllabus level. A new faculty member needs to check with the department chair as to whether the syllabus or course content has specific requirements mandated by the college in terms of accreditation.

NATIONAL AND REGIONAL POLICY

Many music programs (610 in the country) are members of the National Association of Schools of Music (NASM). NASM is the national accrediting agency for music and music-related programs. The NASM web site (nasm.arts-accredit.org) states that one of the goals of the organization is to establish "national standards for undergraduate and graduate degrees and other credentials." It is recommended that new faculty in an accredited department of music become familiar with NASM guidelines. NASM does not mandate specific courses or credits but provides suggestions for content areas to be addressed with the undergraduate curriculum.

Music education programs often participate in a teacher education accreditation (i.e., the National Council for the Accreditation of Teacher Education—NCATE) in addition to NASM. Although most of the policy "dealings" for NCATE will be handled by the department or college of education in conjunction with music education faculty, it is important for all faculty to be aware of the reasons for the strict curricular frameworks for music education programs. Most music education programs must answer to state-level organizations regarding teacher licensure as well. Each of these agencies has different recommendations and requirements for music curriculum design.

LOCAL POLICY

At the local level, most music students must take a minimum of college of university core courses and these can vary from only two or three courses in a conservatory to over 40 credits in some liberal arts programs and state universities. It is important for the new professor to get a sense of the requirements that must be met and the issues associated with fitting the music curriculum into the larger picture of the entire school curricula. Most institutions have a curriculum committee and changes to courses usually need to be approved by that organization. New courses often need extensive course proposals including a detailed syllabus and list of assessment strategies. Even smaller changes such as course titles, number of credits, or grading procedures often need full committee approval.

At the school or department level, instructors are often required to align course learning outcomes and objectives with departmental and institutional outcomes and objectives. In many cases, instructors are then required to submit assessment materials that align with the common language.

CULTURE OF THE SCHOOL AND POLICY

Every music program has a distinct "culture" that may affect course planning, curricula, and assessment. See Kingsbury (1988) and Nettl (1995) for interesting sources on the culture of the conservatory (Kingsbury) and the school of music within a large Midwestern university (Nettl). These issues of culture affect the "macro" levels of curriculum design as well as the issues at the syllabus level mentioned earlier (how busy students are outside of class; quantity and quality of background experiences in music and in school in general, etc.). New professors need to get a sense of the local culture regarding issues such as concert attendance and recitals.

SAMPLE DEGREE PROGRAM OUTLINE FOR UNDERGRADUATE MUSIC DEGREES

Bachelor of Music in Music Education

This is a generic five-year outline. Students will add classes in general studies and teacher education to this course schedule. If a student agrees to take courses on general studies in the summer, then this degree may be completed in four to four-and-a-half years. Course sequences vary among institutions. Check with your institution for specifics.

	Fall	**Spring**
Freshman	Theory I	Theory II
	Aural Skills I	Aural Skills II
	Keyboard I	Keyboard II
	Ensemble	Ensemble
	Applied Lesson	Applied Lesson
		Foundations in Music Ed
Sophomore	Theory III	Theory IV
	Aural Skills III	Aural Skills IV
	Keyboard III	Keyboard IV
	Ensemble	Ensemble
	Applied Lesson	Applied Lesson
	Percussion Methods	
Junior	Music History I	Music History II
	Ensemble	Ensemble
	Applied Lesson	Applied Lesson
	Orchestration	Form & Analysis
	Brass Methods	Vocal Methods

Senior #1	Music History III	Music History IV
	Ensemble	Ensemble
	Applied Lesson	Applied Lesson
	Conducting I	Conducting II
	String Methods	Secondary Methods (choral/instrumental)
		Elementary Music Methods
Senior #2	Ensemble	Student Teaching
	Applied Lesson	Student Teaching Seminar
	Woodwind Methods	
	Senior Recital	

Bachelor of Music in Performance

Students will add general studies courses to this schedule

	Fall	Spring
Freshman	Theory I	Theory II
	Aural Skills I	Aural Skills II
	Keyboard I	Keyboard II
	Ensemble	Ensemble
	Applied Lesson	Applied Lesson
Sophomore	Theory III	Theory IV
	Aural Skills III	Aural Skills IV
	Keyboard III	Keyboard IV
	Ensemble	Ensemble
	Applied Lesson	Applied Lesson
Junior	Music History I	Music History II
	Ensemble	Ensemble
	Chamber Music	Chamber Music
	Applied Lesson	Applied Lesson
	Orchestration	Form & Analysis
		Junior Recital
Senior #1	Music History III	Music History IV
	Ensemble	Ensemble
	Chamber Music	Chamber Music
	Applied Lesson	Applied Lesson
	Diction / Repertoire	Diction/Repertoire
	Conducting	Senior Recital

CURRICULAR TENSIONS

Since it would be rare for one professor to be in charge of the complete music curriculum in a college or university, it is inevitable that the music professor will have to work with other professors on curriculum design and this can often lead to tensions regarding curriculum content. Even choosing a common text for multiple sections of the same course can be a difficult task. Other sources of curricular tension include tonal solfege syllable systems (movable do, fixed do, do-based minor, la-based minor, numbers, etc.) and rhythm counting systems within the theory sequence; baseline piano skills for all music majors; balance of Western Art music and world music in the musicology sequence; appropriateness of various repertoire in the applied studios; the list goes on and on.

It is important for the new professor to recognize that every professor may have a different teaching philosophy and a different approach to the content as well as to the students. Fitting in to the culture of a department and getting a sense of the expected quality of music-making and scholarship is often challenging for the new professor. The next section addresses issues of curricular innovation. However, new instructors are cautioned that change happens slowly and the best thing a new professor can do is get a sense of the "lay of the land" before initiating change.

CURRICULAR INNOVATION

Music curricula in many colleges and universities have changed little in the past 50 years. It is important for the new professor to consider innovative approaches to the preparation of musicians. Some institutions have begun exciting initiatives in providing leadership courses for performance majors along with community outreach activities that allow the music major to explore various career options. Many schools are exploring the role of technology in music performance, composition, and pedagogy as well as the intersections between world music, jazz, and traditional Western Art Music. Curricular change is slow, but the new professor is encouraged to reflect on the needs of the twenty-first century musician and make connections between those needs and undergraduate music curriculum. Discussion about the need for change and curricular tensions often centers on what one might call the "philosophy of teaching" that is represented in the department. The next section addresses this concept of developing your personal teaching philosophy.

DEVELOPING YOUR CURRICULAR PHILOSOPHY

As stated in the preface of this book, we as the authors uphold a philosophy of teaching that is "learner centered." We wish to encourage professors to work against the "transmission" model of teaching and to find creative ways to actively engage undergraduate students in music classes. As you answer the questions for discussion throughout this book, you will begin to see the emergence of your own teaching philosophy. Your beliefs and attitudes about the content of your courses as well as your level of interest and concern for students will form the basis of your philosophy. You may find that your past experience has led you to be more "content centered." It is our hope that reflection on the issues presented throughout this book will assist you in evaluating your philosophy and considering new ideas.

CHECKLIST FOR EARLY COURSE DECISIONS

1. Gather course materials from the last time the course was taught. Was a text ordered for the class? Is there a syllabus from the last time it was taught?
2. Contact the department chair or a department staff member to get a calendar for the academic year.
3. Try to get a sense of your course in the sequence of courses in the degree program.
4. Read the course description in the college catalog.
5. Find out how often the course meets and for how long. Get a sense of how many students are typically in the course.
6. Find out what type of space the class meets in. Be sure that the room can accommodate equipment needs (piano, staff board, music stands, etc.).
7. Begin to ask about the students in the course and try to get a sense of the culture of the school or department.

CONCLUSION

Many decisions regarding course design relate to one another and the professor's understanding of who the students are and what will help the students learn. The choice of text is related to the goals and objectives outlined for the course. If the instructor is interested in teaching the *students,* and not just the content, than he/she should focus on development of pedagogical content knowledge. Many of us have grown accustomed to the "transmission model" of education where the teacher tells and the students listen. Without careful attention to course planning and preparation, we will "fall back" on a linear model of lecture/test for our classes.

The next chapter examines issues associated with assessment in music courses. Instructors are encouraged to reflect on these issues before moving ahead with course descriptions, outlines, or curricular frameworks.

QUESTIONS FOR DISCUSSION AND SUGGESTED ACTIVITIES

1. Discuss your experiences as an undergraduate in music courses. What was the culture of that school or program?
2. On the basis of your experience, what are the positive attributes of successful college professors?
3. On the basis of your experience, what are negative behaviors exhibited by some college professors?
4. Discuss the "culture" of a school or department of music as well as the "culture" of a classroom.

5. Discuss your understanding of the "transmission model" of teaching and think about alternatives for a course that you might teach.

6. Choose a course that you might teach within the undergraduate music curriculum and generate course descriptions and course content statements for that course.

7. Search the web for multiple syllabi for a course you might teach and compare goals and objectives of the same course across various syllabi.

8. Discuss what you believe to be "pedagogical content knowledge" for a course you might teach. How will you consider where the students are in their development as thinkers and musicians?

9. Discuss the list of criteria for reviewing a textbook. What is important to you as the instructor? What do you think might be important for your students?

10. Go online and review possible textbooks for courses you might teach.

11. Discuss the differences between focusing curriculum on teaching versus focusing curriculum on learning.

12. Choose a course and generate some language for an "objectives-based" approach to curriculum design.

13. Choose a course and generate some language for a "literature-based" approach to curriculum design.

14. Choose a course and generate some language for a "skills-based" approach to curriculum design.

15. Choose a course and generate some language for a "knowledge-based" approach to curriculum design.

16. Obtain a copy of the *NASM Handbook* and examine the recommendations for a degree program that you will teach in.

17. Discuss some of the curriculum tensions mentioned in the text (solfege systems, counting systems, repertoire, teaching philosophies) as well as others you can think of.

18. Discuss what you perceive to be the role of the accrediting bodies in shaping music curriculum.

19. Share your thoughts for innovation in music school curriculum. Discuss some of the challenges in implementing music curriculum change.

20. Share what you think might be some of the key aspects of your teaching philosophy. What do you believe about undergraduate music students? How does that interact with your beliefs about your content?

CHAPTER 2

Assessment and Grading in Music Courses

It is difficult to write a syllabus or design curricula for degree programs without considering the assessment outcomes associated with the course or content. However, the linear nature of curriculum development and course design often encourages instructors to write objectives for courses, design a sequence for instruction, and then develop an evaluation or test of the content for the purpose of a grade. In contrast to this model, Fink (2003) suggests that instructors begin course design and curricular planning with the following questions:

1. What are the important situational factors in a particular course and learning situation?
2. What should our full set of learning goals be?
3. What kinds of feedback and assessment should we provide?
4. What kinds of teaching and learning activities will suffice, in terms of achieving the full set of learning goals we set?
5. Are all the components connected and integrated, that is, are they consistent with and supportive of each other? (p. 63)

He goes on to suggest: "Careful readers may note that in the sequence of questions, the one on 'feedback and assessment' comes before the one on 'teaching and learning activities'" (p. 63). In designing this text, we have opted to discuss "learner-centered" pedagogy and "situational factors" of curriculum design in Chapter 1 and then move right on to assessment in Chapter 2. Instructional activities are not discussed until later in the text as we want to model the concept that professors must consider the learners, assessment, and personal teaching philosophy in advance of planning for specific class meetings and interactions.

Grant Wiggins (1998) refers to this sequence for designing courses as the *backward design*. I (Conway) often design my undergraduate music courses by considering the projects, tests, assignments, interactions, readings, and musical skills that I expect from a student who has completed the course. By starting with that information I can "back up" into a 14-week sequence for instruction. When I write the syllabus, I regularly complete the "Course Assignments" and "Evaluation Criteria" sections before writing the course description or the calendar outline. It is difficult when a course is new to you to have a sense of what is appropriate for students in terms of final outcomes. However, we encourage you to focus on this concept of "backwards design" in thinking about your course. This design assumes an understanding that assessment includes feedback and teacher-to-student interaction as well as student-to-student interaction. The next section expands on this notion of assessment in contrast to what might be considered "grading" in music courses.

ASSESSMENT VERSUS GRADING

Early on in the course planning process, the instructor must plan assignments and criteria for grading. It is important to consider the relationship between grading and assessment in music courses. Alfie Kohn (1999) regularly criticizes the practice of grading and states:

> Grades cannot be justified on the grounds that they motivate students, because they actually undermine the sort of motivation that leads to excellence. Using them to sort students undercuts our efforts to educate. And to the extent that we want to offer students feedback about their performance—a goal that demands a certain amount of caution lest their involvement in the task itself be sacrificed—there are better ways to do this than by giving grades. (p. 203)

Kohn has written extensively on this topic and the reader is encouraged to consider his work and the work of others who examine the relationship between grading and motivation. College students need to begin to view learning as the goal and not "good grades." However, this is a difficult concept and one that is deeply rooted in experiences they may have had previous to arrival at the university. Chapter 5 addresses additional issues regarding grading and motivation as they relate to academic growth, development, and maturity.

Early in course design, instructors must consider how to provide appropriate feedback to students during the course of a semester. Whether this feedback is associated with the grade for the course is in some ways less important than planning for how feedback will be provided. Regardless of the philosophical concerns regarding grading, most courses require instructors to give a final grade to reflect the work of students. Good assessment goes beyond the mere reporting of student work and is used to provide feedback to students as well as information to the instructor regarding student learning. In the effort to design useful and meaningful assessment, it is recommended that music classes include a variety of assessment measures so that learners have opportunities to represent their learning in different ways.

Try to have some written exams, some papers, some oral presentations, and some musical skill demonstration in every class that you teach. Not all courses can include all types of assessment but it is suggested that diverse measures of assessment are a goal for instructors. This chapter will present issues associated with grading and assessment in music classes including an understanding of the differences between music aptitude and music achievement; managing assessment in music courses; methods of assessing student learning; criteria for tests and tools for assessment; student-generated rubrics for assignments; sample performance rubrics; and assessment in the learner-centered classroom. Questions for discussion and suggested activities are included as well.

MUSIC APTITUDE AND MUSIC ACHIEVEMENT

Music professors measure and assess musical achievement. Achievement refers to what a student has learned in music. Although most professors will not be involved in testing musical aptitude, it is important to understand the concept of musical aptitude. Gordon (1997) defines aptitude as "a measure of a student's potential to learn music" (p. 41). There are a number of tests available for measuring music aptitude including a measure for adults called the *Advanced Measures of Musical Audiation* (Gordon, 1989). We sometimes hear music colleagues talk about "talent" and often wonder whether talent refers to aptitude or achievement. Gordon suggests

> Most of us have become accustomed to hearing and to using such words as ability, talented, gifted, and musical, but these words only confuse the issue by obscuring the important distinction that must be made between music aptitude and music achievement. Whereas music achievement is intellectual and primarily in the brain, music aptitude is spontaneous and primarily in the cells and genes, that is, in the entire body. (p. 42)

We share this information on aptitude primarily to encourage music professors to accurately use the term "achievement" when referring to what is measured in music coursework. In addition, we encourage instructors for music classes to recognize that musicianship and musical behaviors can, and should, be assessed. We find some music instructors who are somewhat opposed to thinking about assessment of musical skills in favor of a sort of "artistic" view that music is meant to be a communication of whatever the student feels they wish to communicate. Although there are times when this may be the case, in most instances a tool can be designed to document a student's musical growth. Tools for assessment of music performance and other tools for music courses are provided at the end of this chapter.

MANAGING ASSESSMENT IN MUSIC COURSES

In creating the course syllabus and outlining readings, projects, and exams, it is important to include the percentage toward the final grade that each assignment is worth. Some instructors assign a point value to each assignment or a percentage. There are a variety of software programs available to assist the professor in keeping track of student grades in large classes. Check with your institution to see if they have site licenses for any of these programs. There are also good online programs available at very little cost. It is important to keep careful and accurate records of student grades as administrators may ask for this information in the event that a student questions a grade.

Be sure to be clear regarding due dates. If you intend to allow electronic submissions for assignments, give a clear time that an assignment is due. Give a time and then plan your week so that you have several hours available to respond immediately to student work. One of the keys to good assessment is a timely response from the instructor. Later chapters address issues of responding to student written work as well as assessment of applied music.

We have found one of the difficult issues of assessment in music courses to be the assessment of "class participation" that is often a part of a course grade. Although it is often tempting to include "class participation" as part of the course grade, it is sometimes difficult for students to know how this is being assessed. I (Colleen) have found this so problematic that I no longer include "class participation" in grading. Do I expect students to participate? Yes, but I use a variety of instructional strategies to ensure this participation rather than the threat of a lowered "class participation" grade. If you intend to grade on class participation, be sure to provide feedback to students with regard to "how they are doing" on this criteria. There are often issues of gender, culture, and language that have an influence on a students' ability to participate. Be sure to be aware of the issues.

VARIOUS METHODS OF ASSESSING STUDENT LEARNING

A music professor can face several challenges regarding the inevitable task of scheduling tests in courses. Tests are of course a necessary and valuable assessment tool the professor can use to determine many things. These facets can be quite varied, ranging from the student's knowledge of the lesson material at both an outright and inferred level to the instructor's ability to properly convey the said lesson material. As McKeachie and Svinicki (2006) suggest, a teacher should "learn from the test yourself" (p. 103), ensuring that every subsequent test gives the students the best opportunities to succeed.

There are several different kinds of testing procedures a music professor can utilize, and each has its benefits and its downsides. It is important for professors to make sure that they are using the most appropriate procedure that relates to the current lesson material. Music professors typically have different situations than most other college professors, and their choice in testing procedure may differ when considering such things as subject matter, class size, and so on.

I published a study in the *Journal of Music Teacher Education* [Colleen Conway. 1997. Authentic assessment in undergraduate brass methods class. *Journal of Music Teacher Education*, 7 (1): 6–15]. The tools I present for use with my undergraduate students in that study may be useful for others teaching instrument techniques. The article can be accessed through the Music Educators National Conference website at menc.org.

Short Answer Tests

Short answer tests ask direct questions that have a limited scope in the length of acceptable answers. They are typically one to two sentences in length, and require an answer of no more than a paragraph. An example of this type of question on a quiz from a music appreciation course might be: *Briefly describe the difference between an aria and a recitative in opera*; or, *How does a concerto differ from a symphony?*

This type of testing procedure can be very effective in a lecture-based music class such as a survey course or a music history class, but can also be found in theory and analysis, composition, or education courses. The short answer question test provides a good balance between testing the student's knowledge and a relatively simple means of grading for the instructor. There are almost always specific keywords or facts a student can mention that will correspond with the teacher's answer key, and if those are brought up in a relevant and accurate way, the answer can be considered as being correct. Short answer tests enable the students to use their own words to answer questions without the anxiety of having to write an entire essay.

The Essay

McKeachie and Svinicki (2006) say, "I recommend that, if possible, you include at least one essay question on examinations in most college courses" (p. 90). These are essentially longer versions of the short answer question. The student is given a question and asked to provide a well-thought-out and organized answer giving more details and examples than would be expected for a short answer question. This may be the best way to ensure a student's grasp of the subject matter, but is not always the most practical testing procedure, especially in a large class. McKeachie and Svinicki go on to describe a technique they use of giving the students broad guidelines to follow where they would write answers to a logical progression of questions that in essence creates an outline for the essay they would write. This makes it easier to grade and allows the students to remain on task throughout the writing process.

In a music program, it is definitely more customary for essays to be used in lecture-style courses such as history and appreciation. Essays require student confidence in writing ability and this may be challenging for younger students. Some students find it difficult to write an essay within an allotted period of time. Work to create essay prompts that lead to good essay responses from students and be sure that you have clear ideas about the correct answers so that you can create a clear grading rubric for the essay.

Multiple Choice

Of the three testing procedures mentioned in this section, the multiple choice is the simplest and most direct. A question is asked and several answers are given, one of which is correct (or the "most" correct). This obviously is a good means for interpreting the student's understanding of the subject matter—either the answer is correct or not. However, tests made up of all multiple-choice questions would not give the professor the best indication of his student's knowledge. McKeachie and Svinicki say, "They are not likely to assess organization of ideas, conceptual relationships, or many of the skills involved in higher-order thinking" (p. 92). It can also place undue strain on the professor. Creating multiple-choice questions is easy—creating GOOD multiple-choice questions is not.

Multiple-choice questions are often used in music courses. Many courses that use a textbook may have multiple-choice exams provided in the teacher's manual for the textbook. Here are two examples, the first from a music history class and the second from a music theory class.

1. This Shostakovich piece was written after a veiled threat from Stalin that suggested he compose music that is more "Russian" or suffer the consequences.
   a. Op. 49—String Quartet No. 1
   b. Op. 29—Lady Macbeth of the Mtsensk District
   c. Op. 47—Symphony No. 5
   d. Op. 35—Piano Concerto No. 1
2. Which of the following cadences is the only one not to resolve to the tonic?
   a. Plagal cadence
   b. Imperfect Authentic cadence
   c. Half cadence
   d. Perfect Authentic cadence

Many students like multiple-choice questions. It is given that one of the choices is correct, and it is only a matter of selecting the right one. Other students find them extremely stressful. McKeachie and Svinicki remind us: "Learning is more important than grading" (p. 85). Each of the discussed testing procedures can be useful and effective in a musical setting, although care must be taken to make sure that they are being used in an appropriate manner. The professor must have a solid idea of what facts he believes are important for the student to glean from the lessons. The professor must be able to organize and construct an optimal test that has a strong likelihood for student success. The professor must also be able to adapt his tests accordingly, suiting to the needs of the students throughout the years. These keys will help make sure that students have the best chance for success.

CRITERIA FOR TESTS AND TOOLS FOR ASSESSMENT

When designing tests for music classes, it is important to consider the reliability and validity of the test or tool. Reliability refers to the consistency of the tool. Multiple-choice tests that are provided by textbook companies often report the reliability of individual test items. Researchers study the items on these tests and make changes to items based on the data they collect. Tests provided by textbook companies are often quite helpful as they typically include study guides for students as well as answer templates for the instructor. Validity refers to whether the tool is actually measuring what it is designed to measure. This is a particularly important criterion to consider when designing your own test. Sometimes, we may think we are testing musical knowledge but the test itself relies so heavily on some other content (e.g., ability to write) that the test is not a valid measure for music.

Other test criteria questions the professor might ask include: How long will it take for students to complete the test? Is the test an authentic musical activity (i.e., something a professional musician might be asked to do)? How will students learn from taking the test? Can I provide timely feedback to students using this measure?

Within each approach to testing are various options for measurement. Examples provided in this chapter include a checklist, rating scales, and rubrics. It is important to provide students with the grading criteria for tests and assignments. The more the detail provided, the better are the chances of the student doing well. The next section provides some detail regarding having students develop the criteria for grading. Even if you decide not to invite student input, be sure to provide ample detail regarding grading and assignment criteria.

STUDENT-GENERATED RUBRICS FOR ASSIGNMENTS

I (Conway) often have students design the rubrics for assignments in my classes. Although this takes some time at the beginning of the semester, it has multiple advantages. After going over the syllabus, I divide the class into groups and have each group develop criteria and assessment tools for each assignment on the syllabus. While students are in their group work, I visit the groups and assist whenever there are questions. I have found that in 20–30 minutes, the class can develop an extensive list of criteria. The goal is for students to take ownership of the assignments and to feel like they know exactly what the instructor is looking for on each assignment. I remind the students that I need to give them a numerical grade at the end of the term, so their tool must include some sort of point system. I put how much each assignment will be worth toward the final grade but invite students to develop the criteria for the individual assignments.

We have included some of the student-generated grading criteria for various assignments in music education courses. The content here is specific to my courses but we think the spirit of student-generated criteria can be replicated. I find that the dialogue regarding the assignments always leads to interesting responses from the students.

Example 1: Development of a Concert Program for Secondary Instrumental Methods Course

Students were given this on the syllabus:

Submit a "copy ready" program for a high school level concert band and/or full orchestra. Include: (1) a copy of all scores; (2) a cover sheet that describes the school district and ensembles; and (3) a one- to two-page rationale for your literature choices. First draft due on January 15, 2008 (10% of course grade, pass/fail).

After approximately 10 minutes of small group dialogue, the students developed the following criteria for a "pass":

- Attractive appearance and logical layout/program presentation
- Description of scenario (grade level, community, school schedule, time of year)
- Appropriateness of literature choices (varied, difficulty, length, interest)
- Clear explanation of rationale of choices
- Rewrite until program is appropriate. Think about use in teaching portfolio.

In the case of the concert program assignment above, students felt that the program would be something that they want to have for a student teaching portfolio in the future, so they asked to be allowed to rewrite the program until it was acceptable.

Example 2: Curriculum Development Assignment for Elementary Music Education Methods

Students in this course were given the following on the syllabus:

Curriculum Assignment (25% of course grade)

Design a curriculum for a grade level. The curriculum may cover yearly objectives or a specific unit (8-week session, etc.). The final document should be between 15 and 20 pages including a description of the class and the time schedule for the curriculum; a brief music department philosophy; grade level goals and objectives; a list of developmental skills and/or benchmarks; requirements for facilities, equipment, supplies, budget, and scheduling; a list of resources to be used (books, recordings, etc.); sample teaching strategies and sample assessment procedures. Papers will be evaluated on both content and style. Grading rubric to be developed in class.

After about 15 minutes of group interaction, the students developed the following criteria:

Content (60 points)
- Description of the grade level goals (thorough)
- Time schedule for curriculum (realistic)
- Brief music department philosophy (one or two paragraphs)
- Overall program goals and objectives (feasibility/age appropriate)
- List of development skills/benchmarks (shows use of national standards)
- List of requirements for facilities, equipment, supplies, budget, and scheduling
- List of resources to be used (books, recordings)
- Sample teaching strategies and assessment procedures (minimum of two lesson plans with assessment strategies if doing a yearlong unit. Could be more like 15 or 20 lesson plans with assessments for a more specific unit)
- Entire project shows connection to coursepack readings and class discussions

Format (40 points)
- Professionalism
- Style
- Grammar
- Flow/ideas/sequence
- Table of contents
- Cover page
- Page numbers

Rewrite until you get the A or decide to take the B or C. April 17 final deadline.

Example 3: Arranging Project for Instrumental Methods

Students were provided with the following on the syllabus:

Arranging project (20% of course grade)

Write an arrangement for 8th/9th grade string orchestra, full orchestra, or concert band. The composition must be at least 2 minutes in length. Create a full score and all parts using "Finale" or another notation software. Recruit the proper instrumentation for a 20 minute rehearsal to be held in March.

Students developed the following:

Seventy-five points for score preparation/composition
- Clear and well edited, computer generated parts and full score
- Scored for at least four parts
- Piece is at least 2 minutes in length
- Proper use of instruments, good harmonization, and voice-leading
- Developmentally appropriate range/technique/musical challenges
- Musical/interesting parts
- Teachable material.

Twenty-five points for Rehearsal
- Ability to recruit an ensemble
- Effective rehearsal presence
- Rehearsal technique
- Conducting
- Prioritization
- Problem-solving.

Piece may be resubmitted for improved grade if weak on first performance.

Note the level of detail on the student-generated tools. If you are not going to have students develop criteria then be sure to provide this level of detail on the syllabus so that students understand the assignments. Undergraduates often discuss their concern about not knowing how to write a certain paper or how to prepare for an exam. They need more information than "write a five-page paper" in order to know how to best approach the assignment. I find the technique of student-generated assignment criteria to work well in addressing these concerns.

SAMPLE PERFORMANCE RUBRICS

As mentioned earlier in the chapter, we encourage music instructors to use systematic rating scales and rubrics to provide feedback regarding musical skills and musical performances. There are a variety of models for performance assessment available. Many public school organizations have carefully designed performance forms (i.e., New York State School Music Association or the Texas Music Education Association). Students

PER FORMANCE OBSERVATIONS AND INSTRUCTIONAL NARRATIVE
(Rate each category listed below: 1 = Excellent, 2 = Good, 3 = Fair, 4 = Poor)

TONE
Beauty
control
balance

INTONATION
Individual
With
accompaniment

RHYTHM
Accents
precision
rhythmicfigure

TECHNIQUE
Fluency
articulation
fingering
execution

INTREPRETATION
Phrasing
expression
tempo
dynamics
style

TOTAL POINTS   (5–7 = Excellent 8–12 = Good   13–17 = Fair   18–20 = Poor)

Faculty   *Date*

Figure 2–1 Instrument Jury Form

will be familiar with these sorts of assessment tools. Figure 2–1 is one example of an Instrumental Jury Form used to assess student performance.

ASSESSMENT IN THE LEARNER-CENTERED CLASSROOM

Grades are somewhat of a necessary evil in higher education. However, the instructor who is learner-centered aims to design assessments so that students get regular feedback throughout the semester and they know how to improve to do well in the course. Including students to have a role in the grading criteria is just one way to focus on the learners. Allowing students to rewrite or re-present assignments is another way to encourage a focus on learning rather than the grade.

Although the idea of paper drafts may sound like extra work for the professor, Elbow and Sorcinelli (2006) disagree:

> Are we suggesting doubling our responding duties? No. Our time is limited so we need to think strategically: how can we use our response time to do the most good?...If we devote most of our available time to feedback on a draft, we have a better chance of getting students to improve their writing and their understanding of course concepts. By responding to drafts, we are coaching improvement—instead of just writing autopsies on finished products that will never be improved. If we respond only to final drafts, students have a hard time using our feedback to improve future papers (especially if there are no other papers in the course—or if the next paper is quite different). (p. 199)

We have experienced some success in allowing students to rewrite papers and re-present class presentations in music classes. Not all students will opt to improve in this way, but some will and for those that opt to "try again" it would seem to make sense.

It is important for students to have a sense of their grade in the course. Frequent assessment and timely return of feedback is important. We have spoken with many students at the end of the semester at advising meetings, those who are frustrated because of not knowing how they are doing in a course. I always give a written midterm report. This includes attendance, homework grades, writing assignment grades, and class participation grades. At the end of the report, I list the remaining assignments left in the term. I find that knowing that I need to give a midterm report helps me to arrange assignments and evaluations so that at least some grade information is available at the middle of the semester.

CONCLUSION

Institutions are becoming more and more concerned with accountability for learning in higher education. The music professor must have clear and well-articulated policies for assessment as well as grading. Students learn best from timely and regular feedback from professors. Professors need to work to choose testing and assessment strategies that best match the assignment tasks or musical skills. There is a strong connection between course planning, curriculum assessment, and student learning. Just as it takes time to learn to teach, it takes time to learn to use good assessment strategies. Although music professors often avoid detailed measurements in assessing musical products in favor of more subjective tools, it is possible to measure growth in musical skills and we encourage the novice professor to explore the options.

QUESTIONS FOR DISCUSSION AND SUGGESTED ACTIVITIES

1. Choose a music course and discuss what may be the difference between assessment activities versus assignments for a grade.

2. Think about the desired skills and "student products" for a course you might teach. How would you articulate these skills or products as assignments for the course?

3. Choose a music course and discuss how you might use a "backwards design" to focus on outcomes before a calendar of class meetings.

4. Discuss the difference between music aptitude and music achievement and consider how these constructs will interact in your classroom.

5. Go online and examine various software programs for managing assessment. Share what you find with the class.

6. Reflect back on your own assessment experiences specifically in regard to "class participation" grades.

7. Discuss the advantages and disadvantages of testing procedures including short answer, multiple choice, and essay.

8. Choose a course and design several different types of test questions or items including short answer, multiple choice, and essay.

9. Discuss how you might include a student-generated rubric activity in a class that you might teach.

10. Review the performance jury scale in the chapter and share other forms for performance assessment that you are aware of.

11. Consider what would be "authentic assessment" for your field. What are "authentic activities" for music theory; music history; music education; performance?

CHAPTER 3

Understanding the Learners

Although we cannot generalize characteristics, experiences, or needs of all students, research on undergraduate student development does suggest some typical behaviors (Belenky et al., 1997; Gilligan, 1982; Levine and Cureton, 1998; Perry, 1999). On the basis of this research, Barbara Davis (2001) suggests that

> Above all, learning is an active, constructive process that is contextual: new knowledge is acquired in relation to previous knowledge; information becomes meaningful when it is presented in some type of framework. In addition, the acquisition and application of knowledge benefit from social interaction. (p. 177)

Davis suggests that in order to plan instruction with this active and constructive process in mind, instructors must ask several questions about student learning. These include

- How do students select, acquire, and construct knowledge?
- How do students integrate and maintain knowledge?
- How do students retrieve knowledge when they have to use it?
- How do students develop effective learning skills? (Davis, p. 177)

This thinking about the interaction between teaching and learning will enhance the process for both the students and the teacher. The first part of this chapter outlines considerations regarding the learner and learning, including: (1) student intellectual growth; (2) learning styles; (3) motivation; (4) gender; (5) cultural diversity; and (6) individual learning needs. Each section includes a focus on the aspects of general theories that may be most applicable for music students. The second part of the chapter provides more specific information regarding undergraduate music students and vignettes from undergraduate students regarding their experiences in music classes.

STUDENT INTELLECTUAL GROWTH

In his seminal study of student growth, Perry (1970) suggests that in the early stages of growth the learners are "dualistic" thinkers. They are right- or wrong-answer oriented and want their teachers to provide the answer and tell them what will be on the test. Belenky et al. (1986) studied development in women specifically and call this early phase that of "received knowledge," meaning a dependence on authority. Students at this developmental level may not want to think independently and they become uncomfortable when professors disagree. We cannot equate any of these developmental levels with certain ages or years in college. It is possible for students in any class to be "stuck" so to speak in this phase of dualism. However, professors of introductory courses (i.e., theory, aural skills, and music history) and those working with younger students in general need to be aware of the possibility that students may be dualistic in their approach to the class. Students will want clear structure and may have little tolerance for open-ended discussions. This does not mean that discussion should be avoided but that the professor must give clear directions for the tasks and provide a summary at the conclusion of the activity so that students are clear regarding what they have learned (more detail on teaching through discussion in Chapter 6).

For music students, dualistic thinking might appear as an "I already know everything" sort of mindset. Students come thinking they already have the one "right" answer since they were successful in music in high school. When I (Conway) was an undergraduate student at the Eastman School of Music back in the 1980s, the then Dean of Students Paul Burgett (now a Vice President at the University of Rochester) used to refer to entering freshmen at the Eastman School as "regional treasures." We find that many of our undergraduates today still fit this description. Music students who arrive as freshmen were often the best singer or instrumentalist that their local communities had seen in years and they come to music school thinking they are pretty "hot." In some cases, they are not quite ready for the culture of the music department. Burgett used to discuss the practice room as the place for discovery and describe that in August or September of the freshman year, students would practice with the practice room door left slightly open so that others could hear what had "arrived" at the Eastman School. Shortly after the upperclassmen arrived back to school, the freshmen would begin to listen to others practicing and decide to close the practice room door. The story goes that by the end of the first semester these "regional treasures" were covering the practice room window with paper.

Even if they were not "regional treasures" or even if they have had past experiences that have given them a sense of the profession, music majors come to us with a wide variety of academic and musical experiences. Students need to be encouraged to reflect on past understandings of musical concepts. If some of them come to us thinking that they already know what they need to know, then we must find out what it is they think they know. Freshmen need to be taught that peers may have different musical experiences that have led to different musical understandings and that they may be able to learn from these other points of view. Young undergraduates need to learn that knowledge is not something that is collected from those in authority but that knowledge is something students are responsible for constructing.

It may be difficult for music majors to come to terms with a different technique in the applied studio or a different outlook on music education. Their previous experiences are powerful and influential. They may resist alternate perspectives at first. This resistance to change is just part of the ongoing development and needs to be seen as important.

As students progress in their thinking, they begin to recognize that there is not always one right answer and that even experts disagree with one another. They often begin to see all knowledge as a matter of educated opinion. All opinions are considered equally valid. Perry calls this next stage "multiplicity" while Belenky et al. refer to it as "subjective knowledge." Kurfiss (1988) suggests that this stage is dominant among most college students. It is only after faculty work with students to help them understand that opinions must be supported by evidence that students begin to understand that knowledge is contextual and situational. Davis suggests in this stage that "Faculty are now viewed as experienced resources, who teach specialized procedures for reasoning and who can help students learn the skillful use of analytic methods to explore alternative points of view and make viable comparisons" (p. 178).

In the final stages of intellectual development (referred to as "commitment in relativism" by Perry and "constructed knowledge" by Belenky et al.), the learners recognize that there may be multiple answers to questions depending on factors of context. Nothing is right in all cases. They begin to understand that differences of opinion are to be valued and should be considered. Part of the job of the undergraduate professor is to help students make this transition from dualistic (right versus wrong) thinking to relativistic (there is more than one answer) thinking.

The content of music lends itself well to the teaching of diverse thought. Assignments might include listening to multiple recordings and interpretations of the same musical work and justifying the musical decisions made by the performers. Thinking about the effect on performance of the size of an ensemble, the equipment available, and the rehearsal time devoted to the performance can help students consider issues of context. Help students to search for evidence and support for any notions or ideas brought forth. Davis (2001) suggests that "real-world" experiences such as putting theory, history, or introduction to music content into performance settings help students to bridge between abstract and concrete learning. Placing music education students in schools as early as possible helps them to use theories of music teaching and learning in a "real" context.

Since many classrooms may include learners in all stages of intellectual development, try to let students know what they are expected to learn through a well-organized syllabus and an introduction and conclusion to each class meeting. Know that some students will struggle with content that is presented in a different manner from the one they may have dealt with in the past. Be available to discuss these discrepancies with students. Researchers on intellectual development agree that all learners benefit from active learning. When discussions, games, simulations, and other interactive approaches that are discussed in Part 2 of the text are combined with solid assessment strategies (discussed in Chapter 2) and a focus on Pedagogical Content Knowledge (discussed in Chapter 1), students have the best chance of success.

LEARNING STYLES

In addition to consideration of cognitive growth in relation to thinking (dualistic to relativistic), instructors must be aware of the various learning styles exhibited by the students in the classroom. There are multiple models of learning styles (see Claxton and Murrell, 1987 for 16 different models of learning styles, Davis, p. 185), but most studies agree on three primary approaches to learning: aural, visual, and kinesthetic. The learner who is approaching a class aurally is most apt to process material from a lecture or a class discussion while the visual approach requires the student to read material or see it in a graphic. The kinesthetic learner is most comfortable in a very "hands on" approach to the content. Most students will find that they differ across the learning styles at different times and in different courses. No one style has been shown to be better than another. It is in the best interest of the instructor to offer various means of instruction so that all learners have an opportunity to grasp the materials through various approaches. As discussed in Chapter 2, instructors are encouraged to assess learning in a variety of ways (presentations, papers, performance exams, written exams, etc.) and this effort to vary assessment strategies may attend to issues of learning styles as well.

Of particular interest to music professors is the work of Howard Gardner (2004, 1993a, 1993b) that highlights musical intelligence as a separate intelligence in the brain. The music professor must consider that a true "musical" learner may have learned music well but might struggle with the work in a theory, history, or education class that draws from linguistic intelligence or one of Gardner's other targeted intelligences (logical–mathematical, spatial, bodily kinesthetic, interpersonal, and intrapersonal). Or, it may be that a music major has learned music in a "linguistic intelligence" way and struggles when asked to truly process music in a "musical" way (i.e., in aural skills). Gardner discusses tonal and rhythm perception as key elements in musical intelligence and also suggests that sensitivity to music (some might call it aesthetics) is an important but less measurable component of musical intelligence. In her discussion of Gardner's theory in the *Music Educators Journal* back in 1998, Cathy Kassell cautions educators regarding assumptions about Gardner's work: "Gardner's theory has lent itself to classroom activities that exercise different intelligences, but some music activities supposedly based on this theory may be misguided" (p. 29). Gardner's musical intelligence relates to aural abilities and yet some teachers use music in activities to support other types of intelligence but do not focus on the aural nature of music. For example, music teaching that is completely notation-based or music activities that focus on concepts about music (i.e., lives of composers, instruments of the orchestra) focus on skills other than those in musical intelligence. It is not that these activities are bad music lessons, they just are not tapping into musical intelligence. Students entering college now may have worked with music teachers in high school who have used a misguided approach to music learning and this may hinder musical learning style for them in college. As mentioned in the intellectual growth section, it is difficult for younger students to recognize difference in approach from what they have been taught. This may appear in the area of learning styles as well. Students may not have been taught to be aware of learning styles and will need assistance in understanding the particular classroom approach being used.

Talk with students about learning styles. Encourage them to broaden their personal learning style scope. Successful musicians must be able to process music through "musical intelligence" in some way but other "intelligences" or learning mechanisms may open the way for learning as well. In planning courses, think about various delivery strategies that will provide a balance between aural, visual, and kinesthetic approaches to learning. Classes should include a mix of lecture, reading, writing, board work, small group discussion, large group discussion, individual projects, and group projects. When possible in music classes, present musical material in a musical way (singing, listening, composing, or improvising) so that music students are accessing their musical approach to learning as much as possible.

MOTIVATION

Every music professor likes to teach students who attend class regularly, perform well on assignments and exams, and are generally motivated to do well in the course. Research on motivation and learning (Brophy, 2004) suggests that learners value the opportunity to have control over their learning. They value making their own instructional choices and learn more in courses where they are asked to connect readings and lectures to their own work. Hofer (2006) suggests:

> In general, individuals want to be in charge of their own behavior, and they value a sense of control over their environment. We can enhance students' sense of control by offering meaningful opportunities for choice and by supporting their autonomy, which in turn enhances motivation. Quite often these opportunities for choice can be relatively simple things such as a choice of paper topics, test questions, due dates, or reading assignments, yet they go a long way toward acknowledging a student perspective (p. 142).

We find that music students, in particular, value "choice" in their course work. Music student schedules are often dictated by applied lesson and ensemble schedules, so if students have some opportunity to choose projects and deadlines around these other requirements, they are often more motivated to do well. Music professors must be flexible and sensitive to the high-pressure performance schedules in most undergraduate music programs.

Undergraduates also value opportunities to choose musical repertoire or literature for projects so that they can make connections between the work in theory or history classes with their work in applied lessons and ensembles. Music professors must encourage these connections and allowing some student choice can facilitate this. The vignette below highlights the need for choice in upper-level courses.

My upper level theory class was a class deemed "less important" by me in the scope of things. It was a class that I did not enjoy, but could have if the information presented been more applicable to my situation. We spent most of the class going into knit-picky analysis of Bach, Beethoven and other classical composer's piano works. Most of the piano and occasional string quartet pieces we dealt with were those I had never heard of and will probably never encounter again in my life. Had I been given the chance to analyze bassoon sonatas of the classical era or commonly played symphonies that I will no doubt encounter again in my life I think the analysis would have been much more intriguing. The piano music had little relevance for me. It was there to analyze and then it was gone. I would have appreciated the analysis we were doing a lot more had I actually cared about the pieces being studied.

Researchers discuss two types of motivation—extrinsic and intrinsic. Hofer (2006) suggests that

Extrinsically motivated students are likely to engage in the course for reasons of external rewards, such as grades, recognition, or the approval of others (notably instructors and parents). Individuals who are intrinsically motivated, engage in an activity for the value of the activity itself, rather than for an external reward. (p. 142)

She goes on to discuss that although we all would love a class full of intrinsically motivated students, most often students will be motivated by some extrinsic values. This is particularly the case in courses where the content is "new" to students and they are unfamiliar with it. As discussed in Chapter 2, there is more to assessment than giving grades and grades that reflect clear feedback from the instructor may assist a student who is initially extrinsically motivated to lean toward finding intrinsic value in a subject.

Instructors are encouraged to create music classrooms that focus on mastery of the course content. Grades will then be determined using a criterion-referencing system rather than a normative one (grading on the curve). When possible, allow students to rewrite and revise assignments so that the focus is on mastery of learning and not on the grade. As discussed in Chapter 2, be sure that students know the criteria for each assignment so that they are motivated to complete the work and do it well.

Research on college student motivation is closely connected to issues of rapport and classroom culture that will be addressed in Chapter 5. In the effort to encourage students to become self-motivated independent learners, Davis (2001) suggests that instructors can do the following:

- Give frequent, early, positive feedback that supports students' beliefs that they can do well
- Ensure opportunities for students' success by assigning tasks that are neither too easy nor too difficult
- Help students find personal meaning and value in the material
- Create an atmosphere that is open and positive
- Help students feel that they are valued members of a learning community. (Davis, p. 193)

Be sure that students follow the "method to the madness" in your course. Begin class with a "where we were last class" statement and then outline the goals for the day. Conclude class with a summary of class activities and make a connection between the class and the assignment for the next class. This sort of organization will help students to find value in the content and will invite student questions regarding course material and assignments.

In addition to wanting control, students do not want to feel "controlled." Ken Bain (2004) discusses issues associated with grade-based motivation in college classrooms and states:

Investigators have also found that performance—not just motivation—can decrease when subjects believe that other people are trying to control them. If students study only because they want to get a good grade or be the best in the class, they do not achieve as much as they do when they learn because they are interested. (p. 35)

So, the challenge for the music professor is to assure that students are "interested." In some courses (particularly, the required music core courses outside of performance), it is difficult for students to see the connections between the topics and their own work. As mentioned earlier in the chapter, one strategy for maintaining interest is to allow students to choose assignments that are relevant to their own work. Another is to move away from the "transmission model" and to have students actively singing, moving, playing, listening, improvising, analyzing, and/or composing as much as possible in music courses.

SELF-REGULATION

Educators use the term "self-regulation" in referring to how students learn to learn and monitor their own growth. Weinstein et al. (2006) suggest several characteristics that are common to strategic and self-regulating learners in higher education including

- Confidence in ability to succeed
- Diligent, resourceful, and not giving up easily
- Understanding that learning and studying are under their control
- Aware of when they understand content and when they do not.

For students who do not naturally have these characteristics, professors are encouraged to include instruction in these areas as part of class instruction. For example, it may be important within aural skills or music theory to provide some carefully sequenced assignments that allow most students to succeed in the early assignments. This will build confidence for learners who are unfamiliar with the content. Teach students how to practice and how to study so that they can learn to take control of their own learning.

Within music, there is a sizable body of research on musical learning and musical skills development (reviewed by Lehmann and Davidson, 2002). Many of the studies have been conducted by psychologists who were studying prodigies and elite performers. McPherson and Zimmerman (2002) state:

> Although research on prodigies and elite performers provides valuable insight into the nature of expertise in music, more work is needed on "normal" performance before researchers will be in a position to more accurately determine what happens during the many years that it takes to develop instrumental skill, and how different levels of motivation might affect an individual's practice across such a lengthy period. (p. 327)

McPherson and Zimmerman suggest that the study of self-regulated learning may offer more insight into the nature of musical learning in an educational context:

> Self-regulated learning, a field in which some of the most important recent advances in the study of cognitive development have occurred, is a useful paradigm from which to study how learners acquire the tools necessary to take control of their own learning and thereby learn effectively (Bandura, 1991). Like any academic or motor task, learning a musical instrument requires a great deal of self-regulation, which is evident when students become "metacognitively, motivationally, and behaviorally active participants in their own learning process" (Zimmermann, 1986, p. 308). (p. 327).

The chapter by McPherson and Zimmerman (2002) outlines a framework for studying self-regulation in music that includes examination of the motive for playing a musical instrument, the parental support for young players, and the strategies for practicing. A new publication by McPherson (2006) provides practical information regarding young learners. Although there is little research on college-age students in music regarding self-regulation, some of the strategies developed for younger students may be relevant for college students as well. These suggestions include

- Help students to understand the process of skill acquisition
- Encourage a focus on process over product (i.e., lots of high notes, louder and faster)
- Teach students how to listen to their own renderings
- Encourage or require the use of practice journals.

GENDER

In *First Day to Final Grade*, Curzan and Damour (2006) suggest that "issues of gender are subtle, complex, and extremely powerful, and they are at work in every classroom" (p. 16). Music classrooms are also known as "gendered" spaces (Green, 1997). Gender is often stereotypically associated with musical instrument choice as well as conducting.

The vignette from a student below provides a student perspective on a negative classroom situation involving gender

> One of my music education classes was taught by a male doctoral performance degree student with four male undergraduate students and one female undergraduate student in the class. Instead of teaching to his fullest knowledge and potential he used a large portion of class time trying to be "one of the guys" by cracking jokes, cursing, telling stories and supporting degrading jokes about the female gender. One of the culminating moments of disrespect was when the instructor purposefully made a sexual joke when demonstrating how to appropriately strike a gong on the "nipple." This is not only incredibly out of line given a female student was present in the classroom, it is out of line for a teacher to make and support male sexual joking while wasting class time. As the semester continued he took on the role of a follower instead of a leader. Because the teacher was not only willing to come down to a less mature level, but in some cases led the way, the five students walked all over him for most of the class and were able to easily get him off topic and subsequently lessen our learning.

Curzan and Damour provide the following list of suggestions for addressing gender in classrooms:

- Be sure that men and women are equal participants in class discussions; if they are not, consider possible reasons for this and make the necessary changes.
- Be nonsexist in your presentation of material (e.g. using both males and females in your examples).
- Demonstrate that you expect to be respected regardless of your gender by treating all of your students with equal respect.
- While students may come to the class with existing ideas about male or female teachers, they will almost always respond to a teacher's command of the material, regardless of their gender. (p. 17)

Gender is an area that the music professor must consciously consider. Try to reflect on the gender balance and gender relationships in your classes on a regular basis. Ask yourself questions such as "Are there certain students I am calling on more than others?"; "Am I making assumptions about careers in music for these students based on gender?"; "Am I inviting all members of the class to participate equally?"

CULTURAL DIVERSITY

Curzan and Damour (2006) suggest that like gender, issues regarding race and culture are powerful within the classroom. In addition to the strategies for gender cited above they suggest the following regarding race and culture in the classroom:

- Students may be less inclined to respect the authority of minority teachers.
- Depending on the teacher's race or culture, minority students or students who are members of the dominant culture may feel less inclined to speak in class.
- Both students and teachers may exploit the power differential that exists among different racial and ethnic groups.
- Regardless of your race or culture, race and culture dynamics will be at work among your students. (pp. 17–18)

As with gender, try to be aware of potential issues of race and culture in your classes. Most professors are hesitant to highlight issues of race in class. We have found that if the class is going to discuss a topic related to race or culture, you might consider taking minority students aside and letting them know what is to be discussed. You might even invite them to lead the discussion. Occasionally, you may have one or more international students who speak English as a second language. Be understanding regarding the challenges faced by these students and refer them to campus services if additional support is needed.

INDIVIDUAL LEARNING NEEDS

One of the most important tasks for the music professor is to get to know students as individuals. Students value the effort that a professor takes in learning names, instruments, hometowns, and so on. If you are trying to promote a "learner-centered" classroom then it is important to know something about the learners on a personal level. Take notes on the first day of class as students are introducing themselves so that you can begin to review information like where they are from or what instrument they play.

It is also important for the new professor or graduate instructor to be aware of national and university policies regarding accommodating individual learning needs and students with disabilities. In music classes, it may be necessary to move chairs, stands, and risers to accommodate students in need of wheelchairs or other mobility aids. Students with "nonvisible" or "hidden" disabilities including learning disabilities, mild sensory deficits (vision or hearing), and chronic disabilities (diabetes, seizure disorders, or other health conditions) may not always present themselves as disabled at the beginning of the term (although most policies suggest that they should). Professors must be sensitive to needs that arise regarding these students as well.

Curzan and Damour (2006) remind their readers that "There is no relationship between being intelligent and having a learning disability; students with learning disabilities simply have some specific difficulty receiving or communicating information in one or more of the ways that are most common in academic settings" (p. 112). Barbara Davis (2001) discusses federal academic accommodations laws and includes the following list of accommodations that seem relevant to music classrooms:

- An in-class aide to read the test orally or to take down the student's dictated answers to exam questions.

- A separate room that provides better lighting or fewer distractions or that houses special equipment (computer console, video magnifier, text-to-speech converter).
- An extended exam period to accommodate a student's slower writing speed or need to dictate answers to an aide or to equalize a student's reduced information-processing speed.
- Option of substituting an oral exam for a written exam, or a written exam for an oral exam, or a multiple-choice for an essay exam.
- Option of having exam questions presented in written or oral form.

If you have questions about how to accommodate disabilities, contact your institution's student services office. Staff there can provide assistance and answer questions that you may have.

Attending to individual learning needs for music classes might also include the needs of students who are returning to college as older students. These students may have been active as freelance musicians and are returning to school for a teacher certification or a degree. They often have family commitments, outside jobs, and other life issues that make them unique as compared to the typical undergraduate student who enters college directly from high school. Help these students to feel part of the music community and be aware that there are often difficult dynamics between older and younger students (Davis, 2001).

All students will benefit from up-front knowledge about the course. Barbara Davis (2001) encourages instructors to "Determine entry-level knowledge required for students to succeed in your course. Make those expectations explicit in your course description and syllabus, and underscore them during the first class meeting" (p. 55). This is particularly important for music courses that might require a prerequisite understanding of music theory or music history. Listening courses that require a baseline skill level in aural skills can be problematic for students if they do not know about the need for these skills in advance. Students do not always realize that music courses are set up sequentially and in relation to one another such that a junior level conducting or music education course assumes a certain level of comfort with sight-singing and keyboard skills, for example. Help students to realize the relationships between courses and the need to transfer knowledge and skills from one course to another.

MUSICAL GROWTH AND THE CHANGING LEARNER

As was mentioned in the opening of this chapter, it is not fair to generalize the stages or experiences of undergraduate students as they develop and mature at different rates. However, within the music program, we have found some common issues in musical development, student maturity, and student music course expectations. Music professors often work with students at multiple levels (freshmen–senior) and a discussion of the "changing learner" may help the music professor to focus on the students and design instruction to meet individual needs. As was discussed in Chapter 1, different types of music programs will have students with different needs. However, most music programs will have students at both ends of the bell curve in terms of background, experience, and achievement in music. The more select the music school the less "spread" the instructor may experience but there are always individual differences to be addressed regardless of the level of achievement and experience. This chapter presents an overview of the experiences and typical course offerings for freshmen, sophomore, junior, and senior music majors. Each section includes a short vignette writing by an undergraduate music major regarding their experiences. Suggested strategies for teaching underclassmen and upperclassmen are included. The chapter concludes with questions for discussion and suggested extension activities.

FRESHMEN EXPERIENCE

We base this discussion of freshmen experiences on our collective years of working with undergraduates as well as many conversations over the years with music faculty and students. Although it is dangerous to suggest that all freshmen experience the same issues, we have outlined several areas of concern that we believe can be typical.

For some students the freshman year is a scary transition. Leaving the protection of home and getting used to living independently is taxing. Many freshmen experience some signs of depression (unable to sleep, hard time waking, poor eating habits, not getting work done) as they are learning how to live on their own. These students need advisors, mentors, and professors who can help them learn how to manage their time. They often do not know how to study or how to practice. They also need to see good role models and they need to interact with upperclassmen who have made the transition to college smoothly.

Other freshmen have no issues of transition to college. In fact, we have often seen the opposite of the "needy" student in freshmen. Some of these students are almost arrogant and think that they really do not need to be at college since they are already quite good. These students begin early on in the term to talk about getting a transfer to another school where their talents will be put to better use. Within music, it is common for a student to have been a bit of a "regional treasure" and these students often miss the glory they had in their hometowns. In dealing with these types of students, it is tempting to want to "tear them down" or show them how much they do not know. However, we have found that good modeling and a nurturing learning environment is the right remedy for these students as well.

Freshmen in all music courses will come to class with diverse past experiences and the professor for a freshman course has the challenge of bringing students together in a shared new experience. The comments of a freshman (below) highlight some of the unique challenges faced by freshmen music students with regard to career planning and passion for music. Music students have the experience of participating in a performance-oriented field, and this can be stressful for students new to the music department culture.

FRESHMAN MUSIC MAJOR VIGNETTE

The transition from high school to college was daunting at best. I had already tasted independence from the responsibilities I had slowly developed in attaining adulthood. I was prepared for living on my own by the constant "pep talks" from family and friends. I was prepared for the class schedule awaiting me. I bought the extra-special bed sheets for the dorm and the far-too-expensive laptop computer. My mother had already kissed me goodbye. I should be eager to tackle this new life: free from the constraints of living under supervision.

Why was I so apprehensive? What was I looking for? Why was I attempting to be a musician? How was I going to get through this process? After these next four years (or may be five), who would hire me? These doubts were like weights on my legs, draining me as I tried to move forward with my new life.

Aside from the inevitable difficulties of learning to live independently, music, the object of my obsession is such an intangible career choice. Unlike those who chose pre-med or engineering, majoring in music rarely triggers the same comments of respect and esteem. More frequently is the response, "So…what are you going to…do?" Honestly, what am I going to do? I am more in love with music than I ever was with John Stamos or the cast of "Friends" and I can't imagine spending five hours a day on anything other than practicing on my instrument. Where does that put me? How do I reconcile these two issues of loving my work and living off of my work? Does the intense passion I have for music overshadow my desire to support a family?

The answer I've decided to focus on is "yes." Pursuing a career in music is as beneficial as becoming some big-shot doctor or making hundreds of thousands in engineering the next space vehicle. Rarely will you meet someone who finds no joy in the music of their lives, from the Beatles tune on the radio to the classical symphony in the waiting room of the doctor's office. It is the essence of every person's being, regardless of background. Why shouldn't I seek professional status in this field over any other?

My experiences as a freshman music major have been exactly as I imagined, from the exhausting hours in the too-small practice rooms to the terribly intimidating peers within them. Learning to convert this pressure into motivation was challenging, but I learned that if I can just keep swimming, I'll eventually reach the end—hopefully stronger than before.

I can honestly say that the most important mentorship I received all year was in the hour and a half long studio class I received each week. I was surrounded by a group of individuals, each from different backgrounds and at different points in completing their degrees. Each of these unique musicians were there for me, every Tuesday at 8, to offer snippets of their experience in an effort to offer the wisdom they had found so worthwhile on their journeys.

TYPICAL MUSIC OFFERINGS FOR FRESHMEN

Most freshmen music majors will have a schedule that includes applied studio lessons, studio class or music major symposium, large and/or small ensembles, aural skills, written theory, and piano class. Music history courses may begin in the freshmen year for some institutions. Some schools may include a music technology course in the freshmen year as well. Music education majors may be required to take an Introduction to Music Education course or any variety of techniques courses (i.e., strings, winds, brass, percussion). In most schools, students are required to take a freshman English course. This course is often a beginning course and does not always focus on writing. Some freshmen in music courses will not have had a background in writing term papers and using writing style manuals. It is important for the music professor to determine where a student is on the continuum of learning to write.

Music majors have some of their classes (i.e., applied lessons and ensembles) throughout their 4 years and it is important for instructors in these courses to reflect on how the teaching is different for students at various levels. Freshmen in applied lessons and ensembles may not be ready for conversation about musical concepts and sharing of their ideas regarding a musical phrase. Some of them will be ready for this type of interaction but others will need more modeling of these behaviors before they are ready to engage.

SOPHOMORE EXPERIENCES

The reflection provided by the sophomore in this chapter highlights some of the primary issues of the sophomore experience. No longer does the student have the "freshman" excuse. He/she must begin to focus on career choice and life decisions. The story below highlights the student's effort to connect all his courses across campus to his growing career interests and his frustration with the linear nature of course work. In some ways, he wants all the answers right away and has to wait for the next course in the sequence to get what he is after. Courses begin to get harder and the need for a focus in a music major continues.

SOPHOMORE MUSIC MAJOR VIGNETTE

Sophomore year—those words finally meant that I already learned how to live in a dorm, met a ton of people, learned more acronyms than I thought possible, and adapted to work in college. What sophomore year meant for me was a shift away from learning about what college is like, and a shift into what it means to be a future music educator. My college courses actually didn't shift very much; I was still in mainly gen eds, and only had a few methods classes that were preparing me for the numerous education classes to come. However, the new year seemed to make a world of a difference.

Perhaps I'm not the kind of person who takes cliffhangers very well. It seemed that every so often in my studies, I'd get to a cliffhanger: in an early methods class, I can recall learning some tools to structure time in a music classroom to get students coming back for more. I left the class almost feeling cheated—I wanted to spend the next couple of weeks learning about the use of time in the classroom, not practicing on the instrument. It's these little tidbits that have helped confirm my major in music education, simply because my own curiosity won't let me choose otherwise.

Interesting enough, these cravings for knowledge haven't been limited to music education classes. In fact, every general music course I've taken now makes me ask how I can apply it to a future classroom. This goes far beyond the obvious case in rehearsals, where I try to learn from every new conductor I see on the podium. In music theory, I wondered what topics in form, melody, and harmony I could cover in a high school band room without losing time or interest. It applied any time I researched a new composer or era, when I was left wondering how I could introduce the history of a piece without boring the average high school student to death.

This isn't to say that every idea I've had confirmed the idea that I should be a future band director. My continued curiosity of sonata-allegro form, interest in mathematics, and a multitude of other ideas have gotten me wondering which classes to take and which career to pursue. A number of these subjects occasionally have me downright confused over what to do with my life. In the end, these subjects have helped me find my way in the maze of majors and careers, allowing me to fully see what is out there and find my calling. These classes, within my majors, outside my majors, and even outside music, have helped immensely in my search to figure out what I want to pursue.

This sophomore year has been a solid continuation of my college studies; the introduction of my freshman year is over, and I've thoroughly enjoyed building upon the foundation of knowledge that I already have. More importantly, this year has guided me from general music into what will be a focused look into music education.

TYPICAL MUSIC OFFERINGS FOR SOPHOMORES

Sophomore music students often have similar schedules to freshmen. Applied lessons and studio class, large and small ensembles, aural skills, music theory, and piano often continue into the second year. Music history courses will continue or begin. Students may begin to complete more of the general studies courses (or may have completed them in the summer as many music students attend classes in the summer in an effort to complete the degree in 4 years). Music education students may begin to take coursework that includes fieldwork (going out to schools to observe or teach small groups).

SUGGESTED TEACHING STRATEGIES FOR UNDERCLASSMEN

Freshmen and sophomore music students need to be encouraged to discuss their musical experiences previous to their college years. An excellent "first assignment" in any music course is to ask students to create an "autobiography" of their relationship with the topic. They may write about where they first learned something about music history (i.e., short lesson at a summer camp) or when they first were asked to make a theoretical decision in an ensemble or solo. Some students may have no previous experience in a content area and this is important for instructors to be aware of as well.

If writing an autobiographical assignment does not seem relevant, students may simply be asked on the first day of class to discuss their past experiences in a content area. For example, on the first day of my brass or woodwind techniques classes for music education students I often discover that students who major in one instrument have some experience on other instruments because of a family member or a friend playing the instrument. In many cases, they come into the techniques courses with some "previous knowledge" that may be right or wrong but nevertheless it is important that they be encouraged to discuss it so that they can relate it to the content of the course.

Instructors in underclass courses must strike a balance between modeling of the musical decisions that students need to learn to make and then asking students to make some musical decisions. Small group work is encouraged so that students begin to take ownership of content. However, small groups must be set up carefully and it must be clear to students what the goals of the group activity may be. Students must be taught how to interact in groups and what the desired outcomes are.

Be careful not to assume prior knowledge. Some students become music majors with very little comprehensive experience in music. Make criteria for assignments very clear so that students learn how to be successful in a music course. Work to create opportunities for students to interact in class and learn from one another. An important disposition in moving from dualistic to relativistic thinking is recognizing that the professor or instructor is not the only "expert" in the classroom. Assign study teams or classroom workgroups to facilitate this learning.

It is important for underclass students to learn how to self-evaluate music-making and their academic work. Instructors can help students in this process by modeling self-reflection as well as asking students to keep practice journals, writing journals, or "diaries" of experiences. Learning to regulate one's own musical learning as well as managing time to performance are skills that can be learned in the early years. Related to the focus on self-evaluation is an understanding that one is in college to learn and not just "get good grades." Chapter 2 addressed some of these issues and "learning how to learn" beyond worrying about grades is an important underclass concept for music majors.

Finally, help freshmen and sophomores to understand the "big picture" of the music curriculum. Do not assume they will recognize the need for various skills in the life of a professional musician. Highlight the use of comprehensive musicianship skills in your own work as a professor so that students begin to internalize the need for a broad musical education.

Part 2 of this text focuses specifically on teaching and learning and includes more detailed suggestions for planning for class, creating good rapport with students, teaching applied music, instructional strategies for academic courses, and teaching with technology. Most of the strategies suggested in this section are relevant for underclassmen as well as upperclassmen. However, those working with underclassmen must focus more intently on striking a balance between various teaching strategies as younger students are often in more diverse "places" in terms of their individual learning needs.

JUNIOR MUSIC MAJOR VIGNETTE

"What am I going to do with the rest of my life?" This question has been on the back burners of my mind since entering school. I came in my freshman year declared as a bassoon performance and music education major figuring I was miles ahead of all those freshmen with undeclared majors. I did not know specifically what I wanted to do, but I at least narrowed it down to performance or teaching music. People ask me all the time "So do you want to teach or perform?" During my freshman and sophomore year I had no problem with telling them that I had not decided yet. Graduation seemed years away and I figured that I would gain a better idea of what I wanted to do with my life as I progressed through my schooling.

The summer between my sophomore and junior year I had lunch one day with my former high school band directors. As we talked, it hit me that I was only two years away from being certified to do what they do! Watching and listening to them, I did not feel like I was anywhere near ready to teach a band. I didn't even know how to conduct yet, let alone direct, read a score, cue and listen all at the same time! Classroom management? Lesson plans? Curriculum? Those things had not yet crossed my mind! I had already been through two years of college and only had two left before I needed to be able to do what my high school band directors do every day. As I began classes in the fall, my bassoon teacher again asked me "So do you want to teach or perform?" I was not nearly as comfortable responding with an "I don't know." I was a junior. I was halfway through my college career. I needed to start making decisions about what comes next in life. I knew the classes in my junior year would be especially important in helping me answer these questions. I went into my junior year knowing the tedious introductory courses were over and looking forward to the upper level courses where I could finally study issues relevant to my career. I was particularly looking for exposure and experience to and in the music education field in order to help me answer the ever burning question on the back of my mind.

As a freshman and sophomore in college I knew that there would be required courses that had very little to do with my future career. I expected classes like this freshman and sophomore year and did not have a problem bearing through them. Junior year, in my mind, was "down to business" year where I could focus on classes within my major. As a result of this attitude, my tolerance for anything other than information applicable to my bassoon playing or music education was limited.

One of the things that frustrated me the most in junior year were assignments for the sake of assignments. In my view, teachers should design assignments to help highlight the most important aspects of the course. College classes are sometimes an overload of information. Assignments should help channel specific information from the course into a productive and meaningful product for the student.

As a bassoon performance and music education major, I felt the two most important classes I took this year were orchestra and field work. These classes were the practical application of all my other courses! I think it is important that teachers not let up on stressing the importance of such classes and opportunities.

If my goal in life were to play in a professional orchestra, it would be silly for me to practice all the time and take private lessons, but never play with an orchestra. No matter how much I educate myself, there are certain things such as playing in tune with others, balancing to an ensemble or following a conductor, which I cannot learn without the practical application of playing in an orchestra. A person learns to play with the professionals by practicing with many other ensembles first. Likewise, one of the best ways to learn the role of a teacher, is to be put into a teacher's shoes while still in the learning process. In my methods classes and conducting I learned how to conduct, study a score and learned about classroom management and proper pedagogy. However, when I stepped up on the podium to conduct a group of students for the first time in my junior year, it was something like I had never experienced before. All of a sudden I was not entirely aware of what all was going on in front of me. It was hard for me to determine where I should direct my focus. My ideas and lesson plan were not always corresponding with what I was getting from the ensemble. I had to think and listen on my feet. It was scary! But it was so good for me. I still have a lot to learn, but I was glad that first shocking podium experience was in a controlled environment before my student teaching.

The practical experience also helped me make some decisions about what to do with my life. The first day I got up in front of a middle school ensemble, I was scared, and not everything went as planned. But when I stepped down from the podium I realized that I had enjoyed my experience. I was excited to get up there again. This was something I could do with my life! I do not want to be stuck with a job that I hate. It was a relief to be put into a real-world situation and come out of it enjoying myself and realizing I was in the right field of study.

TYPICAL MUSIC OFFERINGS
FOR JUNIORS

As is mentioned in the story above, courses in the junior year often appear to the student as if they are beginning to lead toward the final career. Music education students begin extensive fieldwork in schools. Performance students begin to take auditions for summer festivals and local orchestras and opera companies. The junior year curriculum usually includes some "upper-level" theory and/or musicology courses as well as more focused performance requirements (i.e., chamber music, orchestral rep. class). General studies are often completed by the junior year so that the student begins to focus more intently on the music major.

SENIOR MUSIC MAJOR VIGNETTE

I am sitting in my one bedroom, spartan apartment near my student teaching placement. I'm hardly in college anymore, save for a weekly seminar. And that's hardly collegiate: my fellow student teachers and I mostly rush in, vent, eat, and leave. Like any other student teacher, I'm in between worlds—which hopefully gives me a little perspective on the subject of this piece: my senior year in instrumental music education.

At the University, it seems like everybody I know in Instrumental Ed gets out in four years total. Many students in similar programs take a full five. But not at my school. These students slave away diligently at 17–18 credits a semester for three and-a-half years before student teaching. I am taking four and-a-half for a number of reasons. It was an important choice for me, and one that I think other students should consider. Before I elaborate, let me make one last qualifier: I don't mean that people who did it more expediently are at any disadvantage. It's just that the longer route was the best for me.

Delaying student teaching until my ninth semester allowed me to shape and fill my senior year the way I wanted. I was able to march one year in the Marching Band. It was as difficult and time-consuming as anything I've done, but it showed me a culture of hard work, standards and camaraderie that will inform my teaching in the years to come. I also just did something for me—specifically a class I didn't formally need. The course title was "Journalism Coverage of Terrorism, Conflict, and War." It felt great to have a change of pace, to be reading the newspaper for class, and to be (gasp!) interacting with non-music students (something we music students probably don't do enough). Rounding out each day was senior recital practice, ensemble rehearsal time, and trying to have a life.

These class opportunities were important, but I realize something important in retrospect. It was much more the overall mindset of my senior year, and what having finished my degree requirements allowed me to do in music that most defines the experience.

When my senior year came, I knew if I were going to delay student teaching, I had better step up and spend my time on something really worthwhile. Having spent three summers as a camp counselor, I thought of pairing that area of experience with two areas of inexperience: urban and K-5 music education. Initially, the offspring of the two was blurry at best—some sort of summer music camp in an urban environment. This idea then grew, morphed, and developed over the next five months with the careful guidance and advice of one of my Professors. As June arrived, I had a staff of great musicians, a University grant worth $1,200, a donation of camp t-shirts, a donated gas card, facilities, and high spirits. From July 10–27 we had a blast with elementary school students at our very own not-for-profit camp.

Setting this up, I really felt as though I had taken personal control of my music education knowledge. No longer just a student on assignment, I was creating curricula, working with school administration, and recruiting a staff of colleagues. It felt great, and it wouldn't have happened if I had pushed to get out in four years.

Getting to your senior year in music seems to supply perspective on the previous undergraduate years the way a year into a job clarifies the first hectic days. Not until then could I see the merits (or lack thereof) of certain classes and personal connections I had made. I felt like I could throw away the bad and expound on the good. I also tried to utilize those professors who offered their assistance. In all this, I learned a lot about myself and my abilities.

And I'm not a special case: I'm convinced that all it takes to complete a similar project is motivation, time, and resources. In short, the design of my senior year gave me the room to let intrinsic motivation take over. If you're reading this and trying to figure out what to do with your own senior year, consider a ninth semester. Or if your parents are willing, maybe even a tenth.

TYPICAL MUSIC OFFERINGS FOR SENIORS

This story highlights the individual nature of the senior year. In his case, he took it upon himself to design and implement a senior project, so to speak. Some programs require a senior thesis or a senior project. Most music majors are required to perform a senior recital and many will begin graduate school auditions and teaching job applications. Seniors are often involved in small ensembles and are working to secure performance "gigs" outside of the university environment. Music professors working with seniors are encouraged to model professional behaviors by sharing your work with students so that they have an authentic view into the life of a professional musician. Bring seniors to lectures and performances. Help them to get to know important people in the field. Allow seniors to tailor course requirements to their own interests.

SUGGESTED TEACHING STRATEGIES
FOR UPPERCLASSMEN

We are suggesting that instructors for all courses adopt a "learner-centered" approach to the classroom. However, since the learner may change from freshman to senior year the music professor must be constantly examining teaching practice and considering whether techniques and strategies are appropriate for the learners in the course. Upper-class music students are looking to focus their work towards career goals and need assistance in relating music courses to relevant work in the professional world.

Older students begin to have higher expectations of themselves. If they were taught to self-assess their work as freshmen and sophomores, they will begin to use self-assessment as a powerful tool for improvement. Most upperclassmen begin to take more ownership for learning. They are interested in extension activities and making connections between course content and the "real world" of the professional musician.

Upper-class students are now "experienced" in terms of higher education. They have seen multiple approaches to course design and interaction. We find these students to be much less tolerant of unorganized classes, weak lectures, and poor assessment practices. Most juniors and seniors push for the instructor to set clear expectations and fair procedures. Although it is hoped that all courses will have these characteristics, we believe instructors of upper-class students will experience more student concern if these issues are not well-addressed.

Juniors and seniors have more scary "life" issues. Concerns about car payments, rent payments and life after college often create stress for older students. Of course, "senioritis" can also have an effect on classrooms as seniors do begin to get a sense of where they are heading and are looking ahead to the next phase.

QUESTIONS FOR DISCUSSION AND SUGGESTED ACTIVITIES

1. Discuss the "previous knowledge" about music that students may have acquired prior to beginning college.
2. Think back to your own freshmen year in music school. Were you a regional treasure? What did that mean for your early experiences? What were your early interactions like with faculty and fellow students?
3. Choose an undergraduate music course and discuss the content that may offer opportunities for assisting students in their growth from dualistic to relativistic thinkers.
4. Since not all students in a course will be alike in terms of learning styles, discuss the implications of aural, visual, and kinesthetic learning styles on your course planning and instruction.
5. Discuss your own learning styles and the potential impact of your learning style on your teaching style.
6. Choose a music course and discuss some ways to allow for some student "choice" as a motivational strategy.
7. Discuss the characteristics of "self-regulatory" learners in relation to music courses.
8. Discuss gender issues that you may have seen or experienced in your own school experiences.
9. What are your concerns regarding cultural diversity and teaching?
10. Discuss some of the strategies for getting to know you as a person that your past professors have modeled.
11. Reflect back on your own experiences as a freshmen or sophomore. What do you remember about that time in your own growth?
12. Have coffee or lunch with a freshman or sophomore music student and interview them about their experiences.
13. Discuss challenges associated with teaching courses that include students at multiple ages (i.e., freshmen, sophomores, juniors, seniors). What are the strategies for addressing individual differences in student development in the context of the class?
14. Reflect back on your own experiences as a junior or senior. What do you remember about that time in your own growth?
15. Have coffee or lunch with a junior or senior music student and interview them about their experiences.
16. Consider innovative programs for career development for undergraduate music students. Discuss implementation within schools or departments of music.

CHAPTER 4

The Syllabus

The syllabus is arguably the single most important document for any course you are teaching. It is the document that governs the structure, content, and grading criteria for the course. The syllabus may be described as a kind of "contract" agreed upon by you and the students at the beginning of the course. Consequently, the syllabus must be written with great attention to detail and careful forethought. If you find yourself having to revise your syllabus during the semester, we recommend you do this in conjunction with your students, much like renegotiating a contract. Revising due dates, project requirements, or examination schedules without discussion can lead to poor student–teacher relations. Students lose confidence in teachers who appear to be disorganized. Some students will use the lack of organization on the instructor's part as an excuse to be disorganized in their work for the course. Therefore, we recommend careful consideration of all aspects of the course as you construct your syllabus.

Before you begin to design your syllabus, ask your department chair for sample syllabi and any specific requirements or guidelines required by the department. In particular, check to see if there are specific outcomes and/or assessment requirements. In order to meet state certification requirements, many schools are incorporating assessment tools into their department courses. The information collected by these assessment tools is used to create department-wide reports often required for certification.

Chapter 1 discusses the importance of selecting a text prior to writing the syllabus. The text often dictates the structure of a course, particularly academic courses like theory and history. Applied instructors will want to consider jury repertoire requirements and recital expectations as they write their syllabus. Most departments have requirements and policies in place for applied lessons and it is important to fully understand these policies prior to writing your syllabus.

Many college instructors are now choosing to put their syllabi online. In addition to the ecological benefits of saving a tremendous amount of paper, an online syllabus allows for a document that is always accurate and up-to-date. It also allows for the instructor to provide a tremendous amount of detail in describing assignments, projects and examinations. An online syllabus allows one to create links to other important sites and documents related to the course. If an error is made in the original document or if some part of the syllabus needs more description, the instructor can make those amendments to the online syllabus and avoid making new hardcopies each time there is an adjustment. The benefits of an online syllabus are limited only by one's imagination.

There are drawbacks to the online syllabus. Unless your students all have regular, uninterrupted access to the internet, they may use internet outages as an excuse for not getting assignments in on time. If you provide both a hard copy and an internet syllabus, there will be questions as to which one is right (this will also be an issue if you provide more than one hard copy version of your syllabus during the semester). If you use an online syllabus, it makes it difficult to refer to the syllabus while in class unless you and your students have internet access in the classroom. Often, instructors like to talk through the syllabus in their first class meeting, discussing assignments, projects, and course materials. This can be difficult to do without everyone holding a hard copy. No doubt the day will come when we all will have laptop computers and regular internet access so that you and your students can bring up the syllabus together in class. Until then, the online syllabus will have some growing pains. A hybrid syllabus design that is part hard copy and part online may be the best way to bridge this gap.

Depending on the course and its requirements, some syllabi may be only one page in length while others may be several pages. Regardless of its length, the syllabus traditionally consists of the following six parts:

Course Title and Instructor Information

At the top of your first page, list the course number and title as it is listed by the registrar in the college catalogue. This is important because this is what will appear on the student's transcript in the future. If you decide to call the course something else, the student will have no record of it on their transcript. In order to change the title and/or course number officially, you must work with your department chair and probably have to send your changes to a curriculum committee for approval before the change goes to the registrar. This is often a lengthy and complicated task. Unless you have a very good reason for changing anything about the course as it is listed by the registrar, we recommend you retain the original title and number. Instructor information should include your professional name, office location, office hours, office phone number, and your e-mail address. You should also include the web link to the course web site, if you have one.

Course Description or Purpose

This part of the syllabus is described at length in Chapter 1. The course description or purpose usually consists of two to four sentences that broadly describe the genre and scope of a particular course. Some colleges require the course description in the syllabus to match the description listed in the college catalogue. This is important to the registrar's office for record-keeping purposes. A student's college transcript will reflect a course number and title that the registrar can use as a reference to a specific description listed in college records. If a student chooses to transfer to another college or go on to graduate school, this information can be very important in determining a student's qualifications and standing. Whether your institution requires you to use the official catalogue description or not, we recommend you use it at least as a starting point for your own course description.

Course Content or Objectives

This part of the syllabus was also discussed at length in Chapter 1. The course content or objectives usually consists of a paragraph that describes the various topics to be studied and may include a list of skills, outcomes, or goals expected to be attained by the students by the end of the course of study. Some instructors opt to discuss this part of a syllabus with students in a course on the first day and to negotiate content based on student feedback. The content listed here is what you will assess when you determine grades for your students. It is important that you create a clear connection between your content and your assessment for grading (described at length in Chapter 2). As is discussed in Chapter 2, it is sometimes appropriate to involve students in the design of assessments and grading in an early class meeting.

Required and Recommended Materials

List all materials required for the course. Provide full bibliographic information for texts, scores and compendiums. If you expect students to bring staff paper, be sure to specify what kind you want and be sure the bookstore provides it. We also recommend that you request the college library to have a copy of the texts, scores, and recordings you require on reserve. This provides a safety net to students who lose materials or if the bookstore runs out of something. Be sure to ask the library to put them on reserve for the semester so that a student cannot check them out. Order your texts early at the bookstore. Remember that if you change to a new text, you may be forcing students and the bookstore eat the cost of nonreturnable used texts. While this should not be a determining factor in your choosing a textbook, it might be something to consider if your text change is not absolutely necessary. Recommended materials are just that—they are not materials that you expect the students to buy, but if they wish to augment their knowledge, they may choose to purchase this additional material. Do not list a text as recommended and then expect to make an assignment based on that material. If you decide to use a course pack (a collection of readings that you assemble from a variety of resources) you must be sure to retain the rights to reproduce those materials from the various publishers. Most bookstores will provide this service, but it requires lots of lead time. Contact your bookstore for information about providing a course pack. Under no circumstance should you photocopy excerpts from books or journals and hand them out to your students without attaining the rights to do so. You and your institution are liable for this illegal act.

Grading Criteria

Procedures for developing grading systems are discussed at length in Chapter 2. In short, the process by which you assess and assign grades must be clearly explained. Grading and assessment should be linked directly to the "Course Content" as described above. Students should receive grades regularly throughout the course, not just at the end. Students cannot improve their performance for you if they do not know where you have placed the bar. Some instructors are diligent about grading an assignment early in the semester so that students understand the difference between average, good, and exceptional work.

The requirements for a term paper, project, or field work (observation) are usually provided in the grading criteria section of the syllabus. Provide a detailed description of what is expected for this component of your course, including how it will be assessed and graded. As discussed in Chapter 6, we recommend that students be given the opportunity to write drafts for large papers. Some instructors grade the initial draft to give the student a context for where they are in their writing process. Providing feedback throughout the process of a major project or paper can help a student learn better how to develop their ideas and provide guidance through to the end product.

When assigning final grades, most colleges give instructors the opportunity to assign an "incomplete" to a student who was unable to complete some portion of the course work due the extenuating circumstances. This usually comes in the form of a student not completing a paper or project on time. While this can be a helpful grading option for a student who has experienced a difficult semester, you may find some students who request an "incomplete" regularly due to poor planning on their part. Reserve the use of an "incomplete" for the students who truly deserve it and grade procrastinators appropriately.

Including an attendance policy as part of your grade is important for most courses. However, if the content covered during class time is included in your assessment of student work, students will soon learn that they cannot afford to miss class without their absence taking a toll on their grade. This type of attendance control is fairly easy to implement in music theory, history, or methods course. Chapter 5 discusses attendance issues at length.

Assigning grades in applied lessons presents specific challenges to traditional grading practices. The progress in an applied lesson is difficult to measure by a set standard. Musical growth is often accompanied by emotional growth (some might even say turmoil). Applied teachers must assess each student individually and at the same time maintain a set standard in the studio. Strategies for assessing applied lessons are discussed at length in Chapter 8. Here we will simply say that clear and consistent expectations must be spelled out to each student from the very beginning of EACH term and regular communication about a student's progress in relation to a "grade" is essential.

Course Outline or Calendar

The course outline provides students with a week-by-week outline of what will take place in class. It should include weekly topics or objectives (drawn from the "Course Content" section above) as well as examination dates, due dates for papers, and other important calendar events. Be sure to get a copy of the college calendar before you create this outline so that you may incorporate holidays, special campus events, and college-wide examination schedules. Also be sure to take into account dates for student juries and any special music department events that might need some accommodation such as a master class with a guest artist or large ensemble concert event. Some instructors use the weekly or daily topic(s) listed in their course outline as the header for the lecture notes they create for each class. This helps them align the content of each class with the syllabus throughout the semester.

SAMPLE SYLLABI

The following syllabi are drawn from a wide array of typical music course offerings found in most colleges and universities. While the content varies greatly from course to course, the structure of the syllabi remains fairly consistent. Online syllabi are found easily on the web by doing a simple search.

Applied Music

Instructor's Name:
Office hours: Come by any time between lessons and knock on my door. E-mail me to set up an appointment if you need to meet more privately.
Office phone:
E-mail:

Course Objectives

The ultimate goal for a student of any discipline is to become their own teacher. Once you all have reached that point, you'll continue to cycle through the learning process so fluently that no secondary goal will be unobtainable. The studio objectives listed below will be the means to becoming your own teacher.

- Musicality: Student's musical instincts will be nurtured and discovered.
- Technique: Students will start on their own healthy path towards physical coordination, awareness, and efficiency in relation to their instruments.
- Repertoire: Students will be able to play, recognize, speak, and think intelligently about the cello repertoire. Appropriate repertoire will be assigned depending on the student's goals.

Grading

Musical progress is difficult to assess. It is not reasonable to expect aural and physical proof of progress in every lesson—much like it would be unreasonable to expect a seed to spawn a flower without growing in the earth first. The following criteria will apply to everyone, but case-by-case considerations will be made based on the student's goals and capabilities.

- Attendance 25%
- Attitude 25%
- Quality of Preparation 25%
- Jury or Recital Hearing 25%

Attendance is mandatory for all lessons, studio classes, and recitals held by your studio colleagues. I will take attendance, even if you don't see me doing so! Please find a lesson time that has no possibility of scheduling conflicts—you may not cancel your lesson unless there are extenuating circumstances. Every two absences from studio class or a studio recital will lower your final attendance grade by one letter marking. If you miss a lesson without prior communication with me, your overall grade will be lowered by one letter. Please keep me informed if you can foresee any conflicts.

Attitude and Quality of Preparation are paramount in the learning cycle. Here is how I will grade these two:

Attitude

Grade	Student is...	
A:	Always...	
B:	Mostly...	*positive, supportive, enthusiastic,*
C:	Sometimes...	*open-minded, thinking freely*
D:	Rarely...	
F:	Never...	

Quality of Preparation

Grade	Student is...	
A:	Always...	
B:	Mostly...	*arriving with the correct materials,*
C:	Sometimes...	*prepared technically and musically*
D:	Rarely...	*for lessons, applying concepts from*
F:	Never...	*lessons in the practice room*

Juries are your "final exam" for applied lessons and are held during exam week at the end of each semester. You will need approximately 10 minutes of music prepared for each jury and you will receive written feedback from a panel of string faculty.

Junior and Senior recitals are required of performance majors. Programs and program length will be determined in your lessons. The grade for your recital will be given by a panel of string faculty in a recital hearing approximately 3 weeks before your recital date.

Once a letter grade is determined for each of the four criteria, they will be averaged and that will be your final grade for the semester.

Studio Class

The studio will meet once a week on Tuesdays from 1:30 to 3:30. A sign-up sheet will be placed on my door for the upcoming week's performances. I may suggest a performance to a student in a lesson, or a student may sign-up on their own. Everyone must play at least three times per semester. If students are not volunteering, I will create a permanent rotation schedule for the semester.

Practicing

Everyone is expected to practice everyday! How much to practice may be different for each student. I would suggest, as a rule of thumb, to practice each day for as many credit hours as you are taking applied lessons. Example: 4 credit hours of applied lessons = 4 daily practice hours. Practicing good habits in rehearsals are always encouraged, but rehearsals do not count as "practiced hours".

The most important concept to understand about practicing is that it must always be relaxed, focused, organized, and goal-oriented.

One of my primary objectives during the lesson is to give advice on how to create this healthy environment with your instrument.

Required Materials

Besides your instrument and its accessories, I require my students to have their own of the following:

- metronome (capable of a drone and tempi ranging below 30 bpm)
- a tuner (may be in combination with a metronome)
- a planner to organize rehearsal and practice schedules
- a notebook for practicing, studio class, lessons, master classes, etc.
- when possible, hard copies of current repertoire

Communication

The studio has a great opportunity to get to know one another, create an environment that is conducive to learning and enjoy wonderful musical experiences together. This can happen if we keep the positive and constructive communication at a high level. Feel free to stop by my office with your cello and ask a question. Feel free to e-mail me with problems or concerns at any time. Feel free to knock on your studio mate's practice room to ask for advice or to give a mini-practice-room performance! I guarantee that your experience here will be enhanced if you have a solid network of friends and colleagues who all enjoy the same passion for music.

Music Theory

Instructor's Name:
Office hours:
Office Phone:
E-mail:

Course Description

This is an integrated theory course dealing with perception, writing, analysis, and performance of fundamental musical materials, and stylistic comprehension of music of all periods, with emphasis on the Common Practice Period. Corequisites: Aural Skills class of same level.

Course Objectives

To develop fundamental technical knowledge, skill, and musical vocabulary in the student; to enable the student to approach and understand music from any period or style;

and to develop the ability to discern patterns of music. Music Theory is the language of and gateway to musical understanding of style, composition, arranging, performing, conducting, and mature musicianship.

Required Textbook and Materials

Benward and Saker, *Music in Theory and Practice, vol. 2*, Seventh Ed., McGraw Hill Manuscript (Staff) Paper and pencils.

Attendance and Class Participation

It is expected and required that students attend ALL classes. I will allow one unexcused absence; however, your second unexcused absence will count as two unexcused absences. A third unexcused absence will lower your semester grade by one letter. An excused absence can result from illness (with a doctor's note) or the death of a family member, or another event that the instructor approves at least 24 hours before the absence is to take place. In case of inclement weather, we will follow college policy. This is a lecture/discussion course. Much time will be spent with students working at the chalkboard, discussing the previous and following assignments, listening to lectures, taking quizzes, and generally honing skills. Therefore, you must be present to understand how to get the work done and receive credit.

Assignments

Look ahead daily on the last pages of this syllabus to see what assignment(s) you will be turning in at the BEGINNING of the following class period. All work must be done IN PENCIL on the Xerox sheet provided in the previous class period. Other work may be assigned from your workbook; do it in PENCIL. Your work will be graded on its accuracy, neatness, and your ability to follow instructions.

Academic Honesty

Students are expected to hold themselves to the highest standards of academic honesty. Although you are encouraged to work and discuss topics and ideas with other students, all homework, projects, and exam work must be yours and yours alone. Any evidence of plagiarism, submitting work done by another individual, or doing assignment or exam work for another individual is strictly forbidden, and if discovered, you will receive the maximum penalty, which could include flunking this class. Do your own work. Help others (except during exams), but don't do their work!

Examinations

There will be three written examinations plus the comprehensive final examination. Missing any of these will cost you dearly. There are no make-ups for unexcused absences on Exam days.

Quizzes

These may be given at any time as the instructor sees fit. At your instructor's ultimate discretion, quizzes may count toward your grade or may be used simply for attendance or to prepare the student for an upcoming exam or to understand the homework. Quizzes may be written, aural, or cover basic keyboard skills.

Final Project

This will be an individual analysis or composition project, with details announced further into the semester.

Please Note

As you know from previous Music Theory work, this is not an "easy" class; it will require persistence and tenacity on your part. Expect to spend a couple of hours on each homework assignment, and the grade you receive is the grade you EARN. All aspects of the course (and your musical future) build upon the foundation of knowledge and skill sets acquired with each assignment. In order to cover the material in a timely manner, no homework will be accepted after its due date unless other arrangements have been made directly with the instructor. No work will be accepted during or after Finals Week.

Grading Scale

A = 90–100
B = 80–89
C = 70–79
D = 60–69
F = 59.9999…and below

Final Grade Calculation

Class Participation:	10%
Exam 1:	10%
Exam 2:	10%
Exam 3:	10%
Final Exam:	20%
Homework:	20%
Quizzes:	10%
Final Project:	10%

Course Schedule

This is a tentative outline of the information to be covered over the Fall semester; it is subject to change, so you must attend each class in order to ensure you will stay on top of things.

Date	Class Agenda & Chapter Topics	Assignments (due dates)
Week 1		
M 8/29	Orientation, REVIEW	
W 8/31	Review, 2/Two-Voice 18th-Cent Counterpoint	
F 9/2	2/Two-Voice 18th-Cent Counterpoint	pp. 39–40: 2.1

Week 2
M 9/5   *Labor Day* (no class)
W 9/7   2/Two-Voice 18th-Century Counterpoint   p. 41: 2.2
F 9/9   2/Two-Voice 18th-Century Counterpoint   p. 42: 2.3

Week 3
M 9/12   2/Two-Voice 18th-Century Counterpoint   p. 43: 2.4
W 9/14   3/The Fugue   p. 63: 3.1
F 9/16   3/The Fugue   pp. 64–66: 3.2 (expo only)

Week 4
M 9/19   3/The Fugue   pp. 64–66: 3.2 (remainder of fugue)
W 9/21   3/The Fugue   [receive handout]
F 9/23   3/The Fugue   [handout due]

Week 5
M 9/26   EXAMINATION 1: Chapters 2–3
W 9/28   4/Borrowed Chords
F 9/30   4/Borrowed Chords   p. 75: 4.1

Week 6
M 10/3   4/Borrowed Chords   pp. 75–76, 4.2
W 10/5   4/Borrowed Chords   p. 77: 4.3
F 10/7   5/Neapolitan 6th Chords

Week 7
M 10/10   *Fall Break* (no class)
W 10/12   5/Neapolitan 6th Chords   p. 85: 5.1
F 10/14   5/Neapolitan 6th Chords   pp. 85–6: 5.2

Week 8
M 10/17   6/Augmented 6th Chords   p. 87: 5.3
W 10/19   6/Augmented 6th Chords   p. 101, 6.1, 6.2
F 10/21   6/Augmented 6th Chords   pp. 101–102: 6.3

Week 9
M 10/24   6/Augmented 6th Chords   p. 103: 6.4
W 10/26   6/Augmented 6th Chords   pp. 106–107: 6.6
F 10/28   (Review Chapters 5 and 6)

Week 10
M 10/31   EXAMINATION 2: Chapters 4–6
W 11/2   7/Variation Technique   **Discuss requirements of composition project**

F 11/4   7/Variation Technique   p. 119, 7.1
                                                         Improv over given bass

Week 11

M 11/7	7/Variation Technique	p. 120, 7.2
		Improv over given bass
W 11/9	8/Sonata Form	p. 127, 7.4
		(begin pp. 149–158, 8.1)
F 11/11	8/Sonata Form	
Week 12		
M 11/14	8/Sonata Form	
W 11/16	8/Sonata Form	
F 11/18	8/Sonata Form	pp. 149–158, 8.1
Week 13		
M 11/21	8/Sonata Form	**Composition Project Rough Draft due**
W 11/23	*Thanksgiving Break* (no class)	
F 11/25	*Thanksgiving Break* (no class)	
Week 14		
M 11/28	9/Rondo Forms	
W 11/30	9/Rondo Forms	pp. 167–170, 9.1
F 12/2	EXAMINATION 3	
Week 15		
M 12/5	(review for Final, loose ends)	
W 12/7	**Composition Project DUE**	
F 12/9	(review for Final)	
Week 16		
F 12/16	FINAL EXAMINATION	Friday, noon to 2 pm

Aural Skills

Instructor's Name:
Office hours:
Office phone:
E-mail:

Course Description

This is the first of four courses designed to develop the music student's ability to perceive rhythm, melody, harmony, and form. Through a series of sight reading, listening, and aural dictation exercises, the student will enhance his/her ability to hear and understand musical structure.

Course Content

The course will begin with an introduction to rhythm syllables and solfege. We will then proceed with diatonic intervals, triads, simple melodies, and rhythm exercises. Solfege drills in major and minor keys and rhythmic exercises in simple and compound meters will be a focus for the course.

Required Materials

Text: Ottman, Robert W. *Music for Sight Singing.* 6th edition, (2003).
MacGamut Ear Training Software. 2003 edition w/ 2006 update
Standard, unbarred staff paper available in bookstore

Solfege and dictation quizzes:	50%
Midterm grade:	25%
Final Exam grade:	25%
McGamut assignments:	Pass/fail

Grading

Grading is based on the synthesis of grades accumulated through solfege and dictation quizzes and tests. You must complete ALL McGamut assignments in order to receive a passing grade.

Weekly Outline

Week 1
Introduction to Ear Training
Chapter 1: Rhythm—Simple Time

Week 2
Introduction to McGamut software
Chapter 2: Melody—Solfege in Major Keys

Week 3
Chapter 4: Rhythm—Compound Time
MacGamut SCALES (1): Major/minor ascending form
Solfege quiz

Week 4
Chapters 3 and 4: Solfege in Major Keys; Simple & Compound Time
MacGamut SCALES (2): M/m Asc / Desc notate accidentals
Dictation quiz

Week 5
Chapters 3 and 4: Solfege cont.,
MacGamut SCALES (3): M/m Dorian, Mixolydian

Week 6
Chapters 3 and 4: Solfege cont.,
Introduce Asc intervals: P1, m2, M2, m3, M3, P4, Tri, P5, m6, M6, m7, M7, P8
MacGamut INTERVALS (1): Melodic Asc 3 choices

Week 7
Midterm exam
    Chapters 1–4
    MacGamut SCALES (3) and INTERVALS (1)

Week 8
Chapter 5: Minor keys in simple & compound time
Introduce triads: M, m, d, A
MacGamut CHORDS—(1): Triads, M/m root position

Week 9
Chapter 5: Minor keys, cont.,
MacGamut   INTERVALS (2): Melodic 4 choices (Asc & Desc)
                 SCALES (4): M/m, Phrygian, Lydian

Week 10
Chapter 5: Minor keys, cont.,
Introduce harmonic dictation (V-I cadences)
MacGamut HARMONIC (1): Major (2 primary chords)
Solfege quiz

Week 11
Chapter 6: Melodies in Major and Minor keys
Introduce 1st position triads (M, m, d)
MacGamut CHORDS (2): Triads, M, m, d, A root position
Dictation quiz

Week 12
Chapter 6: Melodies cont.,
MacGamut   INTERVALS (3): Melodic 6 choices
                 SCALES (5): M/m, Dorian, Mixolydian, asc / desc

Week 13
Chapter 6: Melodies cont.,
MacGamut   HARMONIC (2): Major keys (any 2 chords)
                 CHORDS (3): Triads M/m root / 1st position

Week 14
Chapter 6: Melodies cont.,
MacGamut INTERVALS (4); CHORDS (4): Triads root / 1st position

Week 15
Prepare for **Final Examination**
Chapters 1–6

MacGamut		
	INTERVALS (4)	Asc/Desc, all choices listed
	SCALES (5)	M/m, Dorian, Mixolydian, asc / desc
	CHORDS (4)	Triads, root / 1st position
	HARMONIC (2)	Major keys (any 2 chords)

Music History

Instructor's Name:
Office hours:
Office Phone:
E-mail:

Purpose

This course provides music students with an in-depth study of music history and literature of the nineteenth century. The principal composers, genres and forms of the era will be an emphasis. The influence of nonwestern music and relations to other art forms will be identified. Students will also engage in daily listening, analysis, research and writing, and the application of these skills in preparing papers and projects.

Content

The course will begin with a review of the developments in the Baroque and Classical eras that provided the foundation for the music of the Romantic era. References to nonwestern practices and their influence on western music will be incorporated throughout. An in-depth study of Beethoven's compositional style will be followed by an introduction to other composers of the era. The development of "romanticism" shall be studied in orchestral, as well as solo, chamber, and vocal music of the nineteenth century. An in-depth study of opera and the development of the music drama will complete the course.

Materials

Required text:
A History of Western Music, 6th ed. (Grout/Palisca), 2001

Recommended:
Norton Anthology of Western Music, Vol. 2., 4th ed. (Palisca), 2001
Concise Norton Recorded Anthology of Western Music, 4 CDs (Palisca), 2001
Study and Listening Guide, 6th ed. (Burkholder), 2001

Grading

3 exams	45%
Final exam	20%
1 paper	20%
1 oral presentation	15%

Course Outline

Week 1
Overview of syllabus, materials, course outline, and a discussion about how to be successful in studying music history
Review of Baroque and Classical music forms up to the nineteenth century

Week 2
Select topic for paper and presentation
Ludwig van Beethoven
The first and second period

Week 3
Beethoven's third period

Week 4
Examination 1
Symphonic works of the nineteenth century, part 1
Schubert and Berlioz

Week 5
Outline of paper is due
Symphonic works of the nineteenth century, part 2
Mendelssohn, Schumann and Liszt

Week 6
Brahms and Bruckner

Week 7
Symphonic works of the nineteenth century, part 4
Tchaikovsky and Dvorak

Week 8
Examination 2
Music for the piano
Important nonwestern musical practices and developments of the period

Week 9
First draft of paper is due
Chamber music
The development of the Lied, part 1
Schubert

Week 10
Begin oral presentations in class
The development of the Lied, part 2
Robert and Clara Schumann, and Brahms
Choral music

Week 11
Examination 3
Development of opera, part 1
Italy
Nonwestern musical comparisons to opera

Week 12
Development of opera, part 2
France
Giuseppe Verdi

Week 13
Development of opera, part 3
Germany

Richard Wagner and the Music Drama

Week 14
Final Draft of paper is due
Review for final exam ·

Week 15
Comprehensive Final Examination

Survey of Music for Nonmajors

Instructor's Name:
Office Hours:
Office phone:
E-mail:

Course Description

The primary goal of Music 101 is to expose students to a variety of music and musical experiences, both in and outside of class. Topics include: elements of music, common styles periods of concert music (baroque, classical, romantic, 20th century), jazz, popular music, musical theater, movie music, and world music. Every class will include listening as well as small-group discussion of textbook material.

Course Objectives

1) Students will become familiar with common terms used to describe musical elements.
2) Students will learn to identify and describe musical characteristics of concert music drawn from the baroque, classical, romantic, and 20th century eras.
3) Students will attend both a symphony orchestra and an opera performance.
4) Students will learn to identify and describe musical characteristics of select repertoire chosen from jazz, popular, musical theater, and world music.

Required Materials

1) Zorn, J. D., and August, J. (2007). *Listening to music* (5th ed.). Upper Saddle River, NJ: Pearson/Prentice Hall.
2) Opera ticket fee: $10—DUE Thurs. 9/6 in class!

Course Assignments

1) *Listening* to music is the number one most important component of this course. Weekly listening assignments are outlined in detail on the "Course Repertoire List" (passed out separately). Recordings of all required pieces are available on reserve in the music library or online through CTools. (If you are unfamiliar with CTools, please read the attached handout from ITCS or see me after class.)

Please come to class *everyday* prepared with questions and comments about the assigned pieces. This is not a lecture course. Everyone must do the reading and listening ahead of time. Class will include short lectures followed by small-group discussion.

2) *Journal*: All students will be required to keep a weekly listening journal throughout the semester. The journal makes up a significant part of the course grade, and its purpose is to help you become a thoughtful, active listener while learning how to write about music. Some journal assignments will have specific prompts, but most often you will be asked to reflect on the course listening for the week. Entries should be approx. two pages long (typed/double-spaced) and handed in every Thursday at the start of class. Make a connection between the repertoire and the textbook information in your journal. Grading criteria for the journals will be developed during class.

3) *Concerts*: You will be required to attend three concerts this semester. We will not meet for regular class during the week of the concerts but will meet and sit together at the concert.
   a) University Orchestra: Thursday, September 27, 8 PM, Concert Hall
   b) Los Angeles Opera, Puccini's *Madama Butterfly*: Thursday, October 25, 7 PM, Dorothy Chandler Pavillion**
   c) Concert of your choice (must be approved by instructor in advance).

For a list of on-campus concerts, go to the Music Department website at www..., but anything of the "classical variety" will probably count.

You will write two-page reports for each of the above concerts (detailed guidelines to be developed by the class). For the third concert of your choice, please also turn in a program with your signature.

4) *Quizzes*: There will be three short listening quizzes throughout the semester. For each quiz, I will play two pieces from the unit's repertoire list, and you will be asked to identify the piece and comment on the excerpt.

5) *Exams*: There will be two formal listening exams (a midterm and a final) this semester. Both will include listening identification along the same lines as the quizzes, in addition to short answer responses regarding the pieces from the repertoire list. Journals will provide a "study guide" for the exams.

6) *Attendance*: You are allowed 1 absence per semester with no questions asked, but **each additional absence will diminish your grade by 2 percentage points**. Excused absences (per university policy) must be cleared with me in advance, at the very latest **before 9:00 am** on the day of class.

Breakdown of grade:
Midterm: 15%
Final: 15%
Quizzes (3): 10% (lowest grade to be dropped)

Journal: 30%
Concert reports (3): 10% each

Calendar

Week 1—Course Introduction and Overview
Development of Grading Criteria and Tools
Introduction to Elements of Music

Week 2—The Music Process and the Materials of Music
READ CH 1–5
Active Music-Making with Materials Provided (drums, Orff instruments, etc.)

Week 3
No Regular Class Meeting
Attend Orchestra Concert as a Group

Week 4—The Common Style Periods of Concert Music I
Orchestra Concert Report Due
READ CH 6–11
Listening Maps Completed as a Class

Week 5—The Common Style Periods of Concert Music II
Listening Quiz #1 (Baroque, Classical Era)
READ CH 12–15
Prepare for Opera Performance

Week 6
No Regular Class Meeting
Attend Opera as a Group

Week 7
Midterm Listening Exam Review
Midterm Listening Exam—Repertoire from CH 1–15
Opera Concert Report Due

Week 8—The Common Style Periods of Concert Music III
READ CH 16–19
Guest Music Major Performers Presenting Solos from the Romantic/20th Century
Repertoire

Week 9—Music in the 20th Century and Beyond/Classical Music in North America
READ CH 20–24
Listening Maps Completed as a Class

Week 10—Catch-Up/What I Really Want You to Know About Classical Music
Quiz #2 (Romantic/20th Century)

Week 11—Jazz
READ CH 25
Guest Performance—Music Major Jazz Combo

Week 12—Popular Music in America
READ CH 26
Quiz #3—Jazz

Week 13—Musical Theater and Music of the Movies
READ CH 27 and CH 28

Week 14—World Music
READ CH 29
Meet in the Gamelan on Tuesday and in the Percussion Studio on Thursday

Week 15
Final Exam Review
Final Exam
Final Concert Report Due

Brass Techniques

Instructor's Name:
Office hours:
Office Phone:
E-mail:

Purpose

The Brass methods course is designed to provide music education students with the skills to model and work effectively with students on all brass instruments in group beginning instrumental music classes. In addition, students will gain knowledge and skills of instruments for rehearsing large groups of instrumentalists in secondary ensemble settings.

Content

Topics covered will include: basics of group music instruction; instrument assembly; instrument care, maintenance, and repair; basic instrument playing positions; breathing; tone production; articulation; common problems of beginners; techniques for more advanced students (multiple tonguing; muting, vibrato); resources for purchasing of instruments and materials (mouthpieces, etc.); overview of common methods books and solo literature; and basic characteristics of instruments in the secondary ensemble settings.

Materials

Colwell, R., and Goolsby, T. (2002). *The teaching of instrumental music.* New York: Schirmer.

Grading

1) *Attendance and Class Participation*: Attendance is required. More than two absences from class will result in one full grade lower. Each absence after two will result in an additional half grade reduction.

2) *Peer Teaching* [5%]: Each student in the class will demonstrate skills in teaching a beginning brass lesson on November 13 or 20. Grading criteria to be developed in class.

3) *School and Campus Observations* [20%]: Go out to a local school and do an observation of a beginning brass class lesson in a school setting. In addition, make plans to observe campus band, university band or the Michigan Youth band here on campus. An observation protocol will be developed for both visits in class. Logistics of the school observation visit will be handled in class. Send an e-mail reflection or meet with your PhD Buddy before December 4. Be prepared to discuss your reflections with your PhD Buddy on December 4. (Pass/Fail)

4) *Performance Exam (s) [40 %; 10% each]*: (Requirements for each instrument to include: Description of proper instrument assembly, care, and playing position; demonstration of proper embouchure, articulation and tone production; performance of several scales; performance of two or three short folk tunes from the beginning band book.

5) *Final Resource Notebook* [35%]: Include instrument assembly and care; basic playing positions, embouchure, and posture; breathing, tone production, and articulation for all instruments studied (not including primary instrument). Additional topics to include: basic concepts of repair; issues with real kids; techniques for more advanced players; suggested equipment, and choosing literature with the brass in mind (based primarily on guest presentations). Each instrument should include a list of suggestions and tips based on small-group lesson learning. Grading criteria to be developed in class. Due to Dr. Conway on December 12, 2007.

Failure to complete any of the assignments will result in a grade of "incomplete."

Course Schedule
Tuesdays: 11:40–12:30—Brass Class
Thursdays: 10:40–11:30—Small-group lessons on high brass (trumpet then horn)
Thursdays: 11:30–12:30—Small-group lessons on low brass (tuba then trombone)

September 4/6
Tuesday: Course introduction and overview/development of grading rubrics and observation protocols/instrument sign-out
Thursday: Lesson #1 (trumpet and tuba)—Assembly and Instrument Care
READ: Assembly and Care

September 11/13
Tuesday: "Readiness for Instrumental Instruction"
READ: Two articles provided
Thursday: Lesson #2—Posture, Hand Position, Buzzing
READ: Posture, Hand Position and Buzzing

September 18/20
Tuesday: Activities for Rhythmic Readiness
Thursday: Lesson #3—Embouchure, Tone production, Breathing, Articulation
READ: Embouchure, Tone production, Breathing, Articulation

September 25/27
Tuesday: Activities for Tonal Readiness
Thursday: Lesson #4—TONE and Technique

October 2/4
Tuesday: Chamber Music Rehearsal (Brass quartet)
Thursday: Lesson #5—Advanced Techniques (Double-tongue, muting, stopping, transposition)

October 9/11
Tuesday: Brass Instrument Repair
Thursday: Lesson #6—Recommended Instruments, Mouthpieces, and Instructional Literature

Tuesday, October 16
Fall Study Break—No Class

Thursday, October 18
Playing Exams, Lesson Conclusion

October 23/25
Tuesday: 5th Grade Band Demonstration
Thursday: Lesson #1 (horn and trombone)—Assembly and Instrument Care
READ: Assembly and Care

October 30/November 1
Tuesday: Middle School Band Demonstrations
Thursday: Lesson #2—Posture, Hand Position, Buzzing
READ: Posture, Hand Position, and Buzzing

November 6/8
Tuesday: Chamber Music Rehearsal (Brass Quartet)
Thursday: Lesson #3—Embouchure, Tone production, Breathing, Articulation
READ: Embouchure, Tone production, Breathing, Articulation for each instrument

November 13/15
Tuesday: Peer Teaching
Thursday: Lesson #4—TONE and Technique
Tuesday, November 20
Peer Teaching

November 27/29
Tuesday: Choosing Literature with the Brass in Mind
Thursday: Lesson #5—Advanced Techniques (double-tongue, muting, stopping, transposition)

December 4/6
Tuesday: Group discussion of school visits
Thursday: Final Playing Tests

December 11
Final Resource Notebook Due, Course Conclusions
12:00—Chamber Music Performance in Lobby

Woodwind Techniques

Instructor's Name:
Office hours:
Office Phone:
E-mail:

Purpose

The Woodwinds methods course is designed to provide music education students with the skills to model and work effectively with students on all woodwind instruments in group beginning instrumental music classes. In addition, students will gain knowledge and skills of instruments for rehearsing large groups of instrumentalists in secondary ensemble settings.

Content

Topics covered will include: basics of group music instruction; instrument assembly; instrument care, maintenance, and repair; basic instrument playing positions; breathing; tone production; articulation; common problems of beginners; techniques for more advanced students (multiple tonguing; other instruments; vibrato); resources for purchasing of instruments and materials (mouthpieces, reeds, etc.); overview of common methods books and solo literature; and basic characteristics of instruments in the secondary ensemble settings.

Materials

Colwell, R., and Goolsby, T. (2002). *The teaching of instrumental music.* New York: Schirmer.

Grading

1) *Attendance and Class Participation*: Attendance is required. More than two absences from class will result in one full grade lower. Each absence after two will result in an additional half grade reduction.

2) *Peer Teaching* [5%]: Each student in the class will demonstrate skills in teaching a beginning woodwind lesson on November 13 or 20. Grading criteria to be developed in class.

3) *School and Campus Observations* [20%]: Go out to a local school and do an observation of a beginning woodwind class lesson in a school setting. In addition, make plans to observe campus band, university band, or the Michigan Youth band here on campus. An observation protocol will be developed for both visits in class. Logistics of the school observation visit will be handled in class. Send an e-mail reflection or meet with your PhD Buddy before December 4. Be prepared to discuss your reflections with your PhD Buddy on December 4. (Pass/Fail)

4) *Performance Exam(s)* [50%; 10% each]: Requirements for each instrument to include: Description of proper instrument assembly, care, and playing position; demonstration of proper embouchure, articulation and tone production; performance of several scales; performance of two or three short folk tunes from the beginning band book.

5) *Final Resource Notebook* [25%]: Include instrument assembly and care; basic playing positions, embouchure, and posture; breathing, tone production, and articulation for all instruments studied (not including primary instrument). Additional topics to include: basic concepts of repair; issues with real kids; techniques for more advanced players; suggested equipment, and choosing literature with the woodwinds in mind (based primarily on guest presentations). Each instrument should include a list of suggestions and tips based on small-group lesson learning. Grading criteria to be developed in class.

Failure to complete any of the assignments will result in a grade of "incomplete."

Course Schedule

Tuesdays: 11:40–12:30—Winds Class
Thursdays 10:40–11:30—Small-group lessons on flute, oboe, saxophone
Thursdays 11:30–12:30—Small-group lessons on clarinet, bassoon

September 4/6
Tuesday: Course introduction and overview/development of grading rubrics and observation protocols/instrument sign-out
Thursday: Lesson #1—Assembly and Instrument Care
READ: Assembly and Care

September 11/13
Tuesday: "Readiness for Instrumental Instruction"
READ: Two articles provided
Thursday: Lesson #2—Posture and Hand Position
READ: Posture and Hand Position

September 18/20
Tuesday: Activities for Rhythmic Readiness
Thursday: Lesson #3—Embouchure, Tone production, Breathing, Articulation
READ: Embouchure, Tone production, Breathing, Articulation

September 25/27
Tuesday: Activities for Tonal Readiness
Thursday: Lesson #4—TONE and Technique

October 2/4
Tuesday: Chamber Music Rehearsal (Woodwind Ensembles)
Thursday: Lesson #5—Advanced Techniques (Double-tongue, vibrato)

October 9/11
Tuesday: Woodwind Instrument Repair
Thursday: Lesson #6—Recommended Instruments, Mouthpieces, and Instructional Literature

Tuesday, October 16
Fall Study Break—No Class

Thursday, October 18
Playing Exams, Lesson Conclusion

October 23/25
Tuesday: 5th Grade Band Demonstration
Thursday: Lesson #1—Assembly and Instrument Care
READ: Assembly and Care

October 30/November 1
Tuesday: Middle School Band Demonstrations
Thursday: Lesson #2—Posture and Hand Position
READ: Posture and Hand Position

November 6/8
Tuesday: Chamber Music Rehearsal (Woodwind Ensembles)
Thursday: Lesson #3—Embouchure, Tone production, Breathing, Articulation
READ: Embouchure, Tone production, Breathing, Articulation for each instrument

November 13/15
Tuesday: Peer Teaching
Thursday: Lesson #4—TONE and Technique

Tuesday, November 20
Peer Teaching

November 27/29
Tuesday: Choosing Literature with the Woodwinds in Mind
Thursday: Lesson #5—Advanced Techniques (double-tongue, vibrato)

December 4/6
Tuesday: Group discussion of school visits
Thursday: Final Playing Tests

Tuesday, December 11
Final Resource Notebook Due, Course Conclusions
12:00—Chamber Music Performance in Lobby

Percussion Techniques

Instructor's Name:
Office hours:
Office phone:
E-mail address:

Purpose

The purpose of this class is to provide the music education student with modeling skills, teaching techniques, and pedagogy tools on percussion as applied to K-12 music education.

Structure

The course has been structured to provide foundational experiences applicable to most music education positions. Specific, intermediate and advanced experiences will be provided for specific education circumstances, e.g., middle school band, high school orchestra, elementary general music. An effort has been made to provide flexibility so that students may avail themselves of topics, skills, and techniques that are most relevant to their career aspirations and interests.

Objectives

As a result of this course, students will

- demonstrate adequate modeling skills on orchestral and classroom instruments
- learn & apply historical information about percussion instruments & their use in school music
- describe a variety of pitched and unpitched percussion instruments from the listener's perspective
- demonstrate a variety of pitched and unpitched percussion instruments from the educator's and performer's perspective
- improvise using percussion instruments
- arrange/compose for percussion instruments
- interpret percussion parts from an instrumental score
- use percussion instruments effectively and musically in a teaching demonstration
- observe percussion learning, teaching, and performing at a variety of skill levels
- experience the use of percussion instruments in a multicultural context
- design and share teaching strategies and organizational tools
- acquire & organize a wide range of material related to the use of percussion in music education.

Materials

To be purchased:

- Tom Siwe *Percussion: A Course of Study for the Future Band and Orchestra Director*
- One pair of Pro-Mark (TX2B) snare drum sticks (wooden tip) from a local merchant or from www.steveweissmusic.com or www.percussionsource.com

Provided to you:

- Practice pad with stand
- One pair of timpani mallets
- Two pairs of yarn keyboard mallets
- One stick bag
- One pair glockenspiel mallets
- One student glockenspiel

The items above will be checked at the end of the semester for unusual wear and tear and the student may be assessed a fee for repair or replacement. If the equipment is not returned at the end of the semester, a hold will be placed on the student's grades until the equipment is returned or replaced.

Assignments and Assessments

1) *Playing exams and technique quizzes*—Students will have an opportunity to demonstrate significant playing skills on snare, timpani, and mallet percussion, along with quick check-ups on other instruments and skills. (~150 points)

2) *Observations/Teacher's Guide*—Attend any approved event and submit a 1–2 page reflection on the use of percussion and playing techniques at the event, or prepare a teacher's guide on a specific percussion topic. Complete either 3 observations or 2 observations and one project. (50 points)

   a) *If you choose observations*, submit 2–3 pages that include (1) specific instruments and techniques you observe, (2) the ensemble skills and textural devices of percussionists and percussion writing, and, if appropriate, (3) overall relationship of percussion to the total ensemble.

   A partial list of observation examples includes

   • Percussion Ensemble: TR 12:30–2:30
   • Band or Orchestra rehearsals/concerts
   • Marching Drum Line rehearsal
   • World music ensembles that include perc. (GAMELAN: Thurs 4:30–6 & 7–9)

   b) *If you choose to produce a guide* it should include information on history and background, details on the instruments and how they are played, and a discography of music that demonstrates the particular area. Topics could be but are not limited to: Gamelan, East Indian, Central American Marimba, New Orleans Brass Band Tradition, Pacific Islands Percussion, Celtic percussion, West African Drumming (Senegalese or Ghanaian), Japanese Taiko, Electronic Percussion.

3) *Budget Project Outline*—You have just been hired as one of two instrumental teachers to open a new school, Thumbnail Middle School, in a growing, middle class, rural community. You get to buy equipment for a 6–8 school in which students begin instruments in 6th grade. With your colleague, draw up a budget to purchase $15,000 in percussion equipment for the school. Use www.steveweissmusic.com and similar catalogs and websites. You may purchase used equipment if you wish.

   You will turn in a hard copy, formatted either as a table in MSWord or a Spreadsheet. Include all relevant information necessary to purchase the equipment, including make, model, catalog numbers, and cost, including a total. You do not have to factor in shipping or tax. (50 points)

4) *Teaching demonstration*—Plan and execute a musical percussion event that demonstrates your ability to prepare, model, respond to students, and sequence instruction. (50 points)

5) *Written Final Exam*—multiple choice, short answer, and essay. (100 points)

Attendance—Attend each class meeting and participate at a high level. While the class usually meets three times each week, you are required to attend two meetings; thus expect to attend 28 sessions, not including the final. Any absence or any two late arrivals without prior notification will result in a lowered course grade.

Weather—The university does not close, so assume we will have class. If the public schools close, and driving looks dangerous, then we may cancel or reschedule a class. If so, you'll receive an e-mail by 7:30 am.

Grades—Letter grades will be determined based on the point totals (out of approx. 400 possible) with adjustments made for attendance.

Calendar

Attendance at 28 meetings (plus the final exam) is necessary for a perfect grade. In general, everyone attends a lecture/demo once a week and a lab once a week, with exceptions as agreed upon and noted in the course calendar. For every meeting, have all materials and set up bells and pad for class unless otherwise instructed. The readings listed below are drawn from the Siwe text along with handouts provided.

Week One
Course Overview,Types of Equipment, Taking Care of the Equipment,
Logistics/Lockers
Pretest of Skills

Week Two
Some History of the Percussion Family (READ)
Tunes on Mallets/Beginning Snare (Hand Position, Posture)

Week Three
The Snare Drum (READ)
Beginning Rudiments

Week Four
Timpani/Cymbals (READ)
Skills on Timpani/Meet in Timpani Room

Week Five
The Bass Drum (READ)

Week Six
Triangle, Tambourine, and Castanets (READ)
Midterm Skills Review (mallets and snare)

Week Seven
Playing Exams (mallets and snare) and Peer Teaching

Week Eight
Small Wooden and Resonant Metal Instruments (READ)
Discussion of School Observations
Observation Reports Due

Review for Timpani Exam

Week Nine
Marimba, Xylophone, Orchestra Bells, Chimes, Vibes (READ)
Playing Exam—Timpani

Week Ten
Drum Set (READ)
Meet in Drum Set Studio

Week Eleven
Marching Percussion (READ)
Meet in Marching Rehearsal Space

Week Twelve
World Music Drumming (READ)

Week Thirteen
Care and Repair of Percussion Instruments (READ)
Percussion Budget Assignment Due
Review for Final Playing Exam (snare and mallet)

Week Fourteen
Classroom Percussion Instruments (READ)
Advanced Snare and Mallet Exam
Review for classroom percussion exam

Week Fifteen
Discussion of Second School Observation
School Observation Paper Due
Classroom Percussion Playing Exam

FURTHER READING: PART ONE

Course Planning and Preparation

Bain, Ken. 2004. *What the best college teachers do.* Cambridge, MA: Harvard University Press.

Biggs, John. 2003. *Teaching for quality learning at university: What the student does* 2nd ed.). Maidenhead, Berkshire, UK: Open University Press.

Boyle, J. David and Rudolph E. Radocy. 1987. *Measurement and evaluation of musical experiences.* New York: Schirmer Books.

Conway, Colleen 1997. Authentic assessment in undergraduate brass methods class. *Journal of Music Teacher Education*, 7 (1): 6–15.

Curzon, Anne and Lisa Damour. 2006. *First day to final grade* (2nd ed.). Ann Arbor: University of Michigan Press.

Davis, Barbara G. 1993. *Tools for teaching.* San Francisco, CA: Jossey-Bass.

Diamond, Robert M. 1998. *Designing and assessing courses and curricula: A practical guide.* San Francisco, CA: Jossey-Bass.

Eble, Kenneth K. 1988. *The craft of teaching* (2nd ed.). San Francisco, CA: Jossey-Bass.

Fink, Dee L. 2003. *Creating significant learning experiences: An integrated approach to designing college courses.* San Francisco, CA: Jossey-Bass.

Huba, Mary E. and Jann E. Freed. 2000. *Learner-centered assessment on college campuses: Shifting the focus from teaching to learning.* Boston, MO: Allyn and Bacon.

Palmer, Parker. 1998. *The courage to teach.* San Francisco, CA: Jossey-Bass.

Walvoord, Barbara E., and Virginia Johnson Anderson 1998. *Effective grading: A tool for learning and assessment.* San Francisco, CA: Jossey-Bass.

Weimer, Maryellen. 2002. *Learner-centered teaching: Five key changes to practice.* San Francisco, CA: Jossey-Bass.

Undergraduate Development

Belenky, Mary Field, Blythe Mcvicker Clinchy, Nancy Rule Goldeberger, and Jill Mattuck Tarule. 1997. *Women's ways of knowing: The development of self, voice and mind.* New York: Basic Books Inc.

Erickson, Bette Lasere, Calvin B. Peters, and Diane Weltner Strommer. 2006. *Teaching first-year college students* (Rev. and expanded ed.). San Francisco, CA: Jossey-Bass.

Gilligan, Carol. 1982. *In a different voice: Psychological theory and women's development.* Cambridge, MA: Harvard University Press.

Perry, William G. 1999. *Forms of ethical and intellectual development in the college* years. San Francisco, CA: Jossey-Bass.

The Culture of Music Schools

Kingsbury, Henry. 1988. *Music, talent, and performance: A conservatory cultural system.* Philadelphia, PA: Temple University Press.

Nettl, Bruno. 1995. *Heartland excursions: Ethnomusicological reflections on schools of music.* Urbana: University of Illinois Press.

Theories of Motivation and Self-Regulation

Brophy, Jere. 2004. *Motivating students to learn.* Mahwah, NJ: Erlbaum.

PART TWO

Issues in Teaching and Learning

CHAPTER 5

Creating a Culture for Learning

This chapter will assist the new professor in creating a culture for learning in the classroom. We begin with a discussion of the teaching personality, reflection on teaching, power and control in the classroom, and issues of identity as a professor. The middle section of the chapter gets at the "nitty gritty" of preparing for the first day of class; assessing prior knowledge, experience, and interest; weekly class planning; interaction with readings and materials; and student assignments. The final section of the chapter focuses on communication with students and dealing with difficult situations.

TEACHING PERSONALITY

A focus on learner-centered pedagogy and a move away from the transmission model of teaching requires the music professor to create a classroom that is open for questions, dialogue, and learning. Since so much of music instruction focuses on the "apprentice" model that is common in the applied studio it is sometimes difficult for the new professor or graduate instructor to find what might be called their "teaching persona" in a learner-centered larger classroom context. Curzan and Damour (2006) suggest:

> Teaching is a kind of performance, and the person you are in front of a classroom is in some ways different from the person you are the rest of the time. Developing your "teaching persona"—the person you become once you step into the classroom—takes time and experience. (p. 5)

Most musicians have a sense of "performance" as mentioned above, and by focusing on the preparation you do for musical performance you can begin to understand how to prepare for teaching performance. The time and practice put into musical performance is the same sort of time and preparation that is put into course planning.

REFLECTION ON TEACHING

Scholars of teaching discuss the concept of "reflection" as one of the most important skills for the teacher (Brookfield, 1995). Looking back on the class and being able to discern what went well and what could be improved helps the professor to grow as a teacher. Eventually the teacher learns to reflect during the class and make changes as the teaching is going on. The analogy to performance works here as well. A young performer may only be able to present a performance as practiced whereas a more experienced musician is capable of responding to the context (could be in relation to pitch or dynamics) in the midst of performance. Strategies for reflection and growth of reflection are addressed in Chapter 11. However, the earlier the instructor begins to think like a "reflective practitioner" (Schon, 1983) the better the teaching will be. Creating a class culture that encourages questions and feedback about the course is an important link for reflective teaching.

POWER AND CONTROL

True learner-centered classrooms challenge the power structures that are traditional in educational settings. Even the professor who is working to create a classroom culture that is welcoming and open has to consider issues of power inherent in the situation. The professor has chosen the text and the readings, written the syllabus including required assignments and rules; and is in "charge" of weekly discussions and class plans. This automatically gives power and control to the instructor. Students will need to "learn how to learn" in the learner-centered classroom as many students have come from other classroom settings that did not allow for student interaction, dialogue, and contribution. The short vignette from a new professor below highlights this issue.

> The most difficult thing about my first year as a professor has been trying to nestle the type of relaxed, creative teaching I want to do within the structure of a larger, less personal institutional culture. I feel a tension between the adaptive, learner-centered professor I want to be, and what I call the "tyranny of the syllabus." It's also harder than I thought to get some students to accept the idea of a course being a collaborative learning community, and it's hard to run it that way!
>
> I started out the semester with a keen sense of responsibility to the undergraduates. The course I'm teaching is an important, required course for certain majors. The students need to leave with concrete skills, combined with some serious philosophical and theoretical knowledge.
>
> I asked a lot of questions about the "typical" student I'd find in my courses, and read past years' syllabi. I decided the best way to walk the line between practical and theoretical would be to assess both skills and understanding frequently, formally and informally. My intent was to use the information garnered from those evaluations along the way to help me continue to construct and shape the course as we went. I thought this would be responsive teaching. I envisioned a real two-way street between the professor as facilitator of learning, and the students who would bring their best thinking energy to learn the material.
>
> I've been successful for the most part, I think, but I've had two problems. One is the way I feel like I'm railing against the confines of my own syllabus!

It is mandatory in most schools to create a syllabus that clearly spells out a course calendar, with information on policies deadlines, requirements, rubrics for assessment, and how students will be graded. Following the lead of those who had taught this class before, I created a dense and detailed document. Now I look at the syllabus and feel like it's not representative of my teaching philosophy but rather a testimony to the linear transmission model of education! I have topics and assignments spelled out in excruciating detail, and I can't believe I was ever so positive that in Week Seven we would cover This-and-Such comprehensively enough to move on to This-and-Such, Part Two, in Week Eight. It's interesting to me that back in August I was confident enough to make those sorts of decisions, and put them in print. I didn't know who would be in the class, or what their background and strengths were, or how fast we'd move through the material.

Here's what happened: This-and-Such was tough but fun and interesting for the students, and we really wanted to keep going with it for three weeks to explore it in depth. This midsemester course correction required a flurry of emails and handouts about revised readings, assignments, and projects; we've also had to cancel some things here at the end of the semester. The students appreciated the flexibility at the time. But they are also afflicted with a bit of panic now because "we didn't get to everything we were supposed to!"

In other words, the sharing, two-way street I imagined at the beginning of the year can rub painfully against the need of the students to know what's due and when, and their intense desire to know what the 'right' way to answer things is. They seem to want to leave the course feeling like they know everything about the topic, and I, as the professor, am the pacesetter: the gatekeeper who determines how much information is doled out to them. The "coverage" style course structure is still desired by some students.

The other problem I had was related to my vision of a caring, sharing, lively community of learners. Well, my course met at 8:30 am. Need I say more? But nevertheless I find myself seeking laughter and chatter from the class as a marker of how much they are learning and how deeply they are engaged. Silence and quietude to me marks a lack of energy, which in turn denotes a lack of learning, although I know that's probably unfair. A saying evolved in our class: "Professor Stanley requires Mandatory Joy in this class." It's become a joke, but I do use their behavior and attitude to try to monitor what's getting through. Some of the students would probably rather just take a test, instead of engaging in the collaborative, hands-on projects that I know will result in deeper understanding of the theory and practice in this field. My classroom style requires an energetic thinking that some students have a hard time summoning up, and I suspect the atmosphere is different than some of their other courses where positive, active participation might not be "mandatory"!

Despite these questions and issues, I do feel like the students have responded well to my teaching and I wager that they would say they learned a lot. I will say that it's been harder than I thought it would be to break the mold of the "sage on stage." There are university customs still firmly in place, like the syllabus, the march-to-coverage course model, and the stand-and-deliver lecture classroom, that reinforce traditional teaching practice.

In *Learner-Centered Teaching* Maryellen Weimer (2002) discusses what she believes are the historical reasons why professors tend to have so much control in the classroom and suggests:

> We feel the need to be in control and assert our position and authority over students, but we fail to understand that the need results from our own vulnerabilities and desire to manage an ambiguous and unpredictable situation successfully. The idea of giving up control, of involving students in decisions faculty have traditionally made, frightens many teachers. (pp. 27–28)

She goes on to suggest that the first step in learning how to better balance power and control in the college classroom is to recognize and acknowledge the power of the professor. In a more learner-centered classroom, students are more involved in course decisions. Weimer suggests many of the teaching techniques already presented in this text to allow students more involvement in course decisions including: student input on course assignments (Chapter 3), and student-generated grading criteria (Chapter 2). Weimer postures that even small steps towards changing the power culture in classrooms will be valuable. She also states that this change in power is different than the culture in most college classrooms: "These theories propose that faculty, willingly and responsibly, beginning to give up some of their control in the interest of creating motivated, confident, responsible learners" (p. 30).

Music professors must consider where students are on the developmental continua (dualistic to relativistic thinkers) discussed in Chapter 3 in order to decide how much control students are ready to handle. If younger students are given too many course choices, they may make poor decisions and not learn in the course. Weimer agrees when she states:

> The amount of decision-making it takes to motivate students must be weighed against their intellectual maturity and ability to operate in conditions that give more freedom at the same time they also require more responsibility. Most students arrive in college classrooms having made almost no decisions about learning. We have an educational system that creates very dependent learners...With little experience making learning decisions and lacking the sophisticated study skills that characterize effective learners, the chance students (especially beginning ones) will make poor learning choices is high. (pp. 41–42)

I (Conway) teach a sequence of music education courses through the sophomore to junior year and students work with me in some way for four consecutive semesters. By the fourth class, I am able to share much of the course control with students in terms of assignments and deadlines. I provide no required due dates and students always get their work done in a timely manner. However, this behavior is nurtured throughout the four terms and my situation with consecutive semesters is somewhat unique. For the purposes of a new professor it is just hoped that an awareness of power and control will help you to begin to reflect on these important issues.

IDENTITY AS A COLLEGE PROFESSOR

There is a certain identity change that the new professor will feel once a teaching position has been accepted. The sense of "Do I really know enough to do this?" and "Are they thinking I am the professor?" is quite common. The two vignettes below highlight these issues of identity for the young professor.

Identity and Socialization: The Isolation of a New Faculty Member in Higher Education
   It was the first week of school. After a complete career change, two moves with my family across three states, hours and hours of coursework (including many late nights and weekends behind my computer), a comp exam, and the works of a dissertation in progress, I was finally teaching in higher education. It was my first day of class.

I went in and passed out the syllabus and began to teach. At the conclusion of my class, I retired to my office and left my door open expecting to meet some of my students. Not a student came by to ask a question, say hello, or discuss anything relating to my class. With the exception of a few faculty members, it was weeks before anyone stopped in to chat about anything.

As at any new job, I expected some uncomfortable seclusion. My colleagues did their best to introduce me to other faculty. However, I found that I spent each day going to my isolated office, teaching my classes and going home. I had very little as far as a connection to my job and my students. It was very sterile. I began to wonder if I had made the wrong choice with my career change. I became a teacher because of the relationships that are established with students in and out of the classroom.

Before entering higher education, I taught high school where there was a host of students in my office or in the corridors for me to interact with on an informal level. In addition, there was always an event or activity to attend to connect with students, faculty, and other families. In higher education, students do not socialize the same way. There are no families that are extensions of the students. During the school day they are often on the run to the next class. Some of them even commute from outside the city.

Instead of drowning in isolation, I attempted to get involved in student activities. This included volunteering to become a faculty advisor to a student organization. This included a weekly meeting with the officers to strategize about the activity of the chapter, bringing in guest speakers, and organizing special events. I found that being involved also allowed for collaboration with other faculty in my department and across campus. By working with this group I felt as though I was making a real difference on campus life in the school of music and offering true supplemental professional development opportunities for our students. This was one of the reasons for entering higher education.

Now I feel much more connected to my position and to the University. The loneliness that I felt is a thing of the past. I find myself pushing students out of my office when I am late for an appointment. In addition, students often want to chat about my experiences in the field. There is often not enough time for these conversations within coursework. This allows me the opportunity to give more practical advice and direction. I have also been mentoring new music teachers in the field that were involved in my student organization. Some of them I did not have in class. It is hoped that my choice to get involved in campus life will continue to offer opportunities to connect and mentor students in the school of music and across campus.

Shifting Identity

I was at a conference and I had just presented my research. About an hour later I was in the hotel restaurant with a group of highly esteemed researchers in my area. We were talking about my presentation, and several people I'd cited in my talk were sitting around the table sharing their ideas with me. Several people complimented me on my presentation and I really appreciated their thoughts. Then they complimented me on "my" TA's presentation, and how well he'd done! It felt weird, like now by virtue of my position I had been deemed an "expert". I don't want to discount the hard work on my part that got me here, but it was a fast shift from student to professor: a professor who gets some of the credit for the great work done by her graduate assistant!

I do miss grad school. There, I was actually required to wonder, read, write, reflect, and read some more. And everyone in my grad school cohort cared about my field just as much as I do. In my position now, though, I'm the expert. Others on my faculty know a lot about related fields, but I'm the main representative of the research and thinking in my area. My colleagues, my grad students, and my undergrads, ask my opinion and pretty much accept what I say. I set my own research and presentation agenda and don't have to be vetted by anyone. However it's almost a kind of intellectual isolation: I'm trying to be the expert, but one who still has the freedom to question and learn at the same time—But I'm now minus all the support and healthy debate from the graduate student colleagues who are immersed in the same issues. So, back to the table. As I was talking there, I received a text message from my TA and some other graduate student colleagues—close friends of mine from my Ph.D. studies. They were around the corner in the bar and couldn't see me, so they were asking me where I was and what I wanted them to order for me.

I felt strange! I wondered if I should leave and go to the other table, w/my buddies. Or do I stay here? The undergrads at my school would expect to find me sitting right here with the full professors. That's their view of me. My close friends over in the bar would have had no problem infiltrating this table but there were too many of them to move, nor would they probably have wanted to. I felt like I'd been "promoted" but wasn't really sure if it was 100% a good thing!

I felt like the discussion about my research topic might be different at the grad student table, so after a while I moved over there. I sat there and talked to them honestly and frankly, I might add, with a minimum of formal politeness, like friends will do. I flashed forward in my mind to a time in about three or five years when we all have professorships and we are the "grown-up" table, running the conferences, editing the journals, selecting the proposals. We all are going to have to find our own way to be independent scholars and experts, on our own. But we can help each other by staying in touch and keeping it real.

IDENTITY AS A GRADUATE ASSISTANT

Graduate assistants may face the identity issues even more acutely. Not a student and not yet a professor, the graduate assistant is caught somewhere in between, often putting the GA in an awkward place.

Graduate Student One—First Semester, First Year.

It was a bit of a shock for me to quit my job, sell my house, and move 750 miles north to become a student again at the age of 30 in pursuit of a career that will pay less than the one I left. I was used to teaching middle school students and the thought of teaching University students, as a Graduate Student Instructor was a little intimidating. Would I have anything to offer them? Would they respect what I had to say? Would they view me as a student or as a teacher? Fortunately, I found that I had a tremendous amount to offer the undergraduates; much more than I realized. The 8–12 years experience difference between us made for a much larger gap than I had expected. This realization quickly gave me confidence that I could teach college students; I did, in fact, have much to offer. However, this confidence was counterbalanced with the glaring realization that just as there was a wide experience/knowledge gap between the undergraduates and me, there was an equally large gap between my professors and me. I wonder how I will be qualified to join their ranks in such a relatively short amount of time.

I was immediately struck by the sharp contrast of what I considered a frenzied pace of life as a middle school band director with what I consider a reflective pace of a doctoral student. Whereas quantity, speed, energy, productivity, and flexibility were valued in my previous work, now thoroughness, thought, perseverance, and depth are valued in my work. This newfound time to reflect, think, and imagine has given me time to question previously held notions about the nature of my field and about myself. I wonder if I will miss public school teaching and will want to return at some point. I imagine how different my classroom would look as a result of my experience in graduate school. To never return to public education after graduate school almost seems like receiving new toys for Christmas but not having the opportunity to play with them. I wonder how long it will take being employed in higher education before I become disconnected with k-12 students. I wonder how much of the profession involves scholarly pursuits (e.g., publications, presentations) and how much of the profession involves practical application, (e.g., teacher education) and where the two forces overlap. Perhaps, just as with my undergraduate program, I will just have to wait until I am actually in the field to answer these questions.

Graduate Student Two—First Semester, Second Year

As a Graduate Student Assistant for the student teaching seminar, I was struck by the similarities between the student teachers' situation and my own. We are all guests in our cooperating teacher/professor's classrooms. They choose the curriculum, they have the long-term relationships with the students, and they give us opportunities to observe, participate, and occasionally, to teach. I am grateful for these apprenticeships which give me a window into my amazing professors' minds as I am afforded the time and space to contemplate why they have made these choices, what I would choose to emulate, and how I would bring myself and my values to a student teaching seminar, instrumental methods class, or even a graduate level curriculum or psychology class in the future.

When the focus of the student teaching seminar turns to the interview process, I again realize that the student teachers and I are in similar positions. Yes, I have successfully interviewed for a teaching position before, but not in this new area. Not in higher education. I love both teaching public school students and playing my instrument and so much of my life has been spent preparing and doing both. Now, after having made a very conscious and exciting decision to leave my comfort zone and branch out into areas that challenge me, I am constantly aware of the fact that the skills that have brought me here are not the same skills that I need to continue on in this program, or even in this profession!

I feel as if I am ready to begin my career as a professor but the thought of all of the responsibility is terrifying. I enjoy the safety net of my faculty advisors but at the same time, I want to experiment and organize my own classes—I want to put my theories into practice. I have grown so much in these first three semesters. I look forward to guiding the students on their collegiate journeys! But who will be there to edit my papers, meet with me, and guide me? I feel a mixture of enthusiasm, fear, overwhelming responsibility, and anticipation. I will be ready when the time comes but for now, I am thankful for this one last semester of course work, editing, and guidance before I am to leave and face this new world—just like many of the student teachers.

Graduate Student Three—First Semester, Third Year

As a Graduate Student Instructor (GSI), I have assisted with courses during the entire length of my program, as well as teaching one course independently. The fact remains, however, that I am a student at the institution and as such my identity as a student and my identity as a teacher run very close together. Even when I taught an independent course and was responsible for designing the syllabus, planning class meetings, and assessing students, it was still in the shadow of my department faculty.

Going to graduate school in the first place had already seriously challenged my sense of identity. As a teacher for several years in middle and elementary school I felt very comfortable with where I was and what I was doing. I entered my doctoral studies and the rules changed completely. I traded my "teacher hat" in for a "student hat." I was being asked to think and communicate in new ways as well as being, for all intents and purposes, a prestudent teacher. In a sense it felt like a demotion and led to feelings of questioning. Who did I think I was, pursuing a doctorate?

This past year, however, I began teaching as adjunct faculty at two other nearby universities. On a practical level, the responsibilities were similar to my experience teaching an independent class as a GSI. Conceptually, the difference was vast. I was independent of my school and was, to my students' perceptions, another member of the faculty. In fact, I was simultaneously teaching the same course for which I was the GSI at my school. It was almost as though I was leading a secret double life.

As an independent professor teaching at a university, I was doing the job for which I was being prepared to do. More importantly, I found that the feeling of teaching at the other schools kept me grounded in what it was that I was working towards—to become a full-time college professor. Not only were these teaching experiences exciting, they were also reinvigorating. I was able to go back to work as a graduate student feeling confident and focused. It felt strange to switch and put on my "student hat" when I got back to my studies, but I was able to put doctoral work within the larger context of higher education, as I could see much more clearly where my studies were leading.

FIRST CLASS MEETING

The culture that is set on the first day of class often sets the tone for the rest of the course. Once the syllabus is prepared, begin to plan for the first day of class as well as for future class meetings. If possible, obtain the class list and begin to get a sense of the students in the course. Most lists include the student year as well as the major instrument/field. Many class lists now include a student picture as well. Begin to study these lists and pictures in advance of the first class meeting in an effort to learn student names. Although learning student names is difficult in large classes, in most music classes the numbers are small enough that learning student names early in the term is reasonable. On the first day of class be standing at the door as students enter so that you can continue to learn student names. Ask students the correct pronunciation and practice saying the names each week until you get them. Check off attendance right at the door and then look for students you missed once class begins. You might provide nametags for the first few class meetings. If possible, create nametags that you can collect at the end of the first class and save for the next class. Try entering the second class holding the name tags and then try to pass them out as a way of working on student names. Students appreciate knowing that you are trying to learn names and will be forgiving when you make mistakes as long as you continue your efforts until you really learn the names.

Be sure to arrive at the classroom early so as to set chairs in the way you wish for the room to be set. Various ways to set up a classroom will be presented later in the text. Double-check the room assignment and the starting and ending time for the class. At some institutions, classes actually begin 10 (or more) minutes after the printed time in the course schedule to allow students to get from class to class. Check on this policy at your institution. Put the course number and the name of the course on the board or on the door so that if students wander in to the wrong class they can leave before class actually begins. If there are prerequisites for the course, list those on the board as well. If possible, visit the room in advance of the first class to be sure that the space is appropriate for your course. Look for equipment that might be needed (CD player, projector, board with musical staff, piano). Secure keys for any locked equipment. If students are going to play instruments in your course, be sure there is enough room for students, instruments, stands, and cases.

Although it is desirable to begin the first class with introductions, sometimes in large classes (or classes that meet for only 50–60 minutes), you might introduce yourself and get right to the syllabus to be sure that you will get through the syllabus on the first day. In this case, take a quick attendance and let students know that you will do extended student introductions at the next class. In classes of 30 or fewer, we would suggest that "extended introductions," whether on the first day or later, include going around the room and sharing student details such as name and hometown, whether instrument or voice (if music majors), and whether having any previous experience with the course content. You might have students complete an index card with this information on it to hand in to you at the end of class. This helps take away any nervousness that they might feel about talking to the entire class by giving them something to read and it allows you to walk away with more details regarding each student. Break up this activity and do 10 student introductions and then something else and then come back to introductions. For classes larger than 30 you might have small group or paired activities where students do the introductions. If you do these several times with different groups over the first few classes students will begin to know one another and you can go around during the activity to get to know the students. It is important for students to know one another and for you to know them so you can shape the instruction to meet student needs.

If you are struggling with student names, you might bring a camera to class and take group photos. Have students write their names on the photos. This is a good icebreaker activity as well as a way to get to know student names. In seminar style courses, you might make name cards and have students place them on the seminar table for the entire semester. This is a good strategy when bringing guests to class as well. In some classes it might make sense to create a seating chart and ask students to sit in the order until you have learned their names. Encourage them to use the seating chart as a way to get to know each other's names as well.

Work to be sure that students use names when addressing one another. For example, if a student says "I agree with what she says" rephrase to say "Jason agrees with what Susan has suggested." You might make learning other student names a part of first day activities or a first assignment. Barbara Davis (2001, p. 24) suggests that in courses that include writing, the first writing assignment might be a description of another student in the class. Students can develop interview questions in class, or do the interview during class. This allows for the content of the first writing assignment to be relatively easy so students know what to write and the professor can get a sense of baseline issues in the writing. In smaller classes it might make sense to provide a class e-mail and/or cell phone list so that students can be in touch with one another regarding the course. McKeachie and Svinicki (2006) suggest that students learn as much from one another as they do from the professor; therefore it is in the professor's best interest to include getting to know one another early in class interactions.

Although icebreaker activities in the first class itself can be awkward, they do help students to relax and get to know one another. Curzan and Damour (2006) suggest acknowledging that icebreakers are corny while giving your reasons for doing them anyway. They recommend having students introduce a partner as one strategy for "breaking the ice." Have each student pick a partner. Give them about 4 or 5 minutes to interview one another and then each student introduces his or her partner to the class.

While students are interviewing one another, it gives you a chance to review the class list and begin to learn some names.

Be sure to know the school or university policy regarding caps on enrollment and preference for getting into the course. Students who are not yet registered may come to class, or if the class is full, students may come anyway and beg to get into the course. If you are unsure, we suggest allowing the students to stay for the first class and then checking with a department chair.

Take time in introducing yourself. Be sure to let students know what you wish to be called. Most faculty with doctorates have undergraduates address them as "Dr. _____." If you are a faculty member but not yet finished with the doctorate, we recommend "Professor_____." Graduate assistants at some institutions are called by their first names and in other settings are addressed as "Mr. or Ms." Be sure to explore the culture of the school regarding these issues. Let students know your background, where you are from originally, where you went to school, and for what. Share your previous higher education experience and let them know a bit about the position you are in at the university. Share other classes that you teach and some details about your specific research and expertise. State during introductions what might be your course "bias" so that students have a sense of who you are right from the beginning of the course. Let students know where your office is and what your office hours or meeting policies will be.

You might e-mail copies of the syllabus to students in advance of the first class but it is also important to pass out a hard copy of the syllabus on the first day of class. Make these copies before the first day as copy machines seem to always break down on the first day of class.

Be sure to review the syllabus carefully on the first day of class and make course policies clear to students. Some instructors have students sign the syllabus or a course contract. Provide some details about the logistics of the course. Let students know where water fountains and rest rooms are located. State your policy regarding food and drinks in class. Share beeper and cell phone policies. If the class will include a break, let students know in advance. Remind students that you intend to start and end class on time and give the conditions under which directions for late arrival or early departure from class will be allowed.

Davis (2001, p. 22) suggests dividing students into groups and having them develop questions on the syllabus or the course once the syllabus has been presented by the instructor. McKeachie and Svinicki (2006, p. 27) suggest asking for anonymous feedback at the end of the first class. The underlying concept for both of these first day activities is to get a sense of what students are expecting from the course, what they are concerned about, and how you can help.

Check on the availability of textbooks and course packs before the first class meeting. There is nothing worse than assigning readings for the second class meeting and finding out that students do not have access to the readings. Always introduce the textbook on the first day. Discuss why you chose a particular text and mention other texts that you considered. It is also important to give some background on the author and caution the students regarding any potential bias in the text. Save enough time at the end of the class to introduce the material for the next class and/or give suggestions for the readings and assignments. Never let students out early on the first day. If introductions are done and the syllabus has been discussed go immediately into the content of the course with a lecture, discussion, or group activity.

Expect some awkwardness on the first day of class. We both have been teaching for many years and yet we still have "first day of school" stress dreams at the beginning of every semester. It takes time to get to know students and it will take time for them to get to know you. Talk with students informally as they enter the class even though this conversation may feel awkward.

Finally, you should plan for the fact that there will be students who miss the first day of class for one reason or another. One strategy may be to videorecord the first class meeting so that students who miss class may still get the material. Or, create a handout or PowerPoint with key concepts covered on the first day. You might also assign a student on the first day to take careful notes and collect extra handouts for anyone not in class. It is ultimately the student's responsibility to find out what has been missed but we have found that for the first class it helps to plan for students who will be missing class.

ASSESSING STUDENTS' PRIOR KNOWLEDGE, EXPERIENCE, OR INTEREST

In the first class or one of the first classes try to develop an activity that will help you to assess the students' prior knowledge, experience, or interest. This might take the form of a survey or a diagnostic test. It is best if this activity does not give the feeling of a "test" to students. As mentioned above, you might have students share their experience related to a course when they introduce themselves at the first or second class meeting.

This activity might be infused into some sort of icebreaker activity that allows students to get to know one another as well as providing the instructor some information about the students. You might use index cards on the first day and ask a question about previous knowledge. Students provide an answer to the question on the card and do not put names on the index cards. You then collect the cards and shuffle them. Sit in a circle and pass the cards around to get the collective class "answer" to the question posed. Another activity you might use is a board activity where you try to assess as a group what they know and what they do no t know about the content. You could keep this list and come back to it on the last day of class as a way of highlighting what students have learned.

In music classes, try to have some sort of "musical" activity in the first class. Even in nonmajor courses, students should be listening, moving, singing, and responding to music. Try to time the first class such that the musical activity happens at the end so that we can look to future musical interactions as the class continues.

FIRST CLASS MEETING CHECKLIST

- Class roster
- Copies of syllabus
- Copies of other handouts or readings
- Pens and pencils
- Chalk or dry-erase pens/eraser
- Keys for stereo or instrument cabinets

- Index cards for student information
- Clock or watch to keep time
- Copy of text book and/or course pack.

WEEKLY CLASS PREPARATION

It is important to plan carefully for each class meeting. Students know when the professor is unprepared. The short vignette from an undergraduate music student below highlights student frustration when music professors are unprepared.

> I enrolled in a class with a professor who was recommended highly. However, this year he is up for tenure and is completely focused on that instead of teaching. The class is a joke; we stopped following the syllabus after the first week. He emails us the day before he wants something due, and then accepts it late because he barely gave us any warning about it. We have assigned readings that I have yet to read and it has yet to matter. He tries to engage us in "class discussions" which is just a fancy name for him not being prepared. Most of our classes so far this semester are run by guest speakers, who really are boring old friends of my professor. One entire hour and a half class we spent drawing on paper with crayons "brainstorming" for our projects and then shared our drawings with the rest of the class. My professor cancels class for "research days" when he is traveling the country giving talks to try to boost his chances for tenure. On the rare occasion we do have an assignment, he merely reads them and returns them three months later. Needless to say, this class is a waste of my time and I have not learned anything.

We would suggest that you prepare a "minute chart" for each class in which you try to outline how long certain activities or discussions will take. Although it is not possible (or even desirable) to stick to this sort of chart, you will find that the chart helps you to pace instruction. Take notes right after class regarding how long activities have taken and what should be included in the next class. This helps you avoid a "did we talk about this last week?" question at the next class.

You might put a "schedule" for the class time on the board so that students have a sense of the plan for the day as well. Ask students where more time needs to be spent. You might find that posting the schedule helps students to understand the goal of group work and discussion. This will be discussed more in Chapter 7. For lectures, prepare a handout for students with spaces for additional notes. More on lectures is discussed in Chapter 6.

Open the class with announcements and reminders regarding upcoming assignments and projects. Students respond to this better at the beginning of class than at the end when you are coming to closure on the goals for the day. Return student work at the beginning of class so that you can discuss any misunderstandings or suggestions for rewrites. The exception to this might be if there are students who did not do well on the assignment due to poor effort. If the entire class does not need to spend time on the assignment you may wait and hand back low grades at the end of the class so that those students are not distracted the entire time about their grade.

It is common for students to comment on course evaluations that a professor "went off on a tangent" or "got off track." It is challenging to manage a learner-centered classroom and still keep a focus on class goals. There is a balance that must be struck between too much student-led dialogue and not enough attention to student concerns. Try to have a daily goal in mind for each class and work to keep the class focused on that goal. In some cases, you may respond to a student question or comment with "that is interesting and I will make time for it next week" so we can move to the goal for the day. Then work to find time for the student-generated issue. Your students know that you will work to find time for their concerns, so they usually will make a note to themselves about the issue for discussion at a later time. Sometimes students will have a more personal issue to discuss that does not relate to the course or others; you should then suggest that you meet outside of class.

In the middle of the semester, you might issue a revised syllabus that reflects changes necessitated by student request or timing of the course. The student story below reflects the frustration felt by a student when a professor claims to be "going with the flow" of the class but the structure moves so far away from the syllabus that students do not know about requirements and preparation.

When it comes to class organization, students need a bottom line. This bottom line of expectation is often clearly spelled out in a syllabus. In one class I took, a clear guideline of expectations was written into the syllabus; however, the instructor never followed what was on the syllabus. He often spoke about his knowledge of being off topic of the syllabus and painted it to be a "good idea in September but not relevant now" document. When the day came in the syllabus schedule for the students to come in with a lesson plan to teach a sample lesson he was disappointed when none was prepared to do the task. The students in the class had grown accustomed to disregarding what was written in the syllabus and going by what the instructor said was due in the next class. Although technically it is the students' fault for not following what was outlined in the syllabus, instructors who do not follow their syllabus should not expect to get what they had planned.

Specific strategies for planning for various types of class activities (lectures, discussion, etc.) are discussed in the other chapters in this section. In the first few classes try to model many of the types of activities that will be used in class. For example, if you are going to study cases as part of the class, model an examination of a case during one of the first class meetings. If students are going to do presentations based on the reading material, model the type of presentation that is desirable during one of the early classes. In classes that include music-making, try to model the types of musical behaviors that will be assessed in the course. For example, in several of my (Conway) undergraduate music education courses, students must come to the front of the class and teach a song, do a movement activity, teach reading of notation, and early skills on instruments. I try to model all of those activities early in the semester so that assessment of musical skills takes place after students have experienced the activity.

INTERACTION WITH READINGS AND MATERIALS

Ideally, the professor will have had the opportunity to read the entire text and additional reading materials in advance of choosing them for the course. However, the reality of teaching sometimes leads to a graduate assistant or new professor being handed a text and additional readings at the start of a semester. Be sure to read anything that is assigned for students to read. Students get frustrated when it appears as if the instructor has not read the text or course pack materials. Strategies for getting students to read and holding them accountable for reading will be addressed in Chapter 6.

A well-designed syllabus should essentially help the class run itself. If the syllabus lists all reading assignments with due dates, there should be little confusion regarding what to read. In order to keep students focused on upcoming due dates and assignments, try to plan your classes a week (or a class session) in advance. This means that you read the assigned reading assignment and design class activities for the next class before teaching the class that comes before. This allows you to focus discussions in class on where you were going and what you will do next. After class, adjust your notes for the upcoming class based on what was covered. Very often you will run out of time in a class discussion and one reading or concept does not get discussed. When you plan a course, try to work in some flexible classes every couple of classes so that the class can "catch up" if need be. You might leave the class period right before the midterm or final as a "catch-up" day for review or addressing content that got "lost" so to speak. It is important to weave all readings into class interactions in some way. Students often complain that there is a disconnection between readings, class discussion, and exams.

STUDENT ASSIGNMENTS

Include as much detail as possible regarding assignments on the syllabus so that students can plan their time carefully in terms of reading, writing, and studying for exams. With so many ensemble and performance requirements, music students often have the busiest course loads in the college or university and need to be able to plan time carefully. Thus, be sure to provide a due date for every assignment (at least until you have worked with students long enough for them to develop good habits and then they might not need due dates). If you accept assignments via e-mail put the time that the e-mail assignment must arrive on the syllabus as well. The vignette below highlights a music student's reflection on due dates and flexibility.

One of the things I liked the most about being a freshman in college was the ability to manage my own time, and more importantly, finish projects on my own schedule. Sure, give me a final deadline, let me know what I'm responsible for, but please don't dictate to me how I should do it. Finally, if need be, I could rearrange things as needed, rather than being babysat through each process. With time now a more precious commodity than ever, having the ability to be flexible in my preparation was not only much-appreciated, but essential. Perhaps my experience in this regard is unique, but somehow I don't think so. I remember rolling my eyes even in high school and middle school when I would be forced to turn in an intermediary step in a research paper, for example. I would have to force my thoughts, still poorly developed and in early stages of research, into some kind of outline that I would never use in later stages, resulting in hours of work and a late night to no final end. Oftentimes it would come at a time when I had a number of other projects due in their final form, and to have to sacrifice the quality of a final product for that of an unnecessary intermediary step always irked me greatly. That being said, I appreciate the fact that in high school and middle school teachers were trying to teach me how to be organized in writing a paper. When forced to do the same kind of work in c ollege, however, I would get extremely annoyed. I've already learned this, thank you very much. No need to treat me like I'm 13 again.

Professors do need to make students accountable for assignments. We have found that students will complete work that they view to be authentic to the discipline. The professor must work to generate assignments that require students to interact with the course content in the same way that music professionals might. Music theory and history projects that can relate in some way to what the music students are studying in applied lessons or ensembles are good examples of authentic assignments. Of course, not all assignments can be directly relevant to the musical world of the student. Some assignments are for drill or are building skills needed for the future.

Of course there are some students who will not complete assignments. However, we have found that if students have solid, clear directions for the assignment and clear criteria for the evaluation of the assignment, they are more apt to complete the work. As discussed in Chapter 2, you might take time at the beginning of each semester to have students develop grading criteria for each assignment. Type these criteria sheets and get them out to students. However, you will be amazed every semester that you still get e-mails from students (particularly freshmen) right before an assignment is due asking you "what you want" for the assignment. Take the opportunity to remind these students that they already have this information. It sometimes takes several courses/years before some students get organized in this sort of way. Thus, you might e-mail students reminders regarding due dates and big projects coming up.

COMMUNICATION WITH STUDENTS

It is important to let students know how to get in touch with you and what are the appropriate ways of communication. Let students know that they can contact you with concerns about the course in general as well as concerns about their work or grades for the course. Put your e-mail on the syllabus and invite students to communicate with you via e-mail. Let students know how often you plan to check e-mail and within what time frame they can expect a response. I (Conway) include my office phone on the syllabus but I let students know that I only check that phone every few days. I do put my home and/or cell phone on the syllabus with strict directions to use it only in an emergency (e.g., student is a driver for fieldwork and the car breaks down). Although it does not happen often, over the years I have had students abuse the home/cell phone connection and call at inappropriate times with inappropriate questions. You must decide for yourself what your home phone/cell policy will be.

Decide how you will communicate with students as well. My institution automatically sets up a class e-mail list and I use that regularly to communicate with students. If the institution does not create this, you might create a class e-mail or class web site for announcements and reminders. Let students know that this is how you will communicate so that they know to check their school e-mail account or the class web site regularly. If the e-mail list is not university created let students know who is to use the list. I request that students send any information they want on the list through me or my graduate assistant so that party announcements and other more social content does not become a regular part of the class list.

Help students to consider what sorts of issues can be addressed through e-mail and which conversations should be held during office hours or an appointment. Students will often assume you are available before or after class and may come up just before or after class to discuss course issues. If your schedule is tight, you may need to let students know that they must make an appointment in order to catch up with you. You will find that it takes your younger students (freshmen and sophomores) a little time to understand the schedule of the college professor and to learn that they must schedule appointments well in advance. I (Conway) often let students know (either by class announcement or e-mail reminder) that I am currently scheduling in to late next week and if they need to meet, they should get on my calendar.

It usually makes the most sense to meet with students at your office. However, it may also be appropriate to meet for coffee, lunch, or in another public space. Know that students will "keep track" so to speak of these sorts of meetings; so if you offer to meet for lunch or coffee with one student you should make that offer to all. Remember that a public meeting space may not be appropriate for sensitive discussions (i.e., a failing grade in a course). If a student is particularly upset about the course or with you, we suggest meeting in your office and including another colleague in on the meeting.

Occasionally you may come across a student who abuses office hours and meetings. If a student misses your class and then asks for an appointment to discuss what they missed, we would suggest that you ask them to meet with another student. Overall, open and fair communication with students is the key to success in higher education. Learn from mistakes and continue throughout your career to keep up with various strategies for student communication.

POTENTIALLY DIFFICULT SITUATIONS

The best way to avoid most difficult situations is through careful class policies that are stated on the syllabus and discussed with students at the beginning of the course. In order to create a culture for learning, policies must be fair and well-crafted. This section includes discussion of attendance, tardiness, difficult students, cheating, plagiarism, and grade complaints.

Attendance

Know the university or department attendance policy. Some departments have standardized policies. Most have rules regarding religious holidays and student travel for university-sponsored activities such as concerts or tours. There are many issues to consider when thinking about attendance and attendance policies. In a truly learner-centered classroom, there probably will not be an attendance policy. Davis (2001) suggests that we tell students that they should come to class but that grades should not be affected by absences if students are able to complete course tasks. I (Conway) have always had attendance policies in my undergraduate classes as much of my content is discussion based and I find it hard to connect the learning from group work to specific assessment strategies. If you do have an attendance policy, post on the syllabus exactly how many absences are allowed and how grades will be affected by absences. The statement I use on most syllabi is

> *Attendance*
> Attendance is required. More than two absences from class will result in one full grade lower. Each absence after three will result in an additional half grade reduction.

The number of "allowed" absences for me varies depends on how often the course meets. If the class meets only once a week, I allow only one absence. If it meets twice a week, I allow two. We recommend choosing a number and then enforcing the rule. I don't ask for details about "excused" or "unexcused" absences. I just allow the number. If students get very sick, they can provide a doctor's note for additional documentation regarding absence in excess of the limit. I ask students to notify me *in advance* of the class meeting if they will be absent.

Once the policy is established, then you must attend each class and keep careful records. The largest class I teach is a class of 20, so I e-mail students every time they miss my class. This may not be possible in larger classes, although I find that the e-mail does seem to cut down on absences.

It is hard not to take it personally when students do not attend class. Attendance may be related to class activities and motivation. However, it is also possible that there are other factors having an affect on a particular student. Make it clear that in an interactive class it is not possible to "make up" the work and then try to ensure that each class lives up to that statement. In the case of extended illness or other personal issues, the student still cannot pass the class without attending. Authorize a late withdraw or issue an incomplete and negotiate a way for the student to attend the course again the following semester or the following year.

In querying a few undergraduate music majors regarding attendance policies in music classes, here were some responses:

> *Response 1:*
> I believe it depends on the class. Our music ed class that meets only once a week and is based on discussions would be a class where attendance is necessary. Musicology and theory are classes where attendance is not as demanding, due to the fact that there are midterms and finals to test our knowledge. If we pass the test, than we obviously know the information regardless of whether we went to class. Classes that do not have tests and are based on discussions should have required attendance. Then again…the students are the ones paying a ton of money and it technically should be their decision on whether they waste their money.

> *Response 2:*
> Here are my thoughts- if you present valuable material in class that you can't get from the readings or from anything else, then you don't really need an attendance policy because students will be motivated to show up. For instance, I wouldn't dare miss some classes because I think that we talk about a lot of interesting things and I learn a lot, so it would be detrimental to me to miss it. Along with that, another incentive to attend class is by giving hints to assignments or ideas or practice or something on what we have to do, so it is only to our benefit to come to class. I skip classes when I don't feel like I gain anything by being there. So, to sum up what I am saying: if you make class worthwhile to go to, you don't need an attendance

policy. On the other hand, I like being graded on being there because I always go to class and it is a grade booster, but I also do better on assignments because I am in class and know what the professor wants, etc.

Response 3:
For general studies classes attendance should not be required because I have found that showing up to the class doesn't affect the material being learned, just how it is explained. On the other hand it is impossible to learn efficiently in a music class without regular attendance because music is more hands on. For example:

1. Aural theory—back and forth singing
2. Method classes—probably couldn't have learned strings or woodwinds without regular attendance. The "do as I do" teaching works better than looking at pictures in a text book
3. Modeling teaching techniques are much different than reading about them
4. Piano—getting the technique down (I used to be able to play many scales—but using all the wrong fingerings)—all of these things and more contribute a better overall experience in learning music if attendance is required. I don't understand how a student in music would succeed attending only some of these classes. Still, classes like musicology and written theory don't require the student to necessarily be there to understand the concepts. Maybe it depends on the type of music class then?

Response 4:
I think that attendance policies are helpful for motivating extremely busy students to make it to class, but I always appreciate policies that allow the students to miss one or two days without any deleterious effect on their grades.

Response 5:
Although I have often been taken aback by attendance policies, I am beginning to see many benefits. Originally I was of the mindset that if you want your education you have to put in the class time and go after it. Because many of my classes have been either solely discussion based or greatly influenced by class discussion, I see mandatory attendance policies as more of a positive than negative. Discussion-based classes without complete attendance and opportunity for participation lead to less involved discussions and discussions that cannot build upon each other from week to week. Smart students will learn that it is actually less work to go to class than it is to figure out what went on and make up the work. I am weary of the "if you come to class you get an A" grading policy; however, attendance can often be implied such as grading by involvement in discussion and ability to speak on weekly course readings. I think it is also important for teachers to understand that 100% attendance is near impossible as illness, overwork and outside opportunities often come up in college environment. The course syllabus should outline a policy or direct questions to the professor.

Tardiness

Make it clear at what point being late to class becomes an absence (i.e., after 20 minutes in a 2 hour course?). If a student is continuously late to class we recommend speaking to him/her individually and making it clear that the behavior is not acceptable. Announce who is missing from class after taking attendance in the first few minutes so that all students know that you are keeping track.

Difficult Students

Most college students will be respectful and reasonable in their interactions with professors; however, every once in a while, you will have a student who is difficult to work with. Based on McKeachie and Svinicki (2006, pp. 179–188), we outline several "types" of difficult students (attention seekers and students who dominate discussions; inattentive students; unprepared students; students with excuses; angry students; and discouraged students) that may be encountered in music classes and provide a few strategies for working with these students.

Attention Seekers and Students Who Dominate Discussions

Students who dominate discussions are sometimes the brightest students in the class. They have a lot to say and they want to say it. These students are often helpful in getting group discussions going. However, sometimes other students begin to back away from participating if one or two students always take the lead in group discussion. There are several strategies for assuring that multiple participants are involved in group discussion. You may need to institute a "raise your hand" policy so that you can monitor who speaks when and how often. Or, you might need to say "let's hear from someone who has not spoken today" if the "dominator" is always the first to respond. Stanton (1992) suggests that each student in a class be given three markers at the beginning of a class. Each time they speak, they must lay down one of their markers. Once the markers are gone, the "speaking" turns have been used up. He suggests that students can pool markers or bargain for markers when there are ideas that really need to be shared. All of these strategies help students to consider what really needs to be shared. If one or two students continue to try to dominate discussions, you may need to pull those students aside and discuss the need for many students to have the opportunity to participate in the class discussion.

Inattentive Students

Inattention can be manifested in a variety of ways. Sometimes a student will fall asleep in class. Or, several students may start their own conversation and not attend to the lecture or presentation. Students may be checking e-mail, text-messaging, or working on their laptops rather than engaging in class activities. The first strategy for dealing with this issue is to reflect on the teaching and the activities to be sure they are appropriate and engaging. If most students are responding positively and just a few are inattentive, we suggest moving inattentive students closer to the front of the room or engaging them in a small group activity and then staying close to them to assure they stay on task. Again, it may be necessary to pull students out individually and inquire as to why they are inattentive. You may need to monitor laptop activity and have some "no laptop" time in the class if online communication during class becomes an issue.

Unprepared Students

Students who have not done the reading, listening, or score study can present a real difficulty during class interactions. Strategies for getting students to read are addressed in Chapter 6. We have found one of the prime factors in assuring that students come to class prepared is to be sure that students understand the assignment. A detailed syllabus that outlines specific chapters and course pack readings with dates will help. In addition, try to end each class with a reminder of the reading and/or writing assignment for the next class. You may even send an e-mail to the class list a day or two before an assignment is due as a reminder. Hold students accountable for assignments through in-class discussions or quizzes. If a student continues to be unprepared, we suggest an individual meeting with the student to discuss the issues.

Students with Excuses

Some of the most difficult dealings with students center around excuses for late assignments or missing classes. It is sometimes hard not to be suspicious when a student has several grandmothers pass away in one semester. However, McKeachie and Svinicki (2006) suggest: "I believe it is better to be taken in by a fraudulent excuse than to be seen as unfair in response to a legitimate excuse" (p. 183). Caron et al. (1992) studied excuses in college students and found that two-thirds of their respondents admitted to having made at least one fraudulent excuse while in college. Since many of these excuses seem to center around due dates and exams, the best way to discourage excuses may be to have a well-articulated and flexible policy regarding extensions and retakes. By creating a "less pressure" environment, you may save yourself from trying to judge the merit of excuses. Students value a professor who understands that they are people in addition to being students and that life can sometimes "get in the way."

Angry Students

On some occasions students may become angry and take it out on you. Students who are not doing well in the class are the most apt to lash out and blame the instructor for their struggles. Music students in competitive environments have many opportunities for disappointment in terms of auditions, ensemble seating, and performance opportunities, and disappointment can easily lead to anger. Angry students can be dangerous as they can rally other students against you and create a culture of distrust. It is difficult to recommend a "quick fix" strategy for dealing with angry students. However, the following suggestions seem relevant for most situations:

- Allow the angry students to speak their mind and voice their concerns. Listen patiently.
- Consider whether the concerns are warranted. If it is a grading complaint, refer to documented rubrics or class rules.
- If the student has begun to rally other students, take time to address the issues with the class and find out what the class as a whole thinks about the issues.
- If the student continues to be angry, let a department chair or dean know of the situation and possibly include them in on a meeting with the student.

Very often, angry students have lots of other issues to deal with than just your class. They may lash out at you for things that have little to do with you. A clearly articulated syllabus and grading policy will protect you from unwarranted student anger.

Discouraged Students

McKeachie and Svinicki (2006) describe a discouraged student: "Sometimes they come to class late or miss class; often their papers are constricted and lack any sense of enthusiasm or creativity" (p. 186). In music classes, these students are often doubting if they are in the right profession. They stop practicing and stop attending lessons, rehearsals, and classes. It is our sense that it would be rare for a music major to complete an undergraduate degree without some periods of doubt and discouragement although not all of them will miss classes due to this. Professors working with music students need to be prepared to nurture students and assist them through the "low points" of development. Peer leadership within the applied studio can often provide a support network for students. We work at our institutions to partner younger students with older students so that discouraged students have peers to discuss their concerns with. Not all music majors will continue as music majors and many of them are making the right choice to get out of music. Supporting and advising undergraduates as they seek to find their way in a music career is a challenge.

CHEATING AND PLAGIARISM PREVENTION

One of the more difficult issues for the new professor to handle is dealing with cheating on an exam or assignment. It is often difficult to know for sure if a student's eyes are wandering during an exam and many professors are reluctant to accuse a student of cheating when they are not sure. We suggest asking a student to move during an exam if there is a potential question. Go with your hunches and monitor closely the behavior of a student in question. Ask a department chair or Dean for advice and you may find that you are not the first professor to be concerned about a particular student.

Cheating on assignments in the form of plagiarism is even more common in the internet age. However, the same technology that makes it easy to cut and paste content for a paper can also allow the professor to check on the originality of the paper. There are a variety of software programs available to cross check electronic paper submissions with large online databases. In some of my courses the final project or required final notebook changes little from year to year. For example, students in my (Conway) Brass Techniques classes gather materials on trumpet, horn, trombone, euphonium, and tuba each year. I often worry about students passing on the notebook from year to year. I try to combat this by spending time in discussion of the value of compiling the materials and I encourage students to organize the materials in a way that will be useful to them. I do not insist on a template for the assignment. McKeachie and Svinicki (2006) suggest plagiarism is often the result of ignorance and that students must be taught about proper protocol for quotation and citation. They also report a variety of statistics that suggest a large majority of college students cheat in some way in their undergraduate degree work. These cheating examples include paying other students to take exams, paying others to write papers, looking at the papers of others during exams and plagiarizing from online sources.

One of the goals of a learner-centered classrooms is to move the culture of the classroom away from a lecture/test model and high-stakes assessments. However, there are still times for exams and final papers in music courses. New professors are encouraged to know the school and university policies on cheating.

GRADE COMPLAINTS AND GENERAL ISSUES OF FAIRNESS

The keys to avoiding difficulties with grading are careful record keeping and constant attention to issues of fairness. Students who think the instructor has treated them unfairly are apt to complain. The short vignette below from an undergraduate student addresses the concept of fairness:

> One week at college, I got a horrible migraine that was atypical and lasted over a week. My typical medications did not help, and upon the local doctors orders, I went to the ER one night when the pain got to be too severe. Being across the country from my family, my friend drove me to the ER and stayed with me. They thought I had a brain aneurism. After a CT scan, a spinal tap, an allergic reaction to the meds, and four medications, I was released 10 hours later at 8:30 in the morning. My friend stayed with me the whole time and made sure I got up to my apartment and into bed safely. Needless to say, neither of us was able to take our midterm at 8:40 am that same morning. I e-mailed my professor and told him what happened and how my friend had stayed with me and hadn't slept or studied. I told him I had a note from the ER doctor to excuse me, and to please excuse my friend, also. He let me take the midterm a couple of days later, but he gave my friend a lot of trouble. He claimed that even with no sleep you should be able to take the exam and that staying up all night with a friend in the ER was no excuse to miss an exam. However, another kid in my class who had accidentally slept through the exam was able to take it later in the week, no problem. A good college professor realizes that students are people first and treats them accordingly.

Good record keeping regarding grades can be challenging in performance-based music courses. As was presented in Chapter 2, tools must be developed to quantify performance skills if grades are to be determined based on a performance product. Keep students informed about grades by returning work promptly and providing a midterm grade report. This will help to alleviate any surprises at the end of the term for students. However, McKeachie and Svinicki (2006, p. 134) suggest: "No matter how you grade, some student will be unhappy." This is particularly true in courses that are required for the major and may include content that is unfamiliar to the students (i.e., theory and aural skills). If a student persists in questioning a final grade, we recommend getting a department chair or a dean involved in the conversation as early as possible.

QUESTIONS FOR DISCUSSION AND SUGGESTED ACTIVITIES

1. Discuss the analogy that preparing for musical performance is like preparing to teach a class. Reflect on your own preparation for performance and teaching.
2. Discuss the connection between chamber music listening and student-focused teaching.

3. Discuss potential identity issues as you think about becoming an instructor.

4. Share examples from your own undergraduate experience of positive and negative first class meeting experiences.

5. Discuss the strategies for learning student names and add your own ideas or examples from your past experience.

6. Discuss icebreaker activities for courses you may teach.

7. Think about how you will introduce yourself on the first day. What should students know about your expertise and your background? What do you bring to the course?

8. Think about ways to assess prior knowledge for a course you might teach.

9. Discuss examples of ways to interact musically on the first day of class.

10. Think about the types of readings you might assign in a course and how you will manage these and connect them to class activities.

11. Discuss the types of student assignments that might be most appropriate for the courses you will teach.

12. Share your perspectives, experiences, and concerns on communication with students (e-mail, phone, and in person).

13. Discuss the various opinions in the chapter on attendance policies in undergraduate music courses.

14. Share your experiences regarding tardiness in music classes.

15. Discuss your concerns regarding difficult students, managing a classroom, and fairness in the class.

CHAPTER 6

Instructional Strategies for Academic Courses

This chapter outlines strategies most commonly utilized in courses in music theory, musicology, composition, conducting, and music education. However, the suggestions for lecture, discussion, and asking questions may also provide useful information for applied instructors when considering studio class interactions. We begin the chapter with a presentation of information regarding lectures and discussion-based lessons and interactions. The second part of the chapter presents strategies for getting students to read and helping students to write. We conclude with questions for discussion and suggested activities.

LECTURES

We have tried to encourage interactive approaches throughout the book. Whether lectures are "interactive" is the subject of heated debate in higher education. In his study of "What the Best College Teachers Do," Ken Bain (2004) states:

> One side in that squabble [lecture or not] is convinced that research has proven that lectures never work; the other is often passionately devoted to using the ancient pedagogical device. While this debate has no doubt opened some minds to the possibilities of using tools other than a formal lecture, it has just as often produced rigid positions that shed little light on good teaching, each side convinced that they know a simple truth. Our study of outstanding teachers revealed, however, that some people can engage their students with good lectures, helping and encouraging them to learn on the highest level; others can do so with case studies, problem-based learning, powerful assignments, playing guide by the side, conducting discussions, or creating stimulating field work. Yet any of these methods can also fail miserably. (pp. 98–99)

It is important for the music professor to understand how to develop and deliver a good lecture as well as how to make lectures more engaging and interactive. In many music courses, a combination of teaching strategies, including lectures will be most appropriate. There are a variety of different types of lectures ranging from the "expository lecture" where the professor does all of the talking to "short lectures framing discussion periods" (Davis, 2001).

The next section of the chapter includes information regarding setting up the room for a lecture, planning a lecture, delivering a lecture, materials for a lecture, and assessment of lecture content. We conclude the section with a discussion of the advantages and disadvantages of lecture as a teaching strategy.

SETTING UP THE ROOM AND PHYSICAL ENVIRONMENT

In some settings, there will be little choice (i.e., large "lecture hall" with auditorium style seating) regarding the classroom environment. However, the professor should examine the site carefully. Be sure there is enough light for note-taking. Check out the various seats in the room to be sure that all students will be able to see the chalkboard or screen and be able to hear musical examples. Be sure that the room temperature will be comfortable. Music for nonmajors courses and musicology classes sometimes end up being scheduled in these larger spaces. Even in larger classes, you may decide to break students into groups; so get a sense of the options for the space. Can you send students to various sides of the room for breakout sessions? Are there breakout rooms available? We suggest standing in front of the lectern, and not behind it. If a microphone is necessary, explore options for a wireless microphone to allow you to move about the room during the presentation. You may opt to ask students to sit in just certain rows so that they are closer to you or closer to one another. Students often tend to gather at the back of the room in large classes and you may want to insist that they sit closer.

In smaller classes (under 20), a horseshoe shape of chairs/desks allows the instructor to "stand and deliver" in the middle but still have an interactive feel with the class. In particular, do not allow just a few students to sit in a back row if everyone else is in the circle. If you have control over where chairs/desks go in the room, we would suggest changing the set-up every few classes so that students sit near different students. Move students around at least once in a 60-minute class. Even in a primarily lecture course, students will benefit from sitting near other students for the occasional group interaction that might be a part of the lecture. Whatever you decide about setting up the room, make an intentional decision about managing space. Students appreciate when it appears that the instructor has thought about their comfort and their level of interaction.

PLANNING A LECTURE

Planning for a lecture is much like the planning and practicing that goes into a musical performance. Last minute "cramming" does not work for lectures any better than it does for musical performance. Good lectures take careful studying and preparation as well as practice in terms of delivery. If lectures are based on readings (which in music classes they usually are) begin by re-reading the student assignment a week or so in advance of the lecture (ideally you would have read the entire text and course pack over the summer or when you were choosing the materials). As you read, take notes on points to highlight in the lecture. Prepare questions you could ask the students and class activities you could develop based on the content. Of course, there are often other sources not mentioned in the text that need to be incorporated into the lecture to add depth to the presentation of the content.

As you outline a lecture, try to have an "interactive moment" such as a question to the class or an opportunity for small-group interaction every 15–20 minutes. Research suggests that the average student's attention span is between 10 and 20 minutes (Penner, 1984). A change in activities every 15–20 minutes will help to keep students engaged.

One of the biggest challenges for the novice teacher is to time lectures appropriately. Try to put together a "minute chart" for the entire class period in the effort to organize the time. McKeachie and Svinicki (2006) suggest that lecture notes include a minute chart as well as reminders to put material on the board, check for student understanding, or put students in pairs to discuss (p. 62). It takes some practice to decide what level of detail will be comfortable for you in terms of lecture notes. We caution that too much detail (i.e., writing out the complete lecture and then delivering it verbatim) or too little detail are both problematic. A good textbook can help the novice teacher in making decisions regarding how to organize content for a lecture.

We suggest that each lecture begin with an introduction that attempts to situate the content of the lecture into something familiar for the students. In music education courses, you might ask students to share their own memories from K-12 music regarding whatever the topic may be. In theory and musicology, try to relate to a composer or piece that some of the students may have experienced. Then the body of the lecture will include new information. Conclude the lecture with some details regarding how this information fits within the larger structure of the course and the field, and let students know what to expect in terms of assessment of material from the lecture.

CHECKLIST FOR LECTURE PLANNING

- Read the assigned reading and take notes on key points.
- Develop questions for students based on the reading.
- Develop small group discussion activities based on the reading.
- Plan an introduction to the topic that connects to students' past experience.
- Present the body of the lecture.
- Provide a conclusion that puts the lecture in the larger context of the course and the field.
- Provide suggestions for how lecture material will be assessed.

DELIVERING A LECTURE

The short vignette from an undergraduate student below highlights the challenge in timing a lecture so that it stays with the materials, yet does not sound like a "canned" presentation. This student discusses the well-known strategies for students to get the professor to go "off topic":

> Getting a teacher off topic can be great fun for a well knit class. In one of my university classes I had a professor who loved to tell stories. She could wax eloquently about anything on her mind from current events, to her own childhood to her experience as a professor. All it took to get her off topic was an honest sounding question asking for personal experience or opinions. Students in her class quickly found out that if they didn't want homework that night, all they had to do was carefully ask these questions to run down the clock and escape like free birds. We didn't get to the last two weeks of material in the class and the exam at the end of the course was substantially easier because of it. Stories can be a teacher's best friend or their worst enemy. It often depends on how much they like the sound of their own voice.

This student's story highlights every lecturer's fear. In response to the concern about "going on a tangent," many novice teachers plan lectures so carefully that there is no time for "stories." This rigid approach can be equally unattractive to the students. Work to find a balance between presentation, discussion, and interaction in every class. Provide an outline for the lecture to students and write a schedule for the day on the board. Move around the room and keep eye contact with all students, even in large classes. Work to look to the back and sides of the room. Vary your vocal inflection so that lectures are easier to listen to and follow. Be aware of physical gestures and use them to highlight points. Be sure that gestures are intentional. It is possible to practice lecture delivery and we would recommend this for novice teachers. Videorecord your lectures so you can review them as you prepare for future classes. Good lecturing is a learned behavior that can and should be practiced and studied.

Another strategy for lecturing in music is to personalize the presentations in some way. If you are the violin professor who is teaching a musicology class, bring your violin to class to demonstrate some of the concepts being discussed in the course. Even better, ask students to bring instruments and perform works being studied. The focus in all music classes should be music.

MATERIALS FOR A LECTURE

We open this section with a student vignette:

> Students in the 21st Century are becoming increasingly more perceptive to visual learning stimulus. Old style lecture format which places a professor in a purely speaking zone for the duration of the class seems to be less and less effective. The best lectures I have sat through have used a wide range of learning stimulus. They are predominantly verbal but use modeling, media such as PowerPoint, pictures and movies and group discussions. Varying how things are taught is a great way to break up the monotony of a purely verbal based presentation.

We have found that a PowerPoint presentations or handouts will help students to engage with a lecture more readily. Be sure that students know the content of the lecture in advance so that they can read in preparation for the lecture (strategies for "getting students to read" are addressed later in the chapter). Use listening examples or live performance to keep music as the focus. Be sure that students know how lecture content will be assessed. This next student vignette expresses concern when technology is used but the lecture does not follow the slides.

> I've been in a musicology class where the class is great, the professor is enthusiastic, the assignments are well thought out (and dare I even say—relevant). The lectures are just not very good. Mainly, the professor doesn't stick to his slides. I spend half of my thought in this class wondering if the material presented is important since much of it is either talked about but not on the slides, or on the slides but not talked about. It makes note taking seem impossible—there's no way I could process all the information he talks about in class without having some idea of where he's coming from or where he's going.

ASSESSMENT OF LECTURE MATERIAL

As mentioned earlier in this section, it is important for students to know how the understanding of material presented in lectures will be assessed. Have a writing assignment due after the lecture on a particular topic so that you can get some immediate information regarding what students have learned from readings and lectures. Quizzes and tests, of course, provide good assessment of content learned in lectures. Multiple choice, short answer, essay, and group presentation are all assessment measures that work well to examine learning in lecture courses. We recommend various assessments of lectures given regularly throughout the semester so that students are not under pressure at midterm and finals to think back on lecture content that has not been assessed.

ADVANTAGES AND DISADVANTAGES

McKeachie and Svinicki (2006) suggest that lectures are particularly appropriate for the following instructional situations:

- Presenting up-to-date information (There is typically a gap between the latest scholarship and its appearance in a textbook).
- Summarizing materials scattered over a variety of sources.
- Adapting material to the background and interests of a particular group of students at a particular time and place.
- Helping students read more effectively by providing an orientation and conceptual framework.
- Focusing on key concepts, principles, or ideas. (p. 58)

It is quite reasonable to consider that lectures will be a part of the instructional tool box for the music professor. We encourage you to learn how to lecture well. However, we caution that too much reliance on lecture may not lead to true student engagement and understanding. The disadvantage in lectures is that they are often very "teacher-centered" activities. The professor organizes the lecture and delivers it to the class with little concern for student needs. As we are promoting a "learner-centered pedagogy," we suggest combining lecture with other strategies. Good lectures in combination with other strategies are extremely powerful.

LEADING A DISCUSSION

The quote below from an undergraduate music major frames our presentation of discussion:

> It seems that discussion is becoming more and more a part of my university classes. I have sat through many great discussions and some that would be better if they had never happened. The best discussions I have been in are when clear guidelines for discussion are presented. Students must not talk out of turn, get too off topic or forget "personal checking" to make sure they are not dominating the conversation. Bad discussions are often dominated by several students who have few ideas to add, based solely off opinion and not readings, research or new thinking, and are poorly facilitated by the instructor. Also, psychologically students need to know each other in some capacity before a good group discussion can take place. Having already introduced yourself and had the students introduce themselves to each other is important for students to feel safe to participate and know who is in the group.

Discussion-based approaches are quite typical in all music courses. Regarding discussion in general education, Bain (2004) suggests: "The teachers we studied thought a good class discussion could help students focus on important questions, stimulate them to grapple with key issues, help them acquire intellectual excitement, and give them the opportunity to construct their understanding" (p. 127). However, more than one college or university professor has had the unfortunate experience of walking behind a group of students shortly after what was thought by the professor to be an engaging discussion only to hear a student, when asked about what they did in class that day respond with an "Oh nothing, we just talked." The next section discusses the following regarding leading a discussion in a music class: setting up the room for a discussion; planning a discussion; leading a discussion; materials for a discussion; and assessment of discussion material. We conclude this section with advantages and disadvantages of discussion-based teaching in music classes.

SETTING UP THE ROOM FOR A DISCUSSION

Some of the issues regarding setting the room up for discussion are similar to concepts already stated regarding lecture courses or any other class. However, in a discussion, it is, of course, important for students to be able to see and talk with one another as well as with the professor. Sometimes, a discussion is held with the entire class while at other times it is held in small groups. Try to vary the type of discussion (pairs, small groups, larger groups, full group). Space must always be a consideration when trying to provide an appropriate environment for discussion.

PLANNING A DISCUSSION

As mentioned in the lecture session, begin to plan for discussion as you are reading the materials that students have been assigned for class. Try to create topics for discussion as you review the reading. Use writing assignments as a way to plan discussions. You might try having a writing assignment due the day before a class meeting so that you can design class discussions around the questions or issues brought forth in writing assignments. Tell students that one of the goals of the writing assignments is to provide a context for class discussion and encourage them to make suggestions regarding topics for class discussion. This works well in smaller (under 30) classes.

Lesson plans for a class including discussion will consist primarily of questions to be provided to students for full class or group discussion. There are various models for including discussion in class. Sometimes, you might pair students or put them in groups of three and ask them to talk to their partners for just 1 or 2 minutes about something related to the topic of the day. Then, bring them back together as a full group and share the partner conversations. This strategy works well when students are hesitant to speak in the full groups.

Or, you might prepare one discussion question and have various groups of students discuss the same question and then report back so that they can compare how students responded to the same question. At other times, you might have five or six groups (in a class of 18 or so), each working on a different question relating to the topic of the day. One of the primary challenges in planning this sort of interaction is to get an idea of how much time groups will need as well as how much time should be allotted for sharing group discussions. Tell groups how long they have to discuss and then assume 3–4 minutes of "report time" for each group. If you run out of time, you might have groups put highlights of their discussion on the board so that everyone can at least see the points even if you run out of time to present them.

LEADING A DISCUSSION

McKeachie and Svinicki (2006) present the following as barriers to discussion:

- Student habits of passivity
- Failure to see the value of a discussion
- Fear of criticism or looking stupid
- Push toward agreement or solution before alternative points of view have been considered
- Feeling that the task is to find the answer the instructor wants rather than to explore and evaluate possibilities (p. 44)

Discussion-based teaching requires careful preparation and skill from the professor. We worry that because it is somewhat difficult to facilitate discussions, novice music professors often avoid it. Try focused discussion questions for short spans of time at first. Be sure that students are clear on the discussion group task or question. Write discussion questions on the board or on a handout. While students are working in discussion groups, try to be a "fly on the wall," so to speak, and just listen to student conversations. Take notes regarding what one or two groups are discussing so you can reference that when you come back together. You may find that some groups of students work better if you are not in the group. If conversation stops when you arrive, try to move away to another group so that your presence does not freeze the discussion. It is often difficult not to take over the group discussions. Research on this phenomena (reviewed by Brown and

Atkins, 1988) suggests that most class discussions are dominated by instructors. One study documents that instructors dominated 86% of the time. When you come to the group, students will often begin to ask questions directly to you and it is tempting for you to respond. However, practice to respond with an answer such as "We will address that in the full group discussion" so that you do not take over in the small-group discussion.

There may be times that you even leave the room during a discussion. Explain to students that you want them to have ample time to share their insights and you know that if you stay in the room you will be tempted to take over in the conversation. Do not use this technique often. In the occasional class where you have students reading one of your own writings or publications, you might leave the room for some part of the discussion to allow time for honest conversation. When you use the "leave the room" strategy, you will get the sense that students take seriously the responsibility of utilizing the discussion time. It often helps to keep a group on task if you assign a note-taker or a reporter for each group and then those students take the responsibility for assuring that the group has addressed the question or problem. It is important to create a safe environment for students so that they feel that they can speak and respond. Try to use discussion when there are problems to solve or issues to discuss rather than for "right and wrong" type content.

Another difficulty in facilitating a discussion can be when too many students want to respond. You may need to move to a "raise your hand" policy if many students want to speak. Work to include as many students as possible in a discussion. Some classes will have someone who might monopolize the discussion and it is important to speak directly to that student outside of class if it becomes an issue. It is sometimes easy to call on only the more aggressive students or the students whom you agree with. Students will notice if equal time is not given to all students. If this is a struggle, you might keep track of who has spoken during a discussion to allow different students time to speak. By designing classes with a combination of small group (pairs and trios), larger group (6–10), and then full class discussion, you will find that most students will find some time to share their thoughts. Not every student will feel comfortable speaking in the large group, and that is okay.

MATERIALS FOR A DISCUSSION

In music classes, materials to begin a discussion could be recordings, live performance, excerpts from a score, or readings. You will have the most success with group discussion when students know in advance that there will be a discussion and are asked to read and prepare discussion points. The next chapter will address the use of cases, games, and simulations that overlap to some extent with the materials for discussion. Ultimately, it must be clear to students that the discussion was carefully planned and thought out by the professor and that there was a clear goal for the discussion. Begin class with goals for the discussion and conclude class with an overview of what was accomplished in the discussion so that students are clear regarding what they have experienced. Younger students in particular may not always recognize learning that takes place through discussion. Some of them will feel that unless the professor is talking they are not learning. Students must be taught how and what to learn through discussion. The vignette below highlights a discussion model that was perceived as useful for this student:

The way in which the teacher made us utilize class materials and apply them to our specific fields determined how much I enjoyed this course. The teacher of my multi-cultural education class had a set of readings to which we had to write response questions every week. She used those questions to lead class discussions. The majority of our class time was spent discussing issues that we were concerned about. In addition, we were required to write several papers based on the readings and how they applied to our field of study. Many of the readings we dealt with had to do with multicultural issues in the general classroom. I was encouraged to ponder the manifestations of these issues in a different classroom environment: the music classroom. As a result of being challenged to make specific applications, I was interested in the readings and papers.

ASSESSMENT OF DISCUSSION MATERIAL

Similar to courses involving lecture, it is important for students to know in advance of a discussion how their understanding from a discussion will be assessed. They will want to know if they should take notes in the discussion or if ideas from the discussion are to be included in writing assignments or essays for tests. Self-assessment tools often work well in considering the outcomes of a discussion. Asking students what the highlights of a discussion were can often help them come to some conclusions regarding what they have learned. Ultimately, the idea in a discussion is to get students to speak and articulate their thoughts and concerns about a topic. Allow students to share their previous experiences regarding a topic as students come into courses with preconceived assumptions about the content and the course. Discussions are a good place to work through these previous beliefs and assumptions.

ADVANTAGES AND DISADVANTAGES

Advantages of discussions include the following:

- Discussion gives students time to think and form opinions about class content.
- Discussion allows the opportunity for practical application of subject matter.
- Discussion can be more motivating than less interactive approaches.
- Discussion gives students an opportunity to speak in their own words.
- Discussion provides a setting for immediate feedback from colleagues and/or the instructor.

Disadvantages or challenges to discussions include the following:

- Depending on the age of the students and the familiarity of the content, it can be a challenge to get students to participate.
- Content from a discussion can be harder to assess.
- Facilitating a discussion requires the professor to reconceptualize his/her role in the room.
- The professor has less "control" in a discussion and this can be more difficult for novice teachers.

ASKING QUESTIONS

Strategies for asking good questions are needed for both lecture- and discussion-based classes. Davis (2001) outlines different types of questions and suggests that professors begin with exploratory level questions and proceed through a sequence to more difficult questions. The list below is based on her work but includes examples for music classes.

1. Exploratory questions—probe facts and basic knowledge:
   What are the most important issues to consider in choosing repertoire for a middle school band?

2. Challenge questions—examine assumptions, conclusions, and interpretations:
   Who is making the argument for more competition in music education? Who are the stakeholders?

3. Relational questions—ask for comparisons of themes, ideas, or issues:
   How does Beethoven's use of sonata form differ in this quartet than from an earlier quartet?

4. Diagnostic questions—probe motives or causes:
   Why did Bach compose the Brandenburg Concertos?

5. Action questions—call for a conclusion or action:
   If you were the music teacher in this setting, what would you do?

6. Cause and effect questions—ask for causal relationships between ideas, actions, or events:
   If assessment in high school instrumental music were based solely on performance skill, what might happen to the band program?

7. Extension questions—expand the discussion:
   Do you see connections between Stravinsky's orchestration and previous compos ers discussed in the class?

8. Hypothetical questions—pose a change in the facts or issues:
   What if the composer had moved to relative minor there instead?

9. Priority questions—seek to identify the most important issue:
   What are the most important suggestions you would provide to a young saxophone student in regards to tone?

10. Summary questions—elicit synthesis:
    What were the most important voice-leading concepts presented in class today?

When asking questions, educators often discuss the important concept of "wait time" in relation to student response. Train yourself to ask a question and then wait until a student responds. McKeachie and Svinicki (2006) recommend between 5 and 30 seconds as appropriate wait time. Resist the urge to answer a question yourself when no one responds. Try to rephrase the question or ask students to talk with the person next to them in pairs about the question and be ready to respond (chosen at random) in a few minutes. This gives students a few minutes to prepare a response with the help of a colleague. Or, ask students to think on the question and write a response so that everyone will have something to say if chosen at random.

Make some decisions regarding your approach to calling on students. If you intend to call on students at random, let them know this on the first day. If you intend to ask for volunteers, take care in calling on many students and not just the first hand that is always raised. In music classes, it is often necessary to have students perform (sing, chant, play) individually during class. Avoid going around the room in a predictable order (i.e., by rows) as this may encourage student apathy as well as may increase apprehension. Try to alternate between group performance and solo performance so that all students are engaged throughout the "testing" activity.

Outline questions to students as you are reviewing the reading for the class. Davis (2001) provides some additional pointers regarding choosing and preparing questions. She recommends that instructors avoid "yes or no" questions. This is challenging for music classes in that much of our content is "right or wrong" (i.e., "Is there a Bflat in the key of C Major?"). Davis recommends that we rephrase questions into "why or how" questions (i.e., "Why is there no B flat in the key of C Major?"). Avoid questions such as "Do you understand?" or "Alright?" in favor of questions that require students to demonstrate their understanding (i.e., "What chord did he move to in measure 10?" or "What is the concert transposition for the horn?"). Novice professors often ask generic questions when they would be better served by questions that assure them that the students understand. In order to encourage questions, avoid saying, "Do you have any questions?" in favor of "What questions do you have?," which encourages students to ask questions.

GETTING STUDENTS TO READ

McKeachie and Svinicki (2006) suggest that although the demise of the textbook has been predicted for many decades, textbooks are as popular as ever in college and university courses. They suggest that the access of multiple reading sources made available through technology provides an even stronger rationale to make use of textbooks that help students to organize diverse content gathered from a variety of sources. They also suggest that students need to be taught how to read: "We need to teach students how to read with understanding, how to think about the purpose of the author, about relationships to earlier learning, about how they will use what they've read" (p. 32).

Mckeachie and Svinicki suggest providing the following to students as they do the reading for your course:

1. Look at topic headings before studying the chapter.
2. Write down questions they would like to answer.
3. Make marginal notes as they read.
4. Underline or highlight important concepts.
5. Carry on an active dialogue with the author.
6. Comment on readings in their journals. (p. 3)

With regard to reading for music classes, we would add that students should be listening to music that is referenced in the reading so that musical concepts are put into context.

Music courses often include a significant reading component, particularly in courses for nonmajors, music history courses, and music education courses. We have found that the key strategy in getting students to read is to be sure to incorporate readings into class interactions. Let students know exactly how they will be responsible for the readings. You might provide a reading guide or questions to be addressed in class based on the readings. However, in some cases, you may find that this guide restricts student reading in that they consider only the issues on the guide and are less creative in their thinking.

You might open class with a "What did this concept from the readings mean to you?" sort of question. McKeachie and Svinicki (2006) suggest what he calls a "minute paper" as a way to have students write responses to the readings. They suggest giving students a minute to write what they believe to be the key concepts from the reading. If you plan to collect and grade this paper, we would suggest letting students know in advance that this is how reading will be assessed. It would also work to use the minute paper as the strategy for getting a discussion of the readings started. Students might share their papers with a classmate and discuss. The possibilities are endless. The key is do something that connects to the readings, or many students may not read.

The two quotes from undergraduate students as below highlights the need for holding students accountable for readings:

Student One: It shouldn't take long for professors to realize that many students don't do the readings. One of my history classes had discussion of the weekly readings on Fridays for 10 minutes before student presentations. These 10 minute discussions consisted of nothing but cricket noises while the professor tried to elicit a dialogue from the students. As she was an expert in the field many students did not even venture a guess as to what the readings may have said. Because there was never follow through with a quiz or group activity and she did not require the readings to come to class, students were able to go through the whole semester without doing the readings. After not getting a student response she often summarized the readings for students which further solidified the mind set of not having to do the readings.

Student Two: My educational psychology class was a problem. I started out doing the readings and coming to class prepared. However, instead of using class time to discuss the information we read and making practical applications, many classes turned into storytelling sagas. Stories drawn from real life have their place and purpose when a clear point is being made. This particular teacher had two students with special needs so she had a lot of experience with the subject material of the class. However instead of making a point of her stories she would go off on tangents. Then others would start telling stories and before we knew it class time would be over and nothing of importance had been discussed. Class after class was like this. Most of us stopped doing the readings because we were not held accountable for them. Many people just stopped coming to class. About two thirds of the way through the semester the teacher asked us to write an anonymous note to her about why so many of our classmates had stopped coming to class. For me the answer was simple: topics discussed were not relevant to our careers! However, they easily could have been. The teacher just did not lead class in manner in which we were forced to make the practical applications.

In some courses, you may prepare a course pack to provide extensive additional reading that may be helpful for students in the future. In that case, we would suggest that you "scaffold" the readings or divide the course pack readings so that no one student reads all articles on a particular topic. Class time then includes a report from each student regarding the article they read. All students have all articles but they are only the "expert" on the one assigned to them. The advantage in this sort of reading assignment is that students often feel the responsibility to present their article to other students. Of course, the disadvantage is that every student does not read all the articles. This technique works well for readings that are extensions of core content.

Be sure to physically use the textbook or course pack in class discussion each time there is a significant reading assignment. E-mail students to remind them to bring books or course packs to class and then design group discussion around specific quotes or questions in the book. Writing assignments should be connected to reading assignments. In some instances, you might assign a "free writing" journal assignment and ask students just to respond to the readings. In other cases, ask for specific references to readings to be cited throughout a writing assignment.

J. Daniel (1988) shares an interesting technique that would work well in music courses. On the day that a reading assignment is due, he asks student to submit a 3×5 index card with the key concepts from the reading. He collects these cards and reviews them for accuracy and stamps his name on the card. He collects the cards again right before an exam and then passes out the cards with his name on it (so that students cannot submit cards other than the ones done on the day the reading was due) at the midterm or final exam for use during the test. He reported that the number of students completing the reading in his course jumped from 10% to 90% when he began using this strategy.

There are many ways to "scare" students into doing the reading. For example, strategies shared in "When They Don't Do the Reading" (*Teaching Professor*, 1989) include designing an exam question on readings that were not discussed in class as well as giving an extra writing assignment to those students who have not done the reading. However, the "learner-centered" professor is less interested in some of these techniques. The "learner-centered" professor wants to find a way to engage students in the readings and have them share their insights from these readings in their own words.

HELPING STUDENTS TO WRITE

Elbow and Sorcinelli (2006) refer to what they call "high-stakes" and "low-stakes" writing assignments and encourage professors to include many low-stakes assignments in an effort to assist students in improving their writing. High-stakes writing assignments are those that professors use for final papers and grading, while low stakes refer to ungraded class writing assignments and drafts. Elbow and Sorcinelli make the case that in some courses, students just need to get their thoughts down on paper without fear of grading and then they can revise until a "high-stakes" product is created.

You might try having the first writing assignment in any course as a "low-stakes" e-mail response to readings. This would be a pass/fail assignment and it allows students to get thoughts on paper and it allows you to get a sense of the writing of each student. If the assignment is a "fail"—you might allow the student to rewrite after suggestions and corrections are provided. The key to helping students to write well is to be sure that students know the goal of the writing assignment, the purpose of the paper, and how the paper will be assessed. As discussed in Chapter 2, you might try to group students together early in the term to discuss the writing assignments and create grading criteria. Although this is a democratic process, we would suggest talking to students about the importance of "error free" manuscripts for the final draft. By discussing the importance of accurate writing in the lives of professional musicians, you will find that students will assign a fairly high percentage of a final paper grade to grammar, syntax, and writing style.

In addition to an early pass/fail assignment, you might try to assign "journal assignments" or a "dear diary." These are first-person responses to course readings, discussions, or experiences, and they help students to talk about course content in their own words. With regard to high-stakes writing, Elbow and Sorcinelli suggest that "Successful parroting of the textbook language can mask a lack of understanding" (p. 194). You will find that journal or diary writing helps you to get a better sense of student internalization and understanding of course content. In larger classes, you might set up "e-mail journal teams" and have students communicate with one another through this "low-stakes" activity and then an occasional overview sent to you.

Decisions regarding assignments are inevitably tied to class size and professor schedules. Try to plan semesters carefully so that big writing assignments are not due in all your classes at the same time. You will find students quite appreciative of the opportunity to revise writing through drafts. The timing of papers and due dates is extremely important since final papers do not give much opportunity for feedback. It is sometimes even difficult to get students to pick up or read final paper comments. For the professor who is really interested in helping students to write, shorter papers throughout the term are more helpful in providing feedback to students. If you are going to assign a large final paper, we recommend that you plan a class toward the end of the term that is a "paper work session" and then ask for drafts in advance of the work session. These sessions often allow for peer response to writing. Students learn from reading other student's papers and getting feedback from other students. The student in the following vignette highlights the student interest in "choice" for paper topics as has been discussed earlier in the text.

> Like most college students, I'm not usually eager to write papers. I can, however, think of a couple of theory papers that I wrote that I really wanted to get into. What set those essays apart was that the assignment was essentially "Analyze this work as we have done in class. You can use any mix of analytical tools to explore the power behind the music." All of a sudden, this wasn't a paper to do because I had to, but allowed me to explore and decide for myself what was important and what wasn't. I could listen to the music, find what drew me to it, and explore for myself why I thought the music had the power it did.

Very few music professors feel prepared to assist students with their writing in terms of structure and mechanics. For students who really struggle with writing, the best strategy may be to suggest that they get a tutor or visit the school or university writing center. Do not reward weak writing. If you do not know how to help a poor writer, send them to an expert but be sure to grade them accordingly so that they understand the importance of good writing.

There are several strategies for learning to grade student writing objectively. Know that reliable grading of papers is difficult. It is not unlike jury grading or auditions in terms of the level of subjective opinion that can be a part of the grade. You might ask students to include a cover page with their final papers and then have a graduate student number the papers (taking the cover page off) so that you can read the papers without knowing who the authors are. You will be surprised at the "good papers" from "not so good students" and the "average papers" from "good students" that sometimes emerge.

Peter Elbow and Mary Deane Sorcinelli (2006) suggest reading an entire paper before making any comments. They also suggest writing comments on a separate paper (or electronic document) rather than in the margins of the paper. Since many professors are moving to electronic submission and response, this may become more common. The thought is that general comments on a feedback sheet are more useful for future writings than very specific concerns in the margins. In grading final papers, professors are reminded to consider some of the plagiarism concerns discussed in Chapter 5.

SUBSTANTIVE VERSUS REFLECTIVE WRITING

A final topic to consider in relation to student writing is the difference between substantive and reflective writing. Fink (2003) defines substantive writing as

> writing that is focused on a topic and that attempts to present an organized statement about the information and ideas the writer has about that topic. The familiar practice of assigning term papers and essays has been used for centuries to engage students in substantive writing. (pp. 116–117)

Thus far in this section on student writing, we have been discussing substantive writing. Fink encourages the "learner-centered" professor to consider reflective writing defined as "focusing on the writer's learning experience itself" (p. 117) and attempts to identify the significance and meaning of a given learning experience, primarily for the writer. Hence it is quite acceptable in this kind of writing to address more personal issues, such as "What am I learning?"; "Of what value is this to me?"; "How did I learn best, learn most comfortably, and learn with difficulty?"; "What else do I need to learn?" Music education courses often focus on reflective writing since the development of personal reflection is a primary goal for music educators. However, we would suggest that the development of reflection is a primary goal for all musicians.

Fink (2003) outlines several strategies for reflection writing. Many of these are similar to writing strategies already presented. However, the goal of the writing is to have the student articulate what they have learned. She suggests minute papers (also mentioned in the section on Getting Students to Read) for brief reflections. She mentions diaries and e-mail journals (also mentioned earlier) for what she calls an "intermediate form of reflective writing" (p. 118) and she suggests learning portfolios for what she calls an "extended form of reflective writing" (p. 118). In music courses, a learning portfolio that includes student writing about their internalization of the content in a course may help the student bring theory or history concepts into their performance world. Writing prompts might include questions such as How will the information from this course affect your performance practice? Or, How will you approach the music of (add composer) differently now that you have taken this course?

College students will have written papers for courses in high school. However, your class may be the first time they write about music. Beginning with some reflective writing or less high-stakes writing may provide a place for them to learn about writing about music under less stressful circumstances.

CONCLUSION

Professors in all areas of music will have the need to organize content into "lecture-like" presentations, facilitate discussion, and work with students on reading and writing skills. Many musicians have not been prepared for assisting students in writing, so it is important to know of campus resources for writing. Just because you have not been trained in how to help students write, does not mean that you should not insist on good writing for your course. Good lecturing can be learned and practiced as can skills for facilitating discussion. See Part Three of this text for more information on personal growth in teaching and professional development.

QUESTIONS FOR DISCUSSION AND SUGGESTED ACTIVITIES

1. On the basis of your own experiences, make a list of characteristics of a good lecture.
2. On the basis of your own experiences, make a list of challenges you have encountered in lecture-based courses.
3. Choose a music content area and design a 20-minute "mini lecture" to practice the timing and organization of lecture.
4. Review the delivery characteristics of good lectures and practice "delivering" your 20-minute lecture developed in question 3.
5. Choose a music content area and develop questions for facilitating a discussion of that content.
6. Review the types of questions provided in the chapter and provide examples of each type within the content of a class you might teach.
7. Reflect back on your own experiences in undergraduate classes with regard to reading. What strategies assisted you in reading and what procedures led you to be less inspired about reading?
8. Discuss the concept of minute papers, group discussions, and scaffolding as ways to get students to read and interact. What are the advantages and disadvantages of each in a music context?
9. Reflect back on your own experiences in learning to write about music in undergraduate courses. What strategies assisted your growth?

CHAPTER 7

Strategies for Active Learning in Music Classrooms

Instructional strategies that get students thinking, talking, and interacting with one another promote active learning. McKeachie and Svinicki (2006) suggest *"active learning* is the buzz word (or phrase) in contemporary higher education" (p. 35). Davis (2001) relates:

> Students learn best when they are actively involved in the process. Researchers report that, regardless of the subject matter, students working in small groups tend to learn more of what is taught and retain it longer than when the same content is presented in other instructional formats. (p. 147)

In music classes, we might consider the need for music making (singing, moving, chanting, playing instruments, listening, composing, creating, and improvising) as part of active learning. A focus on learner-centered pedagogy and a move away from the transmission model of teaching leads to active learning. We open this chapter with an extended discussion of some of the various types of group work including cooperative as well as collaborative learning groups. Cooperative groups work together on a task that is most often presented or designed by the instructor whereas collaborative groups are often involved in task generation as well as completion. Strategies for grouping students as well as room setup, planning for group work, and assessment of group activities are addressed.

The second part of the chapter provides suggestions for specific types of *problem-based learning* including case-based teaching, games, and simulations. McKeachie and Svinicki (2006) suggest the following regarding problem-based learning: "Problem-based education is based on the assumption that human beings evolved as individuals who are motivated to solve problems and that problem solvers will seek and learn whatever knowledge is needed for successful problem-solving" (p. 222). Fink (2003) suggests:

> Evidence indicates that students learn how to analyze and solve problems much more effectively this way, compared, for example, to the traditional medical school curriculum

of 'learn all the facts' for two years and only then proceed to learn how to apply the by-now-half-forgotten facts. (p. 21)

For music courses, problems may be theoretical analysis problems, performance problems, historical problems, or pedagogical problems. Cases, games, and simulations will be situated within these "problem-areas" for music. The final section of the chapter presents "unifying principles" for "what the best college teachers do" (Bain, 2004) with special attention to strategies for larger classes. Questions for discussion and suggested extension activities are provided.

COOPERATIVE LEARNING

Although there are multiple names used to refer to students working in groups (peer learning, peer teaching, work groups, study groups, learning communities, etc.) probably the most common is the term cooperative learning groups. Davis (2001) makes a distinction between informal learning groups and formal learning groups. She suggests that informal groups represent a temporary group of students that may be brought together in a class period for a single task. The group may be just two students or a larger group. She suggests that informal learning groups may be used in classes of any size at any time to check for student understanding or allow students to talk with one another about the material. Davis uses the term "formal learning groups" to refer to a more established group that is assigned to carry out a project, write a paper, or prepare a presentation. Both types of groups are considered cooperative learning groups. Examples of cooperative learning activities for music theory might include providing a score and asking students to outline the form or provide a harmonic analysis in groups. In music history, we might ask students to discuss the relationship between a composer's work and the political climate of the country the composer was in (most likely based on readings). In a performance, class students may work in small groups on a particular musical passage or a particular skill (i.e., tuning of a certain chord). In music education, cooperative groups may respond to readings on pedagogy or the climate of schools. In most cases the instructor would dictate the task and students would complete it in a cooperative group.

SETTING UP THE ROOM

Although the issues of room setup for cooperative learning are similar to the "setting up the room" for discussion-based teaching addressed in Chapter 6, we thought it important to address setup again in thinking about cooperative learning groups. It is important for groups to have appropriate space for their work. If the room is small and several groups are working at the same time, the noise level in the room can make group work unsuccessful. If possible, secure break-out rooms for cooperative groups or have students make arrangements to meet outside of class for specific projects. Try to have an extra chair in each group so you can visit the groups throughout the activity.

SETTING UP THE GROUPS

Groups of three or four are ideal for most cooperative work. In larger groups, there is less opportunity for students to interact. Vary the grouping techniques so that throughout the semester students get to work with different students in the course. Depending on the task or question, you might create the groups carefully to include an even number of brass players versus woodwind players (or whatever) or even numbers of students who have experience in a certain area versus students with little experience. The groups can also be created at random. The following are various strategies that we suggest to create groups in music courses:

- Have students "count" off and then have the "ones" in a group, the "twos" in a group, and so on.

- On the basis of where students are seated in the room, group three or four together, then the next three or four. The danger in this strategy is that if students often sit in the same seats and you use this strategy often, they will often end up in the same groups.

- Use index cards to group the students. Put numbers or colors on the cards, shuffle the deck, and then pass out the cards. All the "reds" will be in one group, all blues in another, and so on.

- Arrange students alphabetically by name or by month or year of birth. We often use grouping strategies as icebreakers in the first few classes in the semester and month or year of birth works well for that goal.

In some cases, students may choose their own groups. Allow students to choose groups for projects or cooperative activities that will take place outside of class time. The students often have a sense of which students have schedules that may be compatible with their own (often tied to large ensemble), and allowing them to choose their own groups often leads to easier scheduling of group meetings. Do be aware of potential gender and racial issues in grouping. Minority students will tend to group together unless you control for this. Students often group together along gender lines as well. Whatever the strategy, be sure to plan out how groups will be divided in advance of the class. Know how many groups you will use and how many students will be in each group. Know where the groups will work and what the task for each group will be. The student comment below highlights the value of diverse backgrounds in group discussion.

I've had some pretty useless small-group discussions in some of my education classes. The subject matter is abstract and doesn't seem applicable to future teaching, and then we are asked to brainstorm ideas about concrete ways to use the subject in our own content areas. The music education students then get together and basically chat for ten minutes, while one or two of us make up feasible answers. Meanwhile, I've had great small-group discussions when teachers break us up and create teams of mixed content areas. All of the sudden, I have to represent music education for the group. All of us really have to contribute to have a conclusion in the end that shows that each subject area had some input. Plus, I feel that I actually learn from my peers when they come from a totally different perspective.

PLANNING FOR COOPERATIVE LEARNING

The most difficult part of designing cooperative group work is ensuring that the goals of the activity are clear to students and that the task or question is clear to them as well. Many of the strategies for planning cooperative learning overlap with the planning for discussion explained in the last chapter as well as the cases, games, and simulation strategies presented at the end of this chapter. In all of these approaches it is important for students to have a sense of how to be successful in a group learning setting. Have students talk about what makes a good group interaction. Explain why you think group interaction is important. In music classes, it is easy to make the case that music-making is often a cooperative group effort. It is fairly rare for a musician to work completely alone. Thus, cooperative grouping during coursework should be seen by students as authentic to the discipline. The materials used for cooperative learning may be readings, musical examples, cases, games, or any other shared experience that a group may interact with. In cooperative learning, these materials are most often supplied by the instructor.

LEADING COOPERATIVE LEARNING ACTIVITIES

After you give the assignments for the groups, give each group some time to get working on their own. As was mentioned in the discussion section in Chapter 6, faculty often take over in group discussions whereas the goal should be in getting the students to speak. Move around from one group to another and try to stay out of the way. If you feel that groups are talking less (or more) with you in the group, try to move on to the next group. Take notes regarding student discussions and then prepare a summary for discussion when you return to the full group. Timing of group activities can be challenging. Tell groups how much time is allotted for discussion and let them know that if they need more time you will try to accommodate the same. Listen to the groups and try to get a sense of the timing. Davis (2001) suggests that when 25% of the groups have completed the task then the others should be given a "last minute" warning and encouraged to finish their conversations.

Some cooperative group work will include a full group share at the end. This could take the form of notes on the board or a brief verbal overview of the conversation. You might use a group activity to conclude a discussion or as an opportunity to share thoughts regarding a follow-up writing assignment. In that case, there will not usually be a full group follow-up discussion. One of the most important logistical issues in group work is having a signal for bringing students back to the full group. If students have moved to break-out groups, be sure they know exactly what time to return. If groups are working simultaneously in one classroom space, the noise may make it difficult to get student attention. Since music classrooms often have a piano, try an "I V I" chord progression at the piano as the class signal to return from groups. Turning lights on and off also works in this scenario although it is a bit more invasive. Whatever the signal is, be sure to let students know what it will be.

ASSESSMENT OF LEARNING
IN THE COOPERATIVE CLASSROOM

In at least one institution that we are aware of, professors are not allowed to give grades for group assignments. Some professors use self-assessment for group work to allow students to share issues of group interaction that they want the professor to know about. You might consider group assignments that are ungraded or termed pass/fail so as to avoid the difficulties of grading a group project. Sometimes, the group discussion or cooperative group is solely a teaching strategy or learning opportunity and the content and concepts from the group work will be assessed through other course requirements (i.e., tests, quizzes, writing assignments).

If you intend to use cooperative learning in a formal way (as mentioned above by Davis) be prepared that there will be some groups who are unable to work together. Outline a process for students to use if the groups are not working well together. This may include a way for students to regroup or divide. If possible, allow students to work out the group issues without instructor intervention as much as is possible.

Advantages and Disadvantages

We have made the case for cooperative learning throughout the book each time we justify the need for learner-centered, active approaches. The advantages in cooperative learning are the same as these learner-centered objectives that have been presented throughout. One disadvantage in the cooperative learning approach is that it is more difficult to plan and pace classes that are interactive. It is harder to create measurable outcomes that can be tested in a solely cooperative learning environment. However, if cooperative learning is used in conjunction with other strategies, some of the disadvantages can be managed. A final disadvantage to consider with cooperative learning groups is the issue of power and control of learning. As has been discussed previously, a learner-centered professor works to manage the inherent power issues of the class structure. Cooperative learning, although interactive, is still quite teacher-directed. Teachers usually choose the materials for the group, design the tasks, post the deadlines, provide assessment information, and so on. It is sometimes difficult for students to feel as if they are directing their own learning when working within activities that were designed for them. The next section on collaborative learning addresses some of these concerns.

COLLABORATIVE LEARNING

Collaborative learning adjusts the power structure of the classroom and allows for maximum student choice in directing learning (Roschelle and Teasley, 1995). It is often referred to as a "teaching methodology" (Luce, 2001). David Luce (based on Bruffee, 1999) outlined basic principles of collaborative learning that are used throughout the collaborative learning literature.

- Knowledge is socially constructed as a "consensus among the members of a community of knowledgeable peers" (Bruffee, p. xxi).

- The authority of knowledge is shared among members of the community.
- Interdependent personal relationships shape a community of knowledgeable peers.

Luce explains that a knowledgeable peer in a music class can be another student in the class who will have a different experience with a topic than student number one and so these two students share different "knowledge." Classmates are also knowledgeable peers if they have been in the class and have been reading and learning the material (versus a peer who is not in the class). Collaborative learning encourages learning from one another as a primary goal and the professor's role changes from one of leader to one of facilitator and participant.

Hoffman (1991) studied computer-aided collaborative learning in a traditional harmony class at the New England Conservatory of Music. Although the technology he used is no doubt dated, the conclusion that collaborative learning was perceived as advantageous in teaching theory is useful. Hoffman states: "Students virtually teach one another. They reinforce the teacher's instructions, and share in decision-making and in evaluating results. The learning of harmony becomes a shared, ongoing, and externalized process, comparable to a performance" (p. 276). His evaluation of the approach included a questionnaire to students and he reported that student comments were "overwhelmingly positive" (p. 276).

Luce (2001) discusses the wide use of collaborative learning in fields outside of music including medicine, nursing, business, teaching, and counseling and makes the case for consideration of the approach in music:

> Music as essential creative communication permeates all cultures as a collaborative, communally based expression of humanity. Thus, theory, musicology, applied instruction, ensemble performance, and music teacher education all offer inherent opportunities to engage students in collaborative processes. Adopting a collaborative learning approach places renewed responsibility on students to participate, on professors to share the authority of knowledge, and on the combined efforts of a community of knowledgeable peers to maintain the integrity and vitality of music. (p. 24)

We consider examples of collaborative learning activities using the same concepts as were shared for cooperative learning and adjusting them to be more in the spirit of a collaborative classroom. In music theory, rather than providing a score and asking students to outline the form or provide a harmonic analysis in groups, students would generate the group assignment and choose the repertoire to be studied. In music history, students might be asked to discuss what came up in the readings that was of interest to them. In a performance, class students would choose the repertoire to be studied and plan their own rehearsals and practice sessions. In music education, collaborative groups may search for materials that answer pedagogical questions that were generated during class fieldwork. It is difficult in higher education to create a "purely" collaborative classroom, but for our purposes, collaborative learning requires more choice and responsibility for learning on the part of the student.

The collaborative approach is particularly interesting in music since so much of music instruction takes place in the applied studio and the ensemble. Most applied studio settings are set up in an apprentice model where the student goes to the teacher expecting to be corrected and given information on how to improve. That is not to say that good applied teachers do not work to get students thinking independently, but we are just outlining the sort of power structure that is typical in applied music. Most college and university ensembles are on a tight performance schedule and are working to model professional ensemble experiences that typically have the conductor as "boss" so to speak. It is often difficult for music students to break out of the "rely on others" mode in their music classes.

The next section outlines issues associated with setting up a room for collaborative learning, setting up the groups, planning for collaboration, participating as the professor in collaborative groups, and materials for collaboration. We conclude the section with a review of advantages and disadvantages of collaborative learning as a strategy in music courses.

SETTING UP THE ROOM AND FORMING THE GROUPS

Although the issues in collaborative learning setup are, of course, similar to cooperative learning and general small-group discussions, it is important to note that in collaborative learning settings, you will work to give students as much choice possible on who is in their group, where they will meet, what they will work on, and how much time it will take. If you have not worked with students in small groups before, this "free" approach may sound just crazy, but evidence suggests that most students rise to the occasion when given this sort of responsibility and may surprise you with what they can accomplish.

PLANNING FOR COLLABORATIVE LEARNING

One of the most important things a professor can do in planning for collaborative work is to make sure that students understand how to work together in groups. McKeachie and Svinicki (2006) suggest that students be given the following directions for group work:

1. Be sure everyone contributes to discussion and to tasks.
2. Don't jump to conclusions too quickly. Be sure that minority ideas are considered.
3. Don't assume consensus because no one has opposed an idea or offered an alternative. Check agreement with each group member verbally, not just by a vote.
4. Set goals—immediate, intermediate, and long-term—but don't be afraid to change them as you progress.
5. Allocate tasks to be done. Be sure that each person knows what he or she is to do and what the deadline is. Check this before adjourning.
6. Be sure there is agreement on the time and place of the next meeting and on what you hope to accomplish.
7. Before ending a meeting, evaluate your group process. What might you try to do differently next time? (p. 215)

Many of the other decisions that the professor makes in other teaching approaches (goals for the group, tasks in meeting the goal, group roles, timing of meetings) are made by the students in a collaborative setting. As mentioned above, a pure collaborative approach is difficult to accomplish within the typical restraints of a university setting; however, any effort to redistribute the power in a classroom will be valuable for student learning. Collaborative approaches work particularly well with older students in smaller class sizes who have worked together in earlier classes and who have an already comfortable rapport with the instructor.

PARTICIPATING IN COLLABORATIVE LEARNING ACTIVITIES

For most professors, it is difficult to participate in collaborative learning activities without "taking charge." You might try to let groups work completely without your aid for some period of time so that you can get a sense of what they can do on their own. As with all the approaches presented in the book, participating in a collaborative learning environment takes experience and practice. Work to allow students to lead discussion and course directions. Allow for as much student choice as is reasonable for the course.

MATERIALS FOR COLLABORATIVE LEARNING

Collaborative learning encourages student choice for class reading, assignments, and activities. However, in some cases, students do not have enough prior knowledge in a subject area to make informed decisions. The professor must make decisions regarding how much choice is appropriate for students. The learner-centered professor works hard to assist students in securing appropriate materials and does not make assumptions about student interests and backgrounds.

Advantages and Disadvantages

Learning how to be independent thinkers and problem solvers is important for students in music classes. Collaborative learning provides a place for this learning. However, the restrictions of the real world in regard to syllabus, policies, curriculum, and assessment make a purely collaborative approach to teaching music classes difficult. Weimer (2002) devotes a complete chapter in her section on "Implementing the Learner-Centered Approach" to what she calls "Responding to Resistance." Resistance to collaborative learning may come from colleagues and supervisors as well as from students. The struggle between traditional approaches to teaching and innovation is a constant challenge for the college professor.

CASE-BASED TEACHING

The use of cases in instructional settings dates back to the Harvard Medical School in the nineteenth century and is now common in medicine, business, law, and education (Barnes et al., 1994). Within music, there is a body of literature regarding the use of teaching cases specifically for music teacher education (Conway, 1997a, 1997b, 1999a,

1999b; Hourigan, 2006). In my 1999 discussion of the use of the case method in music teacher education, I suggested:

> As practiced in teacher education, the case method of instruction includes a variety of approaches using cases or stories of teachers in real or fictional settings as prompts for students' discussion and reflection. L. Shulman (1992) suggests that "case methods are expected to be more engaging, more demanding, more intellectually exciting and stimulating, more likely to bridge the vast chasm between principle and practice and more likely to help neophytes learn to 'think like a teacher'" (p. 1) than traditional methods of teaching, such as lecture and class discussion of textbook material. (p. 20)

If we adjust the quote above to "approaches using cases or stories of *musicians,* or *composers,* or *performers*" than the use of cases in all music classes makes sense. Cases that are used in music education classes usually provide an example of a situation that a teacher might face when working with K-12 students in a music class setting. Students in a case-based discussion group would identify the instructional issues in the setting and discuss what the teacher might do. There are a variety of published music education textbooks that use the case method and can provide the cases for music education discussion (Abrahams and Head, 2005; Atterbury and Richardson, 1995; Brinson, 1996; Conway and Hodgman, 2003).

Case-based techniques for music theory would be appropriate when examining and comparing two "cases" or pieces utilizing the same compositional technique. Students would be given the cases (or scores) and asked to define the use of the compositional technique and compare the cases. We know of several music history professors who use case-based strategies in having students discuss and compare composers and historical contexts. Real stories of historic composers can provide excellent "cases" for class discussion.

Cases are the "materials" for group discussion (could be cooperative or collaborative). When using cases, the strategies for discussion and asking questions presented in Chapter 6 are appropriate as are the concerns regarding space, goal setting, organization of time, and assessment. In addition to these challenges, the creation of a good case or the finding of a printed case is essential. Good cases include sufficient detail in the story, a problem to consider, as well as questions for discussion. They must be engaging and interesting. Ryan Hourigan's (2006) review of the music teacher education case research led to the following suggestions for teaching with the case method that we believe are relevant for all music courses:

- Use cases in conjunction with other strategies and not as the sole teaching strategy in a course.
- Use cases to provide a shared context for discussion.
- Be sure that students know the goal of the case discussion.
- Try having students write their own cases as a vehicle for reflection.

Case-based Teaching Checklist

1. Outline the content or goal to be addressed through a case.
2. Create or find a case
3. Assign the case. Be sure to give students time to read and reflect before discussion.

4. Refer to strategies for grouping students and facilitating discussions (Chapter 6).

5. Make decisions regarding assessment of content and concepts from the case.

GAMES AND SIMULATIONS

Similar to case-based teaching, games and simulations are problem-based models that include students as active participants rather than passive observers. Games often work well for exam reviews or unit reviews as an opportunity to test content knowledge. They can also help to relieve the stress of an upcoming exam. Begin a "game-based" activity by considering the content and the type of game questions that would work best for that content. There are free online resources for creating *Jeopardy* games and crossword puzzles that allow you to use your own content for the questions and answers. Board games such as Monopoly or Clue can often be adjusted for music-based content. Try having students design a game themselves based on a given content. The generation of the game (usually in groups) works as a review session for the content and then the playing of the games that the class developed can also work as an assessment tool for the professor to get an understanding of student learning. Games work well in most music classes since so much of the content in theory, history, and music education is fact-based. Any game that gets students active in the class will be valuable for their learning.

Simulations are a particular type of game that has students acting or taking on particular roles. Examples for music theory might include a mock debate between two theorists regarding the harmonic analysis of a particular passage, or a mock presentation of a musical work for a pretend theory conference. Examples in music history might include a short student-written play in which each character is a different composer at a dinner party discussing the use of wind instruments in the full orchestra, or a pretend train ride in which a composer and a performer are riding and discussing a musical work. Examples in music education include a debate on the issues of competition in secondary ensembles between two teachers on opposing sides of the issue, a debate on the advantages and disadvantages of various rhythm syllable systems for teaching rhythmic notation, a mock school board meeting in which the music teacher must advocate for the value of music education, or a mock job interview for a position in teaching music. All of these simulations require the student to understand and synthesize content from the course. The mock activity requires them to act as professionals in the field and they will value the authenticity of the simulation.

The advantages of games and simulations are that students enjoy these activities and will be motivated to prepare them and complete them. Planning for games and simulations takes some experience as (just like with all group work) goals of the activity must be made clear. Students must have ample time to prepare their work and have a clear understanding of how the work will be assessed.

TEACHING LARGER CLASSES AND UNIFYING
PRINCIPLES OF TEACHING

Although it is fairly rare for music courses to be extremely large, the new professor may be asked to teach large sections of survey courses for nonmajors. Sometimes, these courses can have more than a hundred students enrolled. It is important to consider that active learning may be achieved in large classes as well. Many professors in large classes feel as if they must lecture for the majority of time, but as has been suggested throughout the book, research has suggested that learner-centered and student-directed models lead to better learning.

In his study of "What the best college teachers do," Ken Bain (2004) has identified seven common principles of good college teachers regardless of the content or the size of the class. Although many of these have already been addressed in the text, we will examine these seven principles below as a conclusion to the focus on teaching and learning in a classroom setting.

1. Create a Natural Critical Learning Environment

A natural learning environment in a music class needs live or recorded music as a part of class activities. Singing, moving, listening, analyzing, evaluating, and creating music are key elements of a music class. A critical environment is one in which students learn the vocabulary for describing music and critically talking about it. In music education classes, a natural critical learning environment is also a place where good teaching techniques and strategies are modeled and good pedagogy is questioned and discussed. Anything you can do to have students interacting in a course in the way that professionals in the field interact will create the environment that Bain found in examining what the best college teachers do. This should be true for nonmajors' classes as well. A student does not need previous musical experience in order to interact with music by moving, singing, listening, and so on. Technology allows for considerable flexibility in this area. Bain suggests that students need to leave a class with more questions about the content than they had before they took the class. Sometimes, knowing what you do not know is as important as knowing a certain body of content. Critical learners are always seeking more information.

2. Get Their Attention and Keep It

Getting their attention in a music class begins with finding out about their musical interests and experiences and then figuring out a way to connect course content to their interests. This concept is important for both music majors as well as nonmajors. Music majors are often solely focused on performance; so the music instructor in theory, composition, musicology, conducting, or music education will need to make a connection between course content and performance. The music nonmajor may have little previous experience with the type of music to be studied in a music course. However, almost all students have musical preferences. Getting their attention may mean starting instruction with something familiar to the students and then moving on to other types of music.

3. Start with the Students Rather than the Discipline

For those of us who have dedicated our lives to becoming musicians, it is difficult to move away from music itself as the singular focus in teaching music. However, a focus on music outside of the context of the students who are trying to learn music will not lead to a learner-centered classroom. It is the nature of student learning as it occurs within the musical context that ought to drive the nature of teaching and learning. This does not mean that music is not central to music learning, but that starting your planning with the students rather than the discipline will hopefully lead to music as the focus of music learning. Understanding the learner (Chapter 3 of this text) must be a part of course planning and implementation. Chapter 11 discusses getting feedback from students and attending to suggestions provided by students and this is an important component of this principle as well.

4. Seek Commitments

Students must be made aware of the commitment needed in a course. Quotes from several of the participants in Ken Bain's (2004) study highlight this issue.

> I tell my students the first day of class that the decision to take the class is the decision to attend the class every time it meets. I also tell them that my decision to teach the class includes the commitment to offer sessions worth attending, and I ask them to let me know if they think I'm not doing that. (Bain, 2004, p. 113)
>
> The decision to take the course is yours, but once you make that decision, you have responsibilities to everyone else in this community of learners. (Bain, 2004, p. 113)

Interactive strategies as discussed in this chapter will help students to understand their responsibility to other students. For younger students, an attendance policy may help them to form good habits. It is important to make the commitment known to the students at the beginning of the course and then to monitor that students are meeting the requirements. As was discussed in Chapter 1, students need a clear syllabus with time commitments well documented so they can plan their time. Music students have busy performance schedules and cannot be expected to add commitments once the semester has begun.

5. Help Students Learn Outside of Class

We have focused throughout the text on strategies for grouping students and encouraging students to learn from one another and Bain suggests this as a key principle in good teaching. Even in larger classes, students can be encouraged to form study groups and learning communities. It is common for students in music classes to have outside-of-class requirements such as concert attendance or school observations (music education). Encourage students to complete these requirements in groups so that they use travel time to and from the events as a time to learn from one another.

6. Engage Students in Disciplinary Thinking

As has been mentioned before, work to create course assignments and class interactions that require students to interact with music in a way that is true to the discipline. Students should be asked to "do as a theorist (or other discipline) does." The degree to which this is possible depends on the course and on the experience level of the students. However, even in an introductory course, it is important for students to model some of the behaviors of professionals.

7. Create Diverse Learning Experiences

No one approach will work for all students. Attending to the individual differences and varied learning styles of students means providing many different types of interactions with music. Assignments should be varied including reading, writing, presenting, and discussion. Class meetings should be a mixture of lecture, discussion, cooperative learning, and collaborative learning depending on the content. Assessment should be a mixture of tests, writing assignments, musical presentations, and other strategies. The music itself should represent diversity in terms of ethnicity and gender when appropriate.

QUESTIONS FOR DISCUSSION AND SUGGESTED ACTIVITIES

1. Reflect back on your own experiences in cooperative group learning. What did the professor do to set up a group so that it worked well? What were things that did not work well?

2. Generate ideas for cooperative group learning for a course that you might teach.

3. Discuss the challenge in creating a collaborative learning environment in music.

4. Generate examples of cases or stories you could use in a class you might teach.

5. Be creative in thinking about music games to review content and engage students.

6. Discuss active learning strategies for a large nonmajors music class. How can you engage these learners in active music making?

CHAPTER 8

Teaching Applied Music

The professional practice of teaching music through private lessons appears at first to be deceptively simple. In reality, the Western tradition of studio instruction is extremely complex. The studio lesson is the interface between the professional community and the individual who aspires to join that community. The studio teacher is the mediator between that professional community and the student. The challenge of studio instruction is that all of the cultural history of the professional community may be presented to the student through the medium of the weekly music lesson. As we advance our understanding of how the fundamental cultural replication unit works, we advance our understanding of the most basic teaching-learning process. This knowledge is important for our understanding not just of how we learn music but of how humans learn anything. (Kennel, 2002, p. 254)

The opening quote from Richard Kennel supports the notion that the applied studio tradition of one-on-one instruction is an extremely important aspect of any consideration of teaching music in higher education. Many music graduate students will secure employment in positions that include applied instruction. Some will be exclusively applied instructors while others will teach applied music as a secondary area of expertise. Some will teach a full studio of 15–20 students while others will work as adjunct applied music instructors with smaller studios. Some applied instructors will work exclusively with music majors; some will have a mix of majors and nonmajors; and still others will work with nonmajors only. The chapter is based on responses from applied music faculty at both Adrian College and The University of Michigan as well as responses from undergraduate students regarding applied lesson study. Quotes from both applied faculty and undergraduate students are included throughout the chapter. We have tried to represent the voice of the applied teacher in this chapter as a way of honoring the very specific culture that is created in every applied studio. We begin with a discussion of the varying contexts for applied music instruction, the diverse goals of the learners in the studio setting, and general characteristics of successful applied music instructors. We then proceed with discussion of one-on-one instruction in music including ways to motivate students and teach to individual differences. The next section of the chapter addresses maintaining a healthy culture in the applied studio. Strategies for working with groups of applied students in studio class are presented as well as logistical issues for applied music including scheduling, accompanists, juries, and grading. The final section of the chapter provides a brief overview of research on the applied studio and encourages the applied instructor to consider the documentation of applied studio teaching interactions as an action research area (action research is addressed in Chapter 13). Questions for discussion and suggested extension activities are included.

SETTINGS AND CHARACTERISTICS OF SUCCESSFUL APPLIED TEACHERS

As mentioned above, applied music instruction is a staple course in the school or department of music as well as a common course for interested nonmajors. The key to success in applied instruction is to be aware of the varied goals for different students and to work to teach to these individual differences. In the effort to learn about the studio in advance, the new applied teacher should try to collect materials from the department office or from former students in the studio including recital programs, senior projects, or studio class programs or syllabi.

Students have very different expectations regarding applied music. Since many applied faculty come from schools of music or conservatories, the transition from that atmosphere to a studio of nonmajors or an institution where applied performance is less intense may be difficult. We suggest having a conversation with each student at the first lesson and creating mutually agreed upon goals for the semester. Be sure to have a sense of the timing of lessons (i.e., half hour versus one hour lesson) and the end of semester performance expectation (i.e., juries). Some colleges and universities require students to perform in studio class or some other music major gathering every term. Be sure you are aware of performance policies and requirements. Know the jury requirements and ensemble audition requirements at the school right from the beginning of the term so that you can plan instruction for students according to these performance outcomes. No student likes to be informed a week before the end of the semester that they will need to perform a jury in order to receive an applied lesson grade.

As discussed in Chapter 3, students have a variety of learning styles as well as varying developmental needs. It is not possible to generalize characteristics of the students in applied lessons. There will be performance majors who do not know how to practice and nonmajors who are stars. However, groups of students in a larger music major studio do tend to have a certain "culture" of their own. The short paragraph from an undergraduate performance student highlights this issue.

Each individual studio has a unique atmosphere and culture, partially from the perpetuation of genuine stereotypes, but equally from the personality of the professor. Curious, however, is why these cultures exist and how everyone in a particular studio shares that particular mindset. I see studio mentalities as a "Which came first, the chicken or the egg?" When adopted into the studio culture as a student, the teacher's attitude and personality becomes part of your own, mostly likely as a method for acceptance. However, when an existing studio of students acquires a new professor, he/she must be able to adapt to the preset mentality, or else the students may not respond as favorably. I recently witnessed the audition process of our new studio professor, and while performance was clearly an important factor, perhaps more pertinent was his personality and outlook. Would he fit in with our studio culture?

The new studio professor must work at the beginning of the year to get to know the students and the studio culture. Of course, the new professor will bring his/her own personality into the culture of any studio but change of this sort takes time and we caution the new professor to make any change slowly. Older students who have worked with a previous teacher for several years may never really "come on board." If you expect this sort of challenge, it is easier to work with it.

Fritz Kaenzig, Chair of Winds, Brass, and Percussion at the University of Michigan suggests that the three primary characteristics of success in applied music instruction include (1) the ability to provide positive motivators to students; (2) to be an empathetic individual; and (3) excellence of pedagogy. As was discussed back in Chapter 1, the professor must make use of pedagogical content knowledge as well as content knowledge. Most doctoral students are well prepared with regard to content knowledge but less well prepared with pedagogical content knowledge. In addition to a solid pedagogical approach to the fundamentals of performance, it is important for the applied instructor to have a carefully considered sequence for etudes, solo repertoire and excerpts (if appropriate). Many state music lists for high school solo contests provide graded solo repertoire and this is a good place to start for a new applied music instructor who does not already have a sequenced list of repertoire. Some applied faculty members provide a sequenced list to their students as a sort of "text" for applied lesson work. Chapter 4 had sample syllabi for applied music.

Nancy Ambrose King, Professor of Voice at the University of Michigan, speaks of the following characteristics of successful applied music teachers:

1. Flexibility—The understanding that each student who comes into your office has a different set of needs, skills, musical background, and learning style. A truly comprehensive teaching method must contain an awareness of each student as an individual with unique goals, perspectives, and musical issues. Student and teacher should clearly define their goals and objectives for the semester and the lines of communication must always be open.

2. The ability to diagnose a fundamental problem and explain the solution in a way that will "click" with that particular student, with a commitment to keep re-phrasing the solution and searching for new analogies if necessary, until the concept finally "hits home" with the student. The teacher's primary function is to help each student find their own voice on the instrument, however the fundamental skills of playing the instrument at a high level must be mastered in order to achieve this.

3. The ability to combine all elements of the musical language into a lesson, including basic fundamentals of the instrument as well as the artistry involved in musical interpretation and expression, and the historical and theoretical knowledge essential to understanding the repertoire.

Elizabeth Major, professor of voice at Adrian College, highlights additional attributes of applied teachers:

1. Ability to create a free-flowing, creative, positive and healthy dialogue with each applied student. This requires the teacher to have to "get over into the space of where the individual

student is." It also requires the teacher to give up any attachment to his or her own agenda as a teacher or any expectation in regards to creating a "great singer, pianist, etc."

2. An ability to nurture each student in the way that will most benefit them as a musician and as a whole person. To create a supportive spacious environment in which a student feels safe, cared for and able to explore his or her own instrument and growth potential. It is only in a compassionate space that a student can start to become intimately involved with his/her musical instrument and create a real connection to it.

3. The continuing effort towards finding new and better ways of communicating the technical tools necessary for skill-building and growth of the student-musician. The teacher must be vigilant in assessing whether his/her ideas are being communicated in a clear way to the student. Technical information must be tailored to each student.

4. Finally, the ability to be PRESENT with each student throughout each lesson. I believe this takes great intentionality and practice. It is very easy to slip into cookie-cutter style teaching and with a heavy load, it is always challenging to stay present and intentional in every lesson with every student.

THE ONE-ON-ONE INTERACTION

Noted educational psychologist Benjamin Bloom (1985, *Developing Talent* in Young People) suggested that the one-on-one instructional model is a useful context for understanding much about teaching and learning. In his chapter reviewing the research on applied music teaching, Richard Kennel (2002) suggests: "Within this simple expert–novice dyad is a complex world of human cultural evolution, including the use of language, symbol systems, tools, and many aspects of human psychology" (p. 243). Most of the teaching strategies discussed so far in the book are relevant to applied studio teaching. Providing a clear syllabus and solid assessment strategies as well as working to meet the appropriate development needs of the students (all on Part One of the text) are important in applied instruction. Suggestions for creating a culture for learning (Chapter 5) as well as strategies for motivating students to read, write, and interact (Chapters 6 and 7) may be useful for the applied instruction. However, motivation in the one-on-one interaction is somewhat unique to music instruction. In addition to applied performance courses, music professors may also provide one-on-one instruction in conducting, music technology, and composition. Within graduate programs, thesis and dissertation work is often what we might consider one-on-one instruction.

In response to motivation in the studio specifically, Associate Professor of Bassoon at the University of Michigan, Jeff Lyman, suggests:

Motivation is achieved through the presentation of an ideal (perhaps a recorded performance, a set of traditions to emulate, a personal goal to reach, a competition) or the demonstration of a need (a deadline, a jury, an audition, a set of technical or musical demands.) It is also important to show activity on my own part (recitals, concerts with ensembles, research projects if applicable) and to bring my experiences into the mix whenever appropriate. Students must understand through my actions how I was in their seat years ago and how I overcame a challenge, and must also see how this musical activity either inspires or motivates me to do this over years and years.

Fritz Kaenzig shares that he motivates students

> By being involved musically at all times. I demonstrate, either by playing or singing. If the students can hear improvement in their playing, interpretation, or skills during the lesson, it motivates them during the ensuing week to integrate the improvements.

One of the particularly unique features of applied instruction is the challenge of teaching to individual differences in students. Fritz Kaenzig suggests:

> I show support for my students during those occasional times in a semester when it is necessary for them to deemphasize practice for academic preparation and I place their career goals and creative aspirations above those sometimes narrowly defined in a performance studio.

The freshmen student below comments on teaching to individual differences from his perspective:

One of the struggles I faced initially regarding my applied lessons was in relation to goals and expectations. My professor would suggest dozens of possible pieces and technical studies, much more than any musician could realistically rehearse all at once. What I have come to realize is that he was offering me a wealth of opportunities. Rather than being spoon-fed a predetermined system of progression, I was being taught to evaluate my own situation, and though I wasn't expected to do everything, it was up to me to determine what was most interesting and effective for my situation.

Although some students may need a "predetermined system of progression," others will rise to the challenge addressed by the student above. No one technique or approach will work for every student. This is what makes applied teaching fun as well as challenging. Although the repertoire and the pedagogy stays somewhat the same, each student is different, so the one-on-one interaction changes for each student.

It is important for the applied teacher to create and maintain detailed records regarding student work. We suggest developing a repertoire record so that you can keep track of what etudes, soles, and excerpts the student has completed as well as documenting a weekly grade for each lesson so that the grade for applied study given at the end of the semester can represent the work of the complete term. Grading in applied lessons is addressed at the end of the chapter.

Elizabeth Major, voice professor at Adrian College, provides some voice-specific considerations regarding one-on-one studio teaching:

I try to help them define their strengths as singers and invest in the building of these strengths. If they feel that there is something special and worth investing in, then they will start to motivate themselves. I try to help them connect with what it is that draws them to pursue the craft of singing. How does it nurture them as people? In many cases, singing is a means of growth in a more global sense for these students; it is a means for them to learn about themselves and how they fit into the bigger world. Singing then becomes a metaphor for their lives. If they learn to nurture themselves as singers, then they can start to nurture themselves as people, and then sometimes, they can go back and forth between the two and truly develop whatever potential exists within them.

I also believe that until a student starts to develop confidence as a musician or as a singer, they will have a hard time with motivation and progress. It is thus my task as the teacher to let them see clearly the confidence I have in what they are doing. If they see that I believe they can sing a particular exercise or phrase, they have a much better chance of developing the confidence necessary to execute that phrase. My confidence in them is linked closely with their own developing confidence.

Most student musicians have a need to express something personal, but it is often loaded with all sorts of baggage or fear. It is my job to identify the fear and to help them acknowledge it but start to find ways of not being controlled by it. If a student can connect with his/her emotional connection to singing and know that it is ok to go to that "feeling" place, they can usually start to experience freedom and confidence in their singing. It is my job to let them know that what they have to say is important and interesting to the listener (whether to me or other students or faculty). It is crucial for students to understand that they are worthy of what they are pursuing. Then is might be possible for them to really focus and get into the nitty-gritty work of learning their craft. They have to get to the place of understanding that technical freedom rewards them with the ability to express something.

Building healthy respect for the gift (talent) and the process of growing as a singer—it is only through my own respect for each students' potential and in-born abilities and the process of building the power and beauty of that voice that my students will develop these qualities in themselves.

MAINTAINING A HEALTHY CULTURE IN THE STUDIO

One of the key issues in studio instruction is helping students grapple with issues of competition in the profession. Nancy Ambrose King suggests:

As the musical profession becomes more and more competitive, I find that students are deeply aware of the need to continually strive and prepare for their career as musicians. The teacher's role in motivating is often one of reassuring them that, yes, they are on the right track and making progress even during the 'rough patches' of their musical training. I feel it is crucial to develop a practice plan and routine for each student so that the inevitable encroachment of their busy schedules does not impact their commitment to practice, and so that they are able to cover all the many aspects of a good practice session. Too often, poor practice habits lead to frustration and hence lack of motivation on the part of the student, which can easily be avoided by an organized and integrated practice routine, as well as clearly defined goals, both short-term and long-term. Finally, encouraging students to take advantage of opportunities such as orchestral and summer festival auditions, competitions, and recital performances is a significant motivational tool.

All of the students who spoke to us discussed the importance of healthy competition. For example,

The studio should be a supportive environment. In music performance, and in all aspects of life, competition is present and inevitable. However, competition is productive, but only in a healthy manner not fueled by arrogance. A studio should be cooperative, rather than torn apart by selfish egotism.

Elizabeth Major, of Adrian College, offers the following strategies with regard to competition in the studio.

1. I try to maintain equality in terms of the time and attention I give each student. I try to stay current with make—up lessons and all students receive extra lesson time jury week.

2. Part of this involves staying current with make—up lessons.

3. In addition, all students receive an extra "last chance" lesson during jury week. I assign repertoire that is particularly suited to the student and hence would be inappropriate for any other student of the same gender in the studio (competition in the voice studio usually revolves around two students of the same gender).

4. I have gender-specific vocal exercises incorporated into my technique/warm-up regimen which I find helps students bond with other students of the same gender. It helps the men of the studio feel connected to each other with relation to the development of their voices as opposed to the female students. The same goes for female-based warm-ups. I also tend to assign certain rep. to younger students which the upper classman have studied when they were underclassmen. I try to encourage the upperclassmen to help the underclassmen with issues connected with this repertoire, even sing it for them in the studio and ask them to talk about their experience with this particular piece of rep. when they studied it.

5. I make it a point for all jury evaluation forms to be withheld until such time as the students can meet with me to go over the comments. This eliminates students comparing each other's evaluations.

6. Studio challenges: Spring semester is the Repertoire Challenge—Each student who wishes may participate in this challenge involving learning and coaching (1) piece of rep. per week. This created a bit of healthy competition last year and motivated some students to really focus on building their repertoire base. I have my own children make a decorative poster/chart and as the students learn repertoire, they fill in the chart as appropriate. The winner or winners are acknowledged at the end of the term.

7. Studio field trips: At least once or twice per year, I try to invite the studio to my home for a meal and attend a concert at U/M. (this year, we attended La Boheme). Hosting students in my home really builds the connection between myself and my students, but also between the students themselves. They all know my children and my children try to come to events at the college and have at times developed close relationships with some students.

STUDIO CLASS INSTRUCTION

A weekly studio class is often the context for working with students in the studio as a group and can be the place to foster collegiality as well as healthy competition in the studio. Professor King suggests:

> I work hard to ensure that our studio class is a positive and beneficial experience for all the students. I encourage discussion of class performances in a way that is helpful to the performer, and which focuses on the positive aspects of the performance as well as the areas which need continued work. I encourage the students to phrase their critiques in a way that is diplomatic, insightful, and helpful to their colleagues. In addition, I try and foster an atmosphere whereby each student feels their importance to the studio and is proud of the perspective they bring to the class. I also encourage younger students to seek help, especially with reed-making, from the older students. This is beneficial for both the younger student seeking extra guidance and the older student who develops mentoring skills. We use studio class to

work on a variety of necessary musical skills: performance skills, pedagogical skills, historical knowledge, reed-making skills, preparing for orchestral auditions, etc. In general the students performing on a particular day will give a brief presentation to the class about the work, giving them practice speaking to an audience. Performing for their peers is often quite stressful and allows them the opportunity to perform under pressure for a knowledgeable audience. They receive comments from me in a master-class type setting, but also receive comments (both positive and helpfully critical) from their colleagues. This encourages active listening by the group and their ability to phrase comments in a diplomatic and helpful way. As oboists, we also spend part of each studio class time working on reed-making skills.

In smaller institutions, there may be some sort of combined studio class for all students. Adrian College combines all instrumentalists in one weekly studio class and all vocalists in another. These studio classes are each supervised by two or three faculty and everyone provides feedback to the student performers. The new professor may end up in a studio class context that is specific to his/her instrument or may find themselves participating in a broader version of the same.

Whether it is instrument-specific or not, the students' comments (two students) below speak to the importance of the studio class concept:

Student 1: As a student who has studied at two undergraduate schools with two different professors I have seen first hand the power of an applied performance studio class. One of my professors did not have a studio class or ever get his studio together for any sort of combined activity. Because of this, I did not even know everyone who was in my same studio. I distinctly remember meeting someone in my studio during the last week of school. Having a "studio family" is important as older students often know how to best work with the professor, learn what they expect and how to process criticism. A second professor I have has mandatory studio class every week. My first week in the studio he made me play and "musically introduce" myself to the studio. He fosters a warm and safe environment in which everyone knows each other, goes to each other to play and seek advice, and demands that everyone know each other not only on a musical level but also on a social level because the music business is a collaborative art form. There are many possibilities with how to set up a studio; however, not having one is not only denying students opportunities but also denying the professor opportunities to better get to know students in a group environment.

Student 2: Studio class is great not only for the comments and experience I get, but it also is a place where I can learn and refine the comments I give to others. The art of giving constructive criticism is one where I need the practice, and due to the great people in the studio, I'm forced to think hard to give insightful comments on par with everyone else. It seems like every studio class I'm reminded of another aspect of playing that I can't forget to look into when evaluating a performance.

Fritz Kaenzig adds:

I primarily use studio class as a performance class, but also create mock auditions, occasional master classes, and address issues that concern performance and related areas. After performances, which are formally presented with bows, stage hands, and lights in the Recital Hall, we turn up the lights in the hall and give our impressions and suggestions for improvement to each of the class performers. I start with the students' comments first and generally give mine after theirs. I ask that a positive comment be made before the suggestions for improvement.

LOGISTICS OF APPLIED MUSIC TEACHING

One of the first challenges for the applied teacher is working out the applied lesson schedule. Unlike an academic course or rehearsal that is set by the department or university, applied lessons are usually left for the student and teacher to work out. In addition, your teaching studio space may be shared with other applied faculty; so fitting your schedule with theirs can be a difficult puzzle. In some cases, a department chair or department administrator may be involved in the lesson schedule and sharing of space. It often takes a week or two for student schedules to be settled and so they are sometimes hesitant to sign up for a weekly lesson time until they know about other courses. We suggest having a sign-up sheet for the first week of lessons so that students are sure to get in for their first lesson. The "regular schedule" for lessons may need to be confirmed in the second or even the third week of the term. Be sure to provide a clear policy for lesson cancellation and make-up lessons. We suggest 24 hours notice if the lesson is to be made up. If you intend to include lesson attendance as a grading criteria for applied music, be sure to have a clear policy on your applied lesson syllabus.

Another issue unique to applied areas is a concern regarding accompanists. Find out from the department chair what the policies are for accompanying services. In some settings, accompanists will be provided for lessons. Of course, this adds another level of complication to scheduling. Ask about accompaniment software (i.e., *SmartMusic*) as this technology is important for students to experience and may help them learn their repertoire in preparation for work with a pianist.

Gather as much information as possible about the jury procedures in the school. Some institutions require juries every semester for all applied study (majors and nonmajors). On the other side of the spectrum are institutions with no juries at all and there is everything in between. As mentioned earlier, be prepared for policies and procedures to be different from what you my have experienced as a student. Find out what the performance expectations are for the juries.

JURY QUESTIONS CHECKLIST

- Who is required to perform?
- How long is the exam?
- Do students perform scales and technique?
- Must they perform from memory?
- Are there certain repertoire expectations?
- How do accompanists work? Must all pieces be accompanied?
- Who evaluates the juries?
- Is there a jury evaluation form?
- How does the jury grade relate to the grade for the course?

GRADING

Grading for applied music is one of the more controversial topics within teaching music in higher education. As mentioned previously, it is important for the applied instructor to keep careful documentation of work in applied music. We suggest a weekly record of work completed, including a weekly grade. You may decide not to discuss grades with students each week but it is important for students to know that you are keeping track of this information. Due to the nature of the one-on-one relationship, it is often difficult for applied instructors to give low grades to students who they feel so connected with. Grade inflation is quite common in the applied studio. Nonmajors have various goals in relation to applied music and if instructors give low grades for applied lessons to nonmajors, those students are most likely going to quit and not be involved in applied work. So, there is a bit of a dilemma for grading with nonmajors. But, for music majors in particular, we encourage instructors to really consider their ethical responsibility to provide an honest evaluation of student work. Regardless of the issues associated with grading, plan to keep careful records so that if a student questions a grade you are able to provide evidence regarding the grading decision. As was discussed in Chapter 2, we like to differentiate between grading and assessment. There are many issues to consider with grading (i.e., nonmajors and continuation in the studio), but at some level, students should be aware of the quality of their progress as to whether their "grade" for applied music is affected or not. The sample performance assessment tools provided in Chapter 2 might be used periodically in lessons so that students can see a quantitative measure of their progress.

RESEARCH ON APPLIED MUSIC

The *New Handbook of Music Teaching and Learning* (Colwell & Richardson, 2002) includes a chapter by Richard Kennel that reviews the research literature in the area of applied music. Studies in the review are organized into the following sections: expert–novice apprenticeship models; efficacy of private instruction; evaluation of instruction; expert–novice problem solving; descriptive studies of the applied lesson experience; experimental studies comparing various applied instruction strategies (i.e., verbal guide, modeling guide, verbal and modeling guide); studies of the applied student; studies of applied teacher expertise; and studies of lesson interaction. Although results of these studies are inconclusive and suggest that the specific context of instruction has a strong effect on instructional needs, readers are encouraged to examine the Kennell review.

Chapter 13 of this text introduces the reader to information on conducting research on teaching. Kennell documents that much of applied music instruction occurs "behind closed doors," so to speak. In order to provide ideas for study, we conclude this chapter with unanswered questions regarding applied music. Some of these ideas might be explored through action research or teacher research designs discussed in Chapter 13:

1. What are student perceptions of the characteristics of successful applied music instructors?
2. What pedagogical tools do applied instructors use to improve performance?
3. How do applied instructors acquire the "pedagogical content knowledge" needed to affect student performance?
4. Are there "generalizable concepts" for applied music instruction across instruments and voice?
5. What techniques do applied instructors use to motivate students?
6. How do applied instructors adjust instruction to meet the needs of individual students?
7. What is the relationship between the music, the applied instructor, and the student performer? What is the role of language in assisting the student in understanding the music?
8. What are the strategies for teaching musicality beyond correct notes and rhythms?
9. What is the role of musical modeling in the growth of students in applied lesson

QUESTIONS FOR DISCUSSION/SUGGESTED ACTIVITIES

1. Discuss what you think Kennel means when he suggests that "all of the cultural history of the professional community may be presented to the student through the medium of the weekly music lesson."
2. Discuss what you perceive to be the differences between nonmajors and majors with regard to applied music instruction goals.
3. As you reflect back on your own undergraduate applied music experiences, what do you view to be the characteristics of successful applied instructors?
4. Reflect back on your own experiences in studio class and outline both your positive and your negative memories.
5. Discuss the issues associated with grading in applied music, particularly in relation to nonmajors.
6. Use the "Checklist for Juries" and find out how the procedures work for the institution you are currently associated with.
7. Begin to sequence a list of repertoire that you might consider to use in applied instruction. What is appropriate for the freshmen?
8. Discuss how you might study some aspect of applied studio teaching in your own setting? What are you curious about? How could your questions be answered?

CHAPTER 9

Learning Technology in Music Classrooms: A Catalyst for Deeper Learning and Creativity

Mark Clague[1]

Technology has already transformed faculty and student interactions in what we might call the hybrid classroom—the traditional physical classroom expanded to take advantage of virtual tools. Yet the fundamentals of great teaching remain the same—sharing experience, coaching skills, and inspiring exploration to help students achieve their goals of personal and professional growth. The challenge for faculty and students alike is how to get beyond the technohype to develop eLearning tools that enrich our lives. The bells and whistles of the latest and greatest application or handheld device that make for a compelling vendor pitch or inspiring faculty workshop easily get in the way of putting technology in the service of learning. Technology in education should be engaging and fun, but ultimately it must help teachers and students alike meet their objectives. The purpose of this chapter is to examine successful applications of technology against the backdrop of research on learning and thereby distill some principles for using computers and online tools to make education more effective—what we might then truly call learning technology (LT). When used to advantage, LT can deepen and broaden student learning, particularly given its ability to inspire, structure, and share student-produced content that can in turn enhance the understandings of peers, instructors, and indeed the world.

For better and worse the liquid crystal display is today's window on the world. Computers, cell phones, mp3 players, and our other electronic companions have fundamentally changed the ways we connect to knowledge and how we engage with each other. Technology has transformed skill definition and acquisition: we have been rewired; we have become eLearners. Even the basic metaphors we use to describe human thought have changed: We download our ideas and save our memories to our own hard-drive

[1] Mark Clague, PhD, is an assistant professor of Musicology and American Culture at the University of Michigan School of Music, Theatre, and Dance. He can be contacted via e-mail: claguem@umich.edu.

brains. Data storage is cheap; remembering discounted. Facts are no more valuable than a few clicks on Wikipedia. Information has become less a thing than a connection. Knowledge is hyperlinked and infinitely interconnected by anecdote as much as expertise; we click to learn, multimedia is routine, multitasking—the norm; and all this takes place in a networked atmosphere running 24 hours each and every day, such that distraction, overload, and even physical exhaustion are constant companions of today's student. Yet, for those who have grown up surrounded by such computing power, none of this is "technology" at all—it is not exceptional, it is just life. As computer pioneer Alan Kay reminds us, "technology is only technology if it was invented after you were born" (quoted in Prensky, 2001, p. 38). What instructors view as the wild frontier is just the typical everyday for many of our students. As Don Tapscott (1999) puts it in *Growing Up Digital*, "Today's kids are so bathed in bits that they think it's all part of the natural landscape." So, the challenge for tomorrow's professor is to enter into the world of our students today, using all our instructional skill, insights into learning, experience, dedication, and creativity to adapt this precarious brave new world in the service of education—in sum, to use technology as a tool for peak learning.

LISTENING BLOGS: AN INTRODUCTORY CASE STUDY

Online listening blogs allow music instructors to link audio resources, faculty insight and guidance, plus listener commentary, in a convenient and interactive tool that hones the music student's primary skill—listening. Progress in aural skills classes, musicology and theory, chamber music rehearsals, even the musician's ability to discuss interpretive decisions in a lesson each depend on listening. Listening blogs not only require active engagement with sound they offer instant publication and peer-to-peer interaction and help students keep pace with assignments. Sharing this work online also encourages high-quality participation because students know their comments will be read not just by an instructor but by their peers. Excited by an interesting musical work, students will write several paragraphs, and week after week, such work can add up to the most substantial writing project of the semester. This practice writing can markedly improve the quality of student concert reports and other more traditional writing assignments. In two musicology classes I taught at the University of Michigan School of Music, Theatre & Dance in the 2008 winter term, students listened to almost 50 musical examples and selected one piece in each of about 15 assignments for comment. The resulting posts added up to over 10 pages of writing per student (see Table 9–1). Such listening sites

Table 9–1 Metrics of Student Participation in Online Listening (Winter 2008)

Course	Words Per Comment	Words Per Student	Total
Freshman Music History Survey (138 undergraduates, 15 assignments)	164	2320	324,903
U.S. Music Survey Course (34 students, 16 assignments)	195	2892	98,319

could be developed for a wide range of courses, including the discussion of orchestral excerpts in a trumpet studio or comparisons of multiple recordings of the same Beethoven sonata in a music theory class devoted to form and interpretation.

Logging into the listening site, students are first directed to a display of the 50 most recent postings—the blog. Once or twice weekly, students are required to visit an assignment page, where they find links to recordings appropriate to the week's topic presented alongside engaging imagery, explanatory text, and discussion questions (see Figure 9–1). After listening to the musical examples, students post at least one comment per assignment, discussing either a specific musical work (e.g., King Oliver's "Dippermouth Blues") or the group of three as a whole (e.g., New Orleans jazz as a style). These comments are automatically added to the online blog (web log), where they can be read by peers as well as the instructor. Participants can also respond to previously posted comments. Typically, completion of the listening assignment is required prior to class as a preview of the day's lecture, although due dates can be adjusted to give students

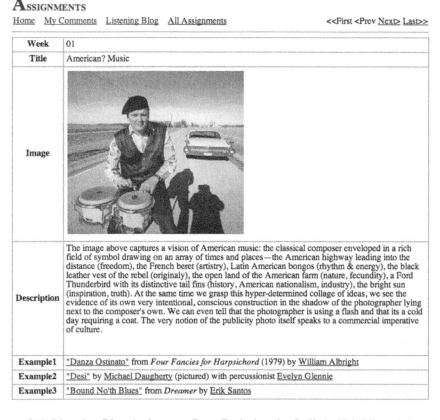

ASSIGNMENTS

Home   My Comments   Listening Blog   All Assignments   <<First <Prev Next> Last>>

Week	01
Title	American? Music
Image	
Description	The image above captures a vision of American music: the classical composer enveloped in a rich field of symbol drawing on an array of times and places—the American highway leading into the distance (freedom), the French beret (artistry), Latin American bongos (rhythm & energy), the black leather vest of the rebel (originaly), the open land of the American farm (nature, fecundity), a Ford Thunderbird with its distinctive tail fins (history, American nationalism, industry), the bright sun (inspiration, truth). At the same time we grasp this hyper-determined collage of ideas, we see the evidence of its own very intentional, conscious construction in the shadow of the photographer lying next to the composer's own. We can even tell that the photographer is using a flash and that its a cold day requiring a coat. The very notion of the publicity photo itself speaks to a commercial imperative of culture.
Example1	"Danza Ostinato" from *Four Fancies for Harpsichord* (1979) by William Albright
Example2	"Desi" by Michael Daugherty (pictured) with percussionist Evelyn Glennie
Example3	"Bound No'th Blues" from *Dreamer* by Erik Santos

Figure 9–1 Listening Blog Assignment Page Exploring the Stylistic Hybridity of American Music and Featuring Composer Michael Daugherty with Explanatory Text and Links to Online Recordings, Listening Questions, and a Comment Form

practice after class in working with a new idea (such as hearing the difference between 12-bar blues and 32-bar song form). Unlike cramming for an exam, the listening blog encourages students to pace their listening work throughout a semester, especially if the original assignments are only available for a brief window of time (e.g., for the week prior to and after the due date). After sorting by author, comments are graded on a check minus, check, and check-plus basis (which requires only limited reading by the instructor). All told, participation in blogging for these classes made up ten percent of the final grade.

By making these listening comments public, rather than part of a personal listening journal, the commonly private experience of listening becomes a shared dialogue in which students learn from each other. A performer with perfect pitch may offer specifics about musical materials that less trained listeners may miss, while nonmusicians often contribute observations that benefit from a broad, nonspecialist viewpoint. Devoted fans of a particular composer or artist may direct peers to "inside info" on a particular recording. Shy students can respond carefully and thoughtfully outside of the classroom context, while the comments of aggressive students do not dominate or overwhelm the class discourse as a whole. As all students gain insight from others, they begin to appreciate the advantages of multiple perspectives.

Ideally, the instructor offers postings as well, helping to model the best responses. The instructor can also read the postings for another purpose—to identify common misunderstandings that should be addressed during class meetings or to glean interpretive trends that can be used to jumpstart class discussion. The listening blog thus enables a class-wide collaboration among students and the instructor to broaden and deepen learning. I have found that when I recognize a "quiet" student's blog post, either online or in the classroom, the feeling of being valued may help that student overcome a reluctance to participate in live discussion and such kudos motivate other students to write thoughtful comments and earn similar praise. LT applications can have a profound effect on the sociality of the classroom, creating a sense of shared purpose and a more supportive face-to-face community. Finally, the blog or discussion tool can be mined for data to facilitate a deeper assessment of student skill levels, learning, and course design.

LESSONS FROM LISTENING BLOGS

Superior eLearning applications leverage convenience and fun to facilitate instruction. Certainly, students appreciate the increased availability of web-based listening and may be more likely to complete listening assignments when they are not limited by library hours. Access to online recordings is becoming increasingly convenient for instructors as well. With the rise of subscription audio services such as Naxos Music Library and Smithsonian Global Sound, using static links to individual tracks covered by institutional licenses may become standard operating procedure and indeed these resources offer instructors immediate access to huge catalogs of audio and even video examples. Some schools also have their own streaming services or allow instructors to post recordings to class websites. Copyright is an essential consideration here. Most campuses treat the course website as an extension of the physical classroom, and thus apply the same Fair Use exemptions used in the real world to the virtual or hybrid classroom.

The online presentation of recordings makes it simple to combine aural examples with explanatory text and other media. Web pages all but require the combination of text and imagery (such as a portrait of a composer). Recordings can be linked to musical scores or listening guides that offer background and suggest listening strategies or questions to inspire musical analysis. Sound can be integrated with text and graphics through online Flash video or even enhanced mp4 files so that when a student plays an audio file in iTunes or on a portable device such as an iPod, the screen can change to announce the appearance of important themes and track the musical form. Such enhanced audio will be available from textbook publishers but can also be created with surprising ease using software such as GarageBand.

More powerful than convenience and media integration, however, is the potential for online tools to encourage students' active engagement in learning by adding their personal observations to a site. User-created content is the hallmark of Web 2.0—the second generation of online sites focused not on delivering information but on encouraging users to post, organize, and link their own ideas as part of a community. (Facebook is a good Web 2.0 example popular on many collegiate campuses.) The most powerful LT tools leverage this user-produced creativity to place students into active learning modes in which they do not just digest information, but describe, contextualize, analyze, interpret, and even create.

Online discussion of listening is only one application of LT that invites engagement and application. Others include online tutorial and quiz tools as well as the increasingly popular classroom response or "clicker" systems. These systems allow instructors to poll students, even in large classes, by asking questions and collecting responses in real time. Results can be tallied instantly and projected in graphs and pie charts. Students find this fun, but more importantly, classroom polling increases engagement, understanding, retention, and even attendance. However, the challenge is to use response technology well—seizing opportune times to ask the most productive questions. One danger with these systems is a side effect of cost. Since polling tools represent large investments by the institution, the students, or both, instructor may feel the pressure to use the system frequently, possibly distorting class goals. Technology should not drive teaching strategies; learning goals drive instruction.

ALIGNING TECHNOLOGY WITH GOALS IN COURSE DESIGN

Rather than an afterthought—say the adaptation of a preexisting course to new teaching gadgets—LT is most effective as an integral part of a thoughtfully planned course design. Benjamin Bloom's taxonomy of learning objectives (Bloom, 1956) continues to offer direction in connecting developments in educational tools to goals. The basic level in Bloom's conception involves the acquisition of knowledge and basic comprehension. Presentation and distribution technology such as PowerPoint, course websites, streaming audio, or automated quizzes and tutorials can aid this objective. As discussed above, online listening can also be integrated into discussion or blogging tools to begin to explore higher levels of Bloom's objectives—such as application, analysis, critical thinking, and collaboration. These as well as Bloom's ultimate goal of synthesis can be maximized by inviting students to create their own online publications or musical

Table 9–2 Applying Technology to Learning Goals (Based on Bloom, 1956)

I. Knowledge acquisition	Presentation & Course Management
	• PowerPoint, Blackboard
II. Application & analysis	Drill & Quiz Tools
	• Custom designed or university supported
III. Collaboration & critical thinking	Streaming Audio & Writing Tools
	• Naxos, iTunes, MP3Trimmer, editing tools
IV. Synthesis	Communication: E-mail and Discussion
	• Mail, chat, threaded discussion
	Editing and Authoring
	• Dreamweaver, GarageBand, Audacity

compositions using website authoring tools and audio applications from editors such as GarageBand and Audacity to notation software including Sibelius and Finale. Table 9–2 offers a summary of possible alignments between LT and common learning goals.

KNOWLEDGE ACQUISITION—PRESENTATION AND COURSE MANAGEMENT TOOLS

PowerPoint and courseware such as BlackBoard, WebCT, or open-source systems like cTools, have become ubiquitous technology of the hybrid classroom. Certainly, these applications invite abuse, but maybe no more than traditional approaches. Key to using these tools effectively is to imagine the student's position as user and perceiver. For both presentation and courseware, the instructor must organize information and resources logically and in ways that emphasize a hierarchy of information. Too much information, delivered at the same level of importance is so much clutter and a guaranteed strategy to confuse. Clarity and simplicity bring information to students in ways that are useful (Figure 9–2).

Strong visual design enhances communication and may indeed be one of the most underappreciated skills in LT. Visual principles of proximity, alignment, repetition, and contrast that make for good concert posters or syllabi are necessary for great PowerPoint slides and course websites. Many LT applications contain templates that use these principles, yet the overuse of templates can also bore students and homogenize the learning experience from one course to any other. Campus workshops as well as books such as *The Non-Designer's Design Book* or *Web Design Workshop* by Robin Williams (1994 and 2001) offer quick ways to improve an instructor's visual skills. Some basic principles for PowerPoint use are summarized in Table 9–3. In classes that regularly use PowerPoint, a daily intro slide shown as students enter the room can display the day's topic, reminders of upcoming due dates, and the title of music playing alongside a picture of the artist or composer (see Figure 9–2).

A shortcoming and potential danger of using PowerPoint in music courses is the software's bias toward image and text. Custom editing tools for words and pictures are excellent in PowerPoint, while music files can simply be linked to play automatically or on click. Essential to any presentation in a music course is the ability to edit audio effectively.

Figure 9–2 PowerPoint Title Slide Used by Author as Students Enter Class

Table 9–3 Ten Tips for Using Presentation Software

1	Variety recruits audience attention; avoid repeating the same slide design or template again and again; successive slides should have a different look; once you become comfortable with presentation software, it may be best to avoid using a design template altogether, so that slides are built individually from a plain white background.
2	Do not display text that is hard to read; a sans-serif font, 24-point or larger is best; avoid underlining and ALL CAPS.
3	Use imagery on most slides; pictures not only fulfill an audience expectation and add another dimension to your presentation, but prevent the error of including too much text on any one slide; images can be scanned, taken from textbook resource disks, or downloaded off the web using such search engines as Google Images <http://images.google.com/>.
4	Use color of text and background to enhance clarity and variety; experiment with single word slides in striking colors to highlight course themes; the repetition of a single word or image can help students recognize and remember central concepts.
5	Integrating text, image, audio, and video into you presentation slides saves class time and lessens the chance of technology failure and the delay of switching between media.
6	Avoid reading slides verbatim and face your audience, not the screen, as you present.
7	Several times during a lecture, put your audience in an active role by escaping the slide show mode to ask a question; PowerPoint can be used like a chalkboard by switching from presentation to edit mode; use a bulleted-list slide and type audience comments onto the display; this approach also creates a record of classroom discussion that can be saved and posted to the course site.
8	Don't get physically tethered to your computer; use a presentation remote to control the slide show, so that you can move around the room and thus make your lecture more dynamic.
9	Make slides available prior to class via file download on the course website; this helps students take notes.
10	Don't use presentation software everyday; even in large lectures it can be good to take a day off from PowerPoint, just to keep variety in your own lecture style.

One option for integrating audio with PowerPoint, and in some ways the best, is to use a separate CD or mp3 player. The advantage of this approach is a separation of control features, such that the instructor can fast forward or rewind the audio or switch slides as the music plays (especially helpful when displaying lyrics or excerpts of a libretto at a

"The Stars & Stripes Forever"
March Form

Figure 9–3 Musical Form Articulated Using the Drawing Tools in Microsoft PowerPoint

legible magnification typically requiring multiple slides). Disadvantages to using a separate player include further limitations on the instructor's ability to move around the room during class and the time wasted in switching media. Every second counts in a lecture and losing even a dozen or two while loading a CD can disrupt a presentation.

I generally prefer having all media (text, images, audio, and video) integrated into a single PowerPoint file. The difficulty with this approach is that all audio and video play from the beginning when clicked and there are no controls to modify playback. Thus, in order to explore a musical track more deeply, the instructor must either shift to another application, such as iTunes, which has playback controls or edit the audio file to feature a single theme from a larger work. When done well, such customized musical examples are elegant and efficient. Shareware applications, such as MP3Trimmer for Mac, offer fast, easy to learn solutions. In a few seconds, the instructor can excerpt a small segment from a longer recording, adding professional fade in/out. This approach works well for listening exams as well, allowing the instructor to begin an example at any point in a piece. Custom sound files can be particularly effective when several are inserted into a single slide containing a form diagram of the work as a whole—illustrating the first and second themes of a sonata, for example. While taking more time to prepare, fully integrating audio and other media into a PowerPoint slideshow preserves lecture time otherwise spent navigating the forward and reverse of a CD or other audio player.

The strong visual tools of PowerPoint and other presentation packages offer great potential in creating quick illustrations for musical analysis. PowerPoint's drawing tools for example, can be quite helpful in explicating musical form, as a different shape can be used for each internal structure and (if used with a separate CD or mp3 player), animation effects allow the instructor to trigger the appearance of each segment as the musical example plays. Figure 9–3 offers an example of march form described in relation to John Philip Sousa's, "The Stars and Stripes Forever" (1897). Each of the symbols used here (including the repeat sign) was built using the shape drawing tools in PowerPoint.

COURSE WEBSITES

Some campuses require that instructors maintain a basic course website, and, if not, most students expect that copies of primary documents (such as the syllabus or assignment instructions) will be readily available online. The course website can serve as a kind of virtual office for participants, allowing them to access documents from anywhere at anytime. If a student at home for spring break wants to catch up on a missed assignment but has forgotten the syllabus, the course website can supply details. Making course documents available in both downloadable pdf format as well as easily accessed html as a simple webpage can serve the needs of both syllabus replacement and a quick assignment confirmation. This can sometimes prevent the instructor from having to spend time responding to a direct e-mail. There is a downside to course sites as well. Wired students also expect the web to answer any and all queries instantly. If the instructor does not regularly update the site to include new documents and schedule changes, eLearners will quickly become frustrated and learning can suffer.

Many campuses use some sort of course management system to provide websites for all courses. While instructors still have the option to create individual sites, using the standard system is efficient and helps students accustomed to campus culture. However, instructors should customize their sites and Table 9–4 offers some suggestions. Rather than use a standard set of tools, select only those most effective for the learning goals of a particular course. Whenever possible, turn unused tools off. This simplifies site navigation and focuses the eLearner's experience. Many systems even allow instructors to customize their course sites by adding graphics (say a class logo) to a homepage or displaying external sites as tools in the navigation bar. For music courses, such custom buttons linking to outside sites can offer a way to incorporate online listening into a system designed more for text-based courses. Taking full advantage of a system's flexibility can promote student learning, not only by giving individual sites a distinctive and engaging look, but also by encouraging instructors to develop custom learning tools and think carefully about eLearning design.

The most frequently used section of a course site is often its Resources area. Here is where copies of course materials are found. Yet-to-be published research from the University of Michigan suggests that student achievement is correlated to the variety and number of course resources. In sum, the more avenues a student has to access and customize learning to his or her strengths, the more learning takes place. Thus, making

Table 9–4 Seven Tips for Using Course Websites and Management Systems

1 Less is more; minimize the tools visible by turning off unused options; this reduces clutter and keeps navigation simple.

2 Customize the site homepage with a class logo or photo/image; especially on campuses where every course uses the same web system; this customization makes your class distinct and confirms the identity of your site.

3 Include the url of your class site on the syllabus, especially for students who are new to campus and do not yet know the courseware system's conventions.

4 Organize the site's Resources area effectively, so that students can quickly and easily find materials; typical folders include: docs, readings, listening, PowerPoint, projects, exams, writing, reference, and extra credit.

5 Use interactive online listening to augment library collections and customize a button on the course homepage to link to this listening area, as well as other important external sites.

6 Use the course site to link students to real-world issues that connect with course themes as well as approved writing and research tools. If your school subscribes to Grovemusic online, for example, a link to this premiere, English language reference tool may serve to check errors found in *Wikipedia*.

7 Enhance the visual appearance and sense of community of your site by taking pictures of guest lecturers or students at work and posting them to the site.

PowerPoint lecture slides available on a course website, adding supplemental readings, using a discussion or blog tool, hosting remote office hours in chat, or even podcasting lectures and discussion can enhance learning. The questions of which resources to share and how best to share them rest on the instructor's course goals and teaching approach.

SYNTHESIS: USING TECHNOLOGY TO INSPIRE AND SHARE ORIGINAL STUDENT WORK

At the top of Bloom's taxonomy are synthesis and evaluation (or creating and evaluating in the revised taxonomy by Anderson and Krathwohl [2001]). These terms refer to the student's opportunity to make learning functional by applying it to new questions and new situations. LT, especially in the user-oriented strategies of Web 2.0, is well suited to make learning active and real. Sound editing programs such as GarageBand, MP3Trimmer, Reason, or Audacity can be used as vehicles for student compositions in music theory and history courses. Even nonmusic majors are often adept at working with these programs to produce mash-ups or beats made of looped audio. Regardless of previous training, any student can explore John Cage's compositional approach using chance operations by randomly applying a program's features for sound manipulation. It could be fascinating, in fact, to give the same audio source to a class of 100 students and see how different the results turn out. Sibelius or Finale notation programs can also be used to manipulate notes and record the results as simulated MIDI files. Rather than printed term papers, students can post research projects as websites (and become HTML literate in the process). One of my favorite web-based learning applications is the oral history database Living Music. Using technology to publish student research results invites a more synthetic, creative expression of learning.

LIVING MUSIC

Begun in the fall of 2003 as a class assignment in oral history, Living Music now comprises a database of more than 700 interviews conducted, transcribed, and posted online by University of Michigan students (see http://sitemaker.umich.edu/livingmusic and Figure 9–4). Students report finding Living Music to be one of the most rewarding projects of their academic careers. They select, contact, and interview a subject who participates in the musical world in some way. These informants may be professional musicians, teachers, arts administrators, publicists, instrument makers, producers, used-CD store clerks, (some combination of these), or even simply members of the audience. Students record the interview and then confront the challenge of transcription. Insight is gained during the transcription process when students must decide whether or not to enter every "ahh" or "um" verbatim, or whether the interview subject is better represented by a translation of spoken language into written that cuts out this verbal filler. Although it results in certain inconsistencies of presentation and format, I do not enforce a single editorial practice in the Living Music project. Rather, each student must make his or her own decision about how the subject is best represented. Interviewers quickly come to understand that they can make their subject appear either the genius or the fool. In confronting such choices, students become more critical consumers of information on

LIVING⬡MUSIC

University of Michigan
School of Music
American Music Institute

Home
Browse Interviews
Search Interviews
View by Scene
View by Role
Nominations
Corrections
Sponsors

Welcome!

LIVING MUSIC offers a snapshot of contemporary musical life throughout the United States and the globe. Linking interviews and questionnaire responses with aesthetic, sociological, and historical responses, the project site offers a collection of first-person commentaries on music today. The interview pages contained here have been produced by student researchers teams at the University of Michigan, especially its School of Music, and edited by musicologists and instructor's assistants also at the University's School of Music.

LIVING MUSIC is currently focused on its initial questionnaire and interview stage. The first round of content became available in December 2003 and is scheduled to run for ten years. LIVING MUSIC is a project of the American Music Institute at the University of Michigan School of Music. Participation is entirely voluntary; no compensation is offered to researchers or informants. We thank all of our volunteers and please be courteous in providing full credit to authors and researchers for any material you use.

Featured Interview...
(Click image for details)

Jazz Vocalist and Club Owner
Susan Chastain

Figure 9–4 Homepage of Living Music Project at http://sitemaker.umich.edu/livingmusic, Here Featuring an Interview with Jazz Vocalist and Club Owner Susan Chastain

the web and, indeed, of history generally, as they experience firsthand just how subjective and ultimately personal are the choices that underlie so-called "objective," "factual" accounts. Further, as interview subjects must approve the transcript before publication, these informants may attempt to exert considerable control over the result. The dynamics of such negotiations often introduce interesting ethical dilemmas into the mix that fuel classroom discussion: what does the researcher do if the interview subject misrepresents or modifies his or her original comments to place them in a more sympathetic light? Is such distortion unusual or characteristic of those who write history?

Not surprisingly, the interview subjects that students find are not generally those covered in popular textbooks and trade magazines. Rather, their projects tend to be the first and only record of their subjects' activities and insights. Living Music informants are remarkably giving of their time and ideas to student researchers, possibly motivated (as are the students) by the prospect of this work being published online. Facebook profiles do not register on Google, but Living Music entries do—and often as one of the top links to a lesser-known artist. Students are excited to see their own original work online and share it with peers, friends, and family. Not simply driven by grades, these projects inspire students' best work and get refined to a more professional degree than a typical paper in several stages of editing. This experience of professional writing as process, rather than product, helps students develop stronger writing and editorial skills.

Living Music entries are created using a contributor's portal with links to instructions and easy-to-use online forms through which students enter biographical data and upload their interview transcripts. Through help pages and other online instructions, contributors learn basic HTML codes in order to add formatting to their transcripts. As the user interface has been improved over the years, I find that the need for classroom training in using the database technology has receded. Now, my primary task as an instructor has become coaching students in interview techniques and using humor and stories of previous student success to bolster their courage. Students usually scoff when I tell them that their main problem as researchers will not be getting an informant to speak, but rather getting them to stop once the interview is underway. But afterwards, they cannot help but agree. Through Living Music, my students have connected with future mentors, coached with prominent composers, learned about their audience, and come to understand more deeply what success in the music profession requires. They even glean a bit about copyright and intellectual property law by having to get a permissions form signed before their work can be made public. Possibly the most important learning outcome, however, is the confidence students gain from getting outside the textbook to engage with music makers in their community. Success in this project (one that can scare students when they first hear about it) nurtures the courage to engage others in their artistic work, whether it be to expand their professional network or to talk with their audiences.

From a teaching perspective, Living Music required a considerable initial investment of time to create the database and the public, contributor, and teacher portals that administer the site. Yet, since I use this project year-after-year in several of my courses, this one-time effort has paid dividends for hundreds of students. Once established, this assignment requires about the same effort to manage as a traditional paper-based project. All student work is graded online and the system automatically generates an e-mail to inform students of any comments made about their work by the instructor, of tasks remaining to be completed, and of their provisional grade. Revisions are especially efficient, although extra attention is needed to collect and register copyright permissions forms. As the site has become larger and richer through further student contributions, I have begun assigning analytical essays in which students consider a group of three previously posted interviews (say of composers, or music therapists, or rappers) to explore such questions as how these professionals make their living, what artistic activities they find most satisfying, what they consider the most important challenges facing the music industry, and many other issues.

Living Music represents an extreme in LT. Few may wish to develop such custom instructional tools, but the power of such tools is limited only by time and imagination. Remember too that the instructor is not alone in this pursuit, campuses vary widely in the availability of computing support, but many have underutilized staff consultants. Schools interested in fostering LT use may have grants available to help develop special tools. Living Music, for example, was aided by University of Michigan consultant Diana Perpich as well as a grant from the school's Center for Research on Learning and Teaching. The technological culture of every campus is somewhat different, but the entrepreneurial instructor with clear goals and the willingness to ask for help may find considerable assistance in the faculty computing center.

THE PROMISE AND PERILS OF LEARNING TECHNOLOGY

While technology offers great promise in facilitating learning, the skill, imagination, and dedication needed for all effective teaching is no less important online. The guidelines in Table 9–5 offer advice for your own exploration of LT. Consider your exploration a personal adventure drawing upon your own leaning skills and creativity. Your enthusiasm for LT can and should be infectious; so, unless you connect with the goals

Table 9–5 Six Guidelines for Using Learning Technology Effectively

1	Learning technology (LT) should not replace but enhance and extend strong teaching methods; no one solution fits all but rather LT must fit the topic and course strategies as well as the instructor's own persona and preferences; build your repertory of LT skills gradually and with a focus on high-value applications used in several courses.
2	LT must be included from the start in course design and must support clearly articulated learning goals—that is, learning drives technology use.
3	Although LT can and should be fun, to be effective LT projects and online discussion must be required course components that are graded; LT should never be add-on busywork, but a substantive and valued aspect of the syllabus design.
4	The learning enabled by any LT application is maximized when the instructor participates in the activity in order to model effective usage, assess instructional impact, and to bring observations from the virtual world into the real-world classroom.
5	While many forms of LT aid teaching, such as presentation software and course websites, tools that invite active student participation are most effective at creating lasting and deep learning by nurturing the creation and sharing of ideas; online publication and peer-to-peer exchange add extra motivation toward excellence.
6	LT use should be continually assessed via course evaluations, online surveys, and the examination of student work; fortunately, most LT applications preserve an archive of student writing, commentary, and creative projects that can be used as the basis for assessment and redesign.

and methods of an LT application, do not use it. Your instructional approach must align with your beliefs, skills, and personality. Continual assessment and refinement is essential. The instructor's quest for great teaching is a lifetime pursuit, and because technology changes relentlessly, both in its specifications and applications as well as in the ways it affects students, teaching strategies using technology likewise must undergo regular revision and reinvention to sustain their learning outcomes.

Fortunately, since LT is highly connected, web searches for "instructional technology," "educational technology," and "learning technology" will yield a host of exemplars. Some of the most useful sites can be found in the "Gallery of Teaching and Learning" maintained by the Carnegie Foundation. The Centre for Learning and Performance Technologies maintains an annual list of the "Top 100 Tools for Learning" that can be both informative and inspiring. The "7 Things You Should Know About ..." series from the EDUCAUSE Learning Initiative provides concise information on emerging learning technologies with a focus on higher education. The Apple Learning Interchange also offers great examples of LT applications, particularly those involving enhanced audio files for iPods. Finally, attending a conference of the Association for Technology in Music Instruction (ATMI) provides a fantastic introduction to the latest thinking in LT for music as well as helpful hands-on workshops (see Web Resources at the end of this chapter for more).

An important caveat to remember is that LT only rarely, if ever, saves the instructor time. Technology may make learning deeper, it may add flexibility to a course, and it may even facilitate routine administrative tasks and thus preserve class time for other activities, but all of these uses require instructor time—for training, planning, and implementation. Rather than saving time, LT will likely increase instructional workload. The question becomes how to balance the time spent on LT with its potential benefits. Table 9–6 offers several caveats to keep in mind when exploring LT applications for your classroom. The seductive attractions of LT or the perceived pressure that

Table 9–6 Seven Caveats in Adopting Learning Technology in Course Design

1	LT should not be adopted unless it fits with the values and goals of the instructor; not every course should include, nor every instructor use the newest technological tools.
2	LT will increase instructor workload for training, planning, and implementation; thus, LT must be incorporated carefully to avoid distorting a course's goals by draining away instructor time needed for other instructional activities.
3	LT will increase student workload, and thus must be added to a course design in ways that have optimal impact on learning; adding an LT application to an already full course design requires removing other requirements.
4	Do not assume that all students are skilled or comfortable with online applications; LT tools should include built-in instructions and problem-solving pages.
5	Using LT creates student expectation that computer learning applications (from email to course websites and chat to web publishing) will be fully supported by the instructor as well as the institution; students quickly become dissatisfied with a course and its instructor if a web application becomes out-of-date or cluttered due to routine neglect or if chat room postings go unanswered.
6	Ethical practices that govern instructor to student interactions in the real world also apply online, even as social networking applications such as Facebook invite sharing personal information; join the group Faculty Ethics on Facebook to contribute to this ongoing dialogue.
7	LT tools are ineffective unless intuitive, efficient, reliable, and flexible; thus using LT well requires all the pedagogical skill, creativity, and insight emblematic of any great teaching; LT is not a short-cut to learning.

if another instructor is using online discussion or podcasting lectures that your course should too, is not the reason to adopt LT. LT is simply a tool, not a goal in itself.

TECHNOLOGICAL LITERACY

Technology is increasingly fundamental to full participation in artistic endeavors. This need for technological expertise is especially acute for musicians who need low cost methods to market and sell their products and services. Yet, accreditation procedures for most schools of music leave little time in the curriculum for electives. Schools often cannot spare the faculty time necessary to teach specialty courses in technology, nor do students have the free electives to take them. Yet, a basic facility with HTML authoring, audio editing software, and music notation programs is arguably essential to today's professional musician.

A potential solution is to incorporate technological skills as learning goals into traditional coursework in music theory and music history or even the applied studio. Theory homework might be done using Finale or Sibelius. Musical notation for assignments, for example, could be given to students not as a photocopied handout, but via an electronic download at the course website. Students could then be asked to correct errors previously inserted into the notation, save the corrected version, and submit their work electronically. Writing pedagogy can benefit from student / instructor exchanges using word processing files. By using a "track changes" feature, an instructor's editing of an electronic manuscript can be marked clearly and comments added to the text. Peer editors can likewise be added to the collaborative mix. Such efforts might be effective primarily in small, writing intensive courses or advising—yet, the learning dividend may be well worth the effort. In such strategies, students gain not only knowledge of the traditional subject, but familiarity with the technological tools used to learn. Today, familiarity with such tools is less a rare talent than a standard component of literacy: a required skill for effective communication in the digital age. So, LT not only facilitates traditional learning goals but also helps satisfy an urgent need to provide music and other college students with the computer skills needed to thrive in the digital age.

CREATIVITY IN THE CLASSROOM: LEARNING TECHNOLOGY AS CATALYST

While more studies of the effectiveness of particular LT tools are urgently needed, technology's most important contribution to education may well be the challenge it offers to our creativity. The possibilities offered by LT have inspired both faculty and students to explore countless and ever changing strategies and enhancements to traditional learning environments. To engage with LT requires that faculty reassess learning goals and teaching techniques to align ends with means. New opportunities arrive regularly: how might online social sites such as del.icio.us or Flickr be leveraged to enhance learning? LT offers an ongoing challenge to those who use it. While technology provides intriguing opportunities, it offers problems and incompatibilities that dare the user to invent creative solutions. While I continue to feel the responsibility to give my students the traditional benefits of a music history course (the knowledge of ideas, events, and trends that characterize the musical past), I feel that my teaching can have even broader impact on my students in part through technology. By creating an environment that encourages students to develop new problem-solving skills, I hope that in the future not only will they be able to find historical information quickly and use it well but that they will also unlock their own creativity as researchers and thinkers. By inviting student expression and connecting it to the web, I hope to nurture creative engagement with the world. Creativity is one of the most powerful aspects of art and the artist's most valuable ability. Yet, music programs, especially at the collegiate level, too often emphasize fulfilling the expectations of tradition over creativity. Schools of music can nurture this widely transferable skill simply by recognizing creativity's value and fostering the independent artist and thinker within each of our students. I hope that developing this creative potential will aid students in inventing their own careers, opportunities, and art long after they graduate. If LT encourages the growth of such creativity, in even a small way, its benefits go well beyond the classroom to influence the very basis of our art.

QUESTIONS FOR DISCUSSION AND SUGGESTED ACTIVITIES

1. What were your best and worst experiences with LT? What general tips or principles about using LT can be distilled from your answers?
2. How might course listening at your school be improved using LT?

3. How could LT enhance an ensemble rehearsal or private studio?

4. When does technology begin to detract from learning and why?

5. How do you feel about faculty using Facebook and other social networking sites in teaching?

6. Make a list of words that pop into your mind when you think of LT. Exchange this list with a peer and discuss. What emotions do your words reflect: hope, excitement, fear? What implications for your own use of LT might these words capture?

7. After coming up with three to five themes essential to a hypothetical course you might teach, go on a webquest to find sites that might connect these themes with real-world problems or applications. If you prefer, you might search for sample course syllabi or videos to enhance a lecture.

8. Use several online tools to have a conversation about LT (see questions above), especially chat, blogging, and a threaded discussion. Then switch topics to discuss the advantages and disadvantages of the different online conversation tools.

9. Visit one of the sites listed in the Web Resources section of Chapter 9 (the Top 100 Tools for Learning works well) and put together a report for the class on one LT tool.

10. Design and execute your own webquest.

11. Design a short questionnaire study about student and faculty experiences with LT and administer it to your class or school-wide among your peers.

BIBLIOGRAPHY/FURTHER READING

Anderson, L. W., & Krathwohl, D. R., Eds. 2001. *A taxonomy for learning, teaching and assessing: a revision of bloom's taxonomy of educational objectives: complete edition*. New York: Longman.

Bloom, Benjamin S. 1956. *Taxonomy of educational objectives: the classification of educational goals*. New York: Longman.

Brown, David G. 2001. "PowerPoint-Induced Sleep." *Syllabus*, pp. 14, 17.

Funaro, Gina Maria and Frances Montell. 1999. "Pedagogical Roles and Implementation Guidelines for Online Communication Tools." *ALN Magazine* Available at http://www.aln.org/publications/magazine/v3n2/funaro.asp

Naidu, Som. 2005. *Learning and teaching with technology: principles and practices*. London and New York: Routledge.

Prensky, Marc. 2001. *Digital game-based learning*. New York: McGraw-Hill.

Rocklin, Tom. 1999. PowerPoint is not evil. Available at http://www.ntlf.com/html/sf/notevil.htm.

Tapscott, Don. 1999. *Growing up digital: the rise of the net generation*. New York: McGraw-Hill.

Thérèse Laferrière, Ed. "Time Saving Strategies and Tips for Instructors Using Online Discussion Forums," 2000. Available at http://www.tact.fse.ulaval.ca/ang/html/timesaver.html.

Williams, Robin. 1994. *The non-designer's design book* (3rd Ed.). Berkeley, CA: Peachpit Press.
Williams, Robin, John Tollet, and Dave Rohr. 2001. *Web design workshop*. Berkeley, CA: Peachpit Press.

WEB RESOURCES

Apple Learning Interchange at <http://edcommunity.apple.com/ali>
Association for Technology in Music Instruction (ATMI) at <http://atmionline.org>.
Educational Resources Information Center http://www.eric.ed.gov.
Educause Learning Initiative, a nonprofit learning technology site for higher education at <http://www.educause.edu>.
Faculty Ethics on Facebook, global discussion group on Facebook.com to explore faculty activities on the Web.
"Gallery of Teaching and Learning" maintained by the Carnegie Foundation at <http://gallery.carnegiefoundation.org/>
Living Music Oral History Project at <http://sitemaker.umich.edu/livingmusic>.
MP3Trimmer is available at http://deepniner.net/mp3trimmer/
Music Portal of Merlot [Multimedia Educational Resource for Learning and Online Teaching] at <http://music.merlot.org/>
Occasional Papers in Education Technology at <http://www.usask.ca/education/coursework/802papers>
Online/Virtual Learning Environments (links for Learning Technology) at http://64.71.48.37/teresadeca/webheads/online-learning-environments.htm
Pew Internet and American Life Project Reports on Education <http://www.pewinternet.org/PPF/c/10/topics.asp>
Read/Write/Web (blog community about technology issues that has educational postings) at http://www.readwriteweb.com/
"Top 100 Tools for Learning" maintained by the Centre for Learning and Performance Technologies <http://www.c4lpt.co.uk/>
WebQuest.org at <http://webquest.org> (An group nurturing inquiry-based learning techniques utilizing the Web)

FURTHER READING: PART TWO

Music Teaching And Learning

Colwell, Richard. (Ed.). 1992. *The handbook of research on music teaching and learning.* New York: Oxford University Press.
Colwell, Richard and Carol P. Richardson (Ed.). 2002. *The new handbook of research on music teaching and learning.* New York: Oxford University Press.
Gordon, Edwin E.. 2007. *Learning sequence in music.* Chicago: GIA Publications.
White, John D. 1981. *Guidelines for college teaching of music theory.* Metuchen, NJ: Scarecrow Press.
McPherson, Gary E., and Barry J. Zimmerman. 2002. Self-regulation of musical learning: A social cognitive perspective. In R. Colwell and C.P. Richardson (Eds.) *The new handbook of research on music teaching and learning* (pp. 327–347). New York: Oxford University Press.
Maehr, Martin L., Paul R. Pintrich, & E. A. Linnenbrink. 2002. Motivation and achievement. In Richard Colwell and Carol P. Richardson (Eds.) *The new handbook of research on music teaching and learning* (pp. 348–372). New York: Oxford University Press.

Natvig, Mary. 2002. *Teaching music history.* Burlington, VT: Ashgate.

Rogers, Michael R. 2004. *Teaching approaches in music theory: An overview of pedagogical philosophies.* Carbondale: Southern Illinois University Press.

Applied Music Instruction

Abeles, Harold F. 1975. Student perceptions of characteristics of effective applied music instructors. *Journal of Research in Music Education,* 23: 147–154.

Barry, Nancy H., and Vincent McArthur. 1994. Teaching strategies in the music studio: A survey of applied teachers. *Psychology of Music and Music Education,* 22: 44–55.

Brand, Manny. 1992. Voodoo and the applied music studio [Special issue]. *Quarterly Journal of Music Teaching and Learning,* 3 (2): 3–4.

Donovan, A. J. 1994. The interaction of personality traits in applied music teaching (Doctoral dissertation, University of Southern Mississippi, 1994). *Dissertation Abstracts International,* 55: 1499A.

Geringer, John M., and Marilyn J. Kostka. 1984. An analysis of practice room behavior of college music students. *Contributions to Music Education,* 11: 24–27.

Kennell, Richard. 1989. *Three teacher scaffolding strategies in college applied music instruction.* Unpublished doctoral dissertation, University of Wisconsin, Madison.

Kennell, Richard. 1997. Teaching music one-one one. *Dialogue in Instrumental Music Education,* 27 (1): 69–81.

Kennell, Richard. 2002. Systematic research in studio instruction in music. In Richard Colwell and Carol P. Richardson (Eds.) *The new handbook of research on music teaching and learning* (pp. 243–256). New York: Oxford University Press.

Rosenthal, Rosanne. 1984. The relative effects of guided model, model only, guide only and practice only treatments on the accuracy of advanced instrumentalists' musical performance. *Journal of Research in Music Education,* 32 (4): 265–273.

Schmidt, Charles P. 1989. Applied music teaching behavior as a function of selected personality variables. *Journal of Research in Music Education,* 37: 258–271.

Issues In General Teaching and LearningBarkley, Elizabeth, Patricia Cross, and Claire Howell Major. 2004. *Collaborative learning: A handbook for college faculty.* San Francisco: Jossey-Bass.

Duckworth, Eleanor. 1996. *"The having of wonderful ideas" and other essays on teaching and learning* (2nd Ed.). New York: Teachers College Press.

Light, Greg, and Roy Cox. 2004. *Learning and teaching in higher education: The reflective professional.* Thousand Oaks, CA: Sage.

Palmer, Parker J. 1998. *The courage to teach: Exploring the inner landscape of a teacher's life.* San Francisco: Jossey-Bass.

Paul R. Pintrich (Ed.). 1995. Understanding self-regulated learning. New Directions for Teaching and Learning, no. 63.

Sawyer, Keith. 2006. *The Cambridge handbook of the learning sciences.* Cambridge and New York, Cambridge University Press.

Schunk, Dale H., and Barry J. Zimmerman. (Ed.). 1998. *Self-regulated learning: From teaching to self- reflective practice.* New York: Guilford.

Sousa, John Philip. 1897. *The stars and stripes forever.* Washington, DC: Library of Congress, 1998.

Stanley, Christein A., and M. Eric Porter. 2007. *Engaging large classes: Strategies and techniques for college faculty.* San Francisco, CA: Jossey-Bass.

Svinicki, Marilla D. 2004. *Learning and motivation in the post-secondary classroom.* Bolton, MA: Anker.

PART THREE

Growth in Teaching Practice and a Future in Higher Education

CHAPTER 10

The Job Search in Higher Education

This chapter includes information regarding how to find employment postings in higher education and how to interpret some of the language in the postings. We provide suggestions for writing cover letters and preparing curriculum vitae as well as gathering other possible materials that may be needed. Sample interview questions are presented and discussed. We conclude the chapter with a discussion of strategies for teaching and performing at the interview as well as information about the negotiation process in higher education. Questions for discussion are included at the end of the chapter.

FINDING THE JOBS AND UNDERSTANDING THE POSTINGS

Although word of mouth is probably the strongest strategy for finding music positions in higher education, there are several other sources that are helpful. The College Music Society (CMS) (http://www.music.org) publishes a comprehensive list of higher education positions in a newsletter called the Music Vacancy List. We suggest that graduate students become members of the CMS and watch the job listings carefully. The Chronicle of Higher Education (available online at http://chronicle.com) also posts higher education positions.

The postings often use a variety of terms to describe the positions. We have listed some of the posting language here with commonly used definitions. This is not a comprehensive list of terms, but may still be useful for those searching for jobs within music in higher education.

- *Full time*: This usually means a position that includes full benefits and is often tenure track (although not always). In some cases, "full time" positions include restrictions regarding time away from campus or outside performance obligations. Most full time positions in higher education require a completed doctorate or ABD (all but dissertation).

- *Half time*: Some half time positions include full benefits. This is an important question to ask if the posting does not state that information. In some rare cases, half time positions may be "tenure track" but in most cases they are not. Half time positions usually require committee work and advising in addition to teaching duties.
- *Part-time or adjunct faculty*: The pay for part-time teaching is usually per credit. Some colleges will offer many credits of teaching to part-time faculty (often even more classes per semester than a full time faculty member). Be careful of exploitation.
- *Tenure track*: This means that the position includes a regular review procedure (more in Chapter 12 on tenure and promotion) with the possibility of tenure. Most institutions have yearly reviews for untenured faculty and an extended third year review process for faculty in a tenure track position. This type of position usually requires a doctorate and on-going research and professional activity.
- *Nontenure or "clinical faculty" track*: This means that the position is not in a faculty line that leads to tenure at the institution. There are a variety of other types of positions. Some are contracted from year to year. Others are multiple year contracts. Some institutions have "clinical faculty" positions that are primarily "teaching only" positions and do not include tenure. For the most part, tenure track positions are more desirable than nontenure track ones. However, there are exceptions. For example, an athletic band position is often in a "clinical faculty" line since it would be difficult for a person in that position to have time to complete the necessary scholarly work required in a tenure track position. Nontenure or clinical faculty lines usually do not require a completed doctorate.
- *Lecturer*: Most lecturer positions are part-time or are nontenure track. This title is often used for faculty who have not yet completed their doctorates but have been hired into tenure track lines. They remain at a "lecturer" title until the doctorate is completed.
- *Assistant professor*: When an institution searches at the "assistant professor" level, they are looking for someone fairly new to the field of higher education. Most of you will apply for assistant professor positions. Some of the postings will state that the candidate must hold a completed doctorate. Some will state a certain number of years of college teaching experience preferred. The posting will usually state whether the position is tenure track or not. In most cases, if the posting was listed as "Assistant Professor," the institution cannot make a hire at a rank higher than assistant (i.e., Associate or Full). They usually can make a hire at a lesser rank (i.e., Lecturer).
- *Associate professor*: In most cases, an associate professor has achieved tenure and moved from assistant professor to associate professor. In some cases, a faculty member will be hired at the Associate Professor level but without tenure. This is usually in institutions that have unionized faculty and set salaries. In order to attract a candidate in terms of salary, it may be necessary to make the person an Associate Professor. If the posting is Associate Professor, the institution is probably looking for an experienced person. However, since it is usually possible to hire at a rank lower than

the posting (i.e., Assistant), an Associate Professor posting should not necessarily discourage you from applying.

- *Full professor*: A posting for full professor usually means that the institution is looking to hire a very experienced and well known person in the field. This is someone who has achieved associate or full professor in another institution and who has a proven record as a performer or researcher in the professional circle.
- *Visiting professor*: A visiting professor posting often means that the position is available for just one academic year. However, sometimes institutions will hire a person into a "one-year" position and then run a search for a tenure track position the following year. This often happens when a personnel change happens too late in the school year for a tenure track line search to be held. It is appropriate to ask about these sorts of details of the position before applying for a visiting professor position.
- *Open rank*: Some searches will post "open rank," meaning they will consider any level (lecturer, assistant, associate, full). This gives the institution the freedom to hire at any level and hire exactly the right person for the job regardless of rank.
- *Other duties based on candidate's expertise*: Many of the postings include language such as "other duties based on candidate's expertise." It is in your best interest to consider what areas in music you might be able to teach beyond what you might consider your "primary" area. Applied music faculty and conductors often teach theory, aural skills, music history, instrument methods courses, or music for nonmajors. Academic area faculty are often asked to teach applied music or nonmajors courses as well. Knowledge of music technology is often very desirable as a secondary area of expertise.

COVER LETTERS

We suggest sending a specific cover letter to each job you are applying for rather than a generic cover letter that goes to all. Use the name of the University you are applying to and reference some of the details of the specific job description in the cover letter. Each cover letter that you write may be slightly different to accommodate for the needs of the job. Open the letter with a statement of your intention (i.e., I write to apply for the position of assistant professor of music theory at the University of ...). Provide some details as to your qualifications for the position (i.e., I have recently completed my PhD in music theory at the ...) and give some of your background experience (i.e., I have been working as an adjunct lecturer in music theory at ...). State in the cover letter that your curriculum vitae and any other documents that were requested are enclosed.

RESUME OR CURRICULUM VITAE

Most jobs will ask for a resume and/or curriculum vitae. Some may use the term "vitae" short for "curriculum vitae." A resume is usually shorter (some say keep to one page) and vitae is more extensive. Unless it is specified that the resume be only one page, we would suggest a four to six page vitae. We recommend that resumes or vitae be created on plain white paper without lots of fancy graphics. Use a 12-point font. There are numerous templates available for resume creation. Many of these begin with an "Objective." In higher education, the objective is to seek a position as a music professor, so we are not sure of the necessity of including this on a music resume. Some templates will also provide a space for statement of philosophy. Unless the job asks for this information specifically, once again we would suggest using the limited resume space for information regarding your background and experience rather than your philosophy. There will be time to discuss philosophy in an interview or on the job application. Religious-based colleges often ask for a statement of faith or a philosophy of teaching at a faith-based institution.

Be extremely accurate on all the documents you submit. There can be no typographical errors. Be sure to have multiple people read your materials carefully before you send them out. Proofread, proofread, and then proofread again. Not all curriculum vitae need to look exactly the same. We outline possible sections of this document here.

1. Contact Information and Format

Be sure to list all of your contact information (name, address, telephone, e-mail) clearly at the top of the document. Be sure that the e-mail listed is one that you check regularly. We recommend creating a header or footer for the document that includes your name and page numbers for the document.

2. Education

List all degrees earned starting with the most recent degree. Write out the name of the degree (i.e., Doctor of Musical Arts). You might include your grade point average within each degree if it is impressive. Include the primary applied teacher (or conductor or researcher) that you worked with in each degree. Include any graduation with honors or distinction. List any additional studies, institutes, or certifications you have completed in this section as well (i.e., Tanglewood Fellow or Suzuki Pedagogy certification).

3. Teaching Experience

If the position in higher education is primarily a teaching position, you should list your teaching experience first. If it is an "Artist in Residence" sort of position, you might list performance credentials ahead of your teaching work. List all teaching positions held and include a short description of the duties in that position including the names of courses you have taught. Include any honors your students have received and any teaching fellowships or awards in the teaching section. Include assistantships or Teaching Assistant positions you held as a graduate student. If you have had a private studio, list that as well. Be sure to include dates for all positions.

4. Performance Experience

List your professional performance experience first before your work in degree programs. Be sure to include dates and places for performances. Include performance competitions and awards in this section as well. In some cases, you may list "performance highlights" as it may not make sense to document every performance.

5. Scholarship (Publications, Presentations, and Master Classes)

List any publications in this section. Be sure to include whether the paper was for a referred journal (meaning a blind review); peer-reviewed (not necessarily blind) or invited. It is fine to list publications in review as well as works in progress in this section. Include any conference presentations, paper presentations, master classes, or other events in which you were the primary figure.

6. Service in the Profession

Service may include an office held in a national music organization, review board work, work in planning conferences or performances or a variety of other jobs. Many graduate students may have assisted professors in service work and it is fine to list this as well. Be sure to list your role in the work.

7. Honors and Awards

If you have received any honors or awards as a student, or a teaching assistant, list those here. If you do not have any awards, just leave this section out.

8. Repertoire List

Many postings for positions in applied music and conducting will ask for a repertoire list. Be sure to include dates of performances in this section.

9. Professional Organizations

List your membership in professional music organizations (i.e., International Trumpet Guild, International Horn Society, American Choral Directors Association) Write out the name of the organization and include any office you may have held in a local or national chapter of these groups.

10. References

We would suggest listing four or five professional references right on the resume. Some resume templates suggest "references available upon request." However, we think that potential employers are happy to have this information supplied. Be sure to contact anyone whom you intend to list as a reference to be sure they are willing to be a reference for you. List the name of the person and their title (in relationship to you). Include the person's address, telephone, and e-mail. Do not list more than four or five references even if you have 20 people who are willing to be a reference for you. The employer does not want to have to choose from a long list. You might change the list of references depending on the job.

TRANSCRIPTS

Many employers will ask for "official" transcripts from your college or university. These are usually ordered through the college or university registrar's office and may take several weeks to process. There is usually a fee for sending transcripts. Be sure to leave time for the process as you consider application deadlines. Purchase an "unofficial" transcript for yourself so you can bring it to an interview in the event that your official ones have not arrived. Many institutions have a campus placement office or credential file center. These centers will often send your resume, transcripts, and recommendation letters out to any employer upon your request. Contact the student services office at your institution to see if there is such an office and to get details regarding setting up a placement file.

LETTERS OF RECOMMENDATION

Most jobs require three letters of recommendation. They will often stipulate that the letters be "confidential." This means that the person who wrote the letter sent it directly to the placement office or the school and knew that the applicant (you) did not see the letter. Ask someone to write you a confidential letter only if you are sure that the person writing the letter will be completely supportive of you and your work. If you are not sure, do not ask for a confidential letter.

It is fine for the references on your resume to be the same people who write your letters of recommendation. Be sure to give them time to write the letter. We suggest three to four weeks. We would suggest providing a copy of your resume so that the letter writer can be reminded of your background and accomplishments. In most cases, you will leave a letter cover sheet for the person. The person will complete the cover sheet and the letter and then send the letter directly to the placement office or the school. You should provide the letter writer with a stamped envelope so that there is no cost to the letter writer. Many placement offices are now doing recommendation letters in an online format. Either way, be sure to give the person time to write and be sure to follow up with a thank-you letter for writing the letter.

COMMUNICATION WITH THE INSTITUTIONS

Most institutions will not begin calling candidates for interviews until after the application deadline for the position. It is fine to contact the institution to be sure that all your materials have arrived. However, we would suggest that you do not contact the school more than once before the application deadline. After the deadline, search committees will begin to contact candidates for interviews. They will often interview several rounds of candidates before letting applicants know that the position has been filled. What this may mean is that weeks (maybe even months) may go by before you hear anything from some of the institutions where you have applied.

It is appropriate to contact the school to inquire about where they are in their search. If they have begun interviews, they may let you know that. Or, they may not. As frustrating as it may be, there is a lot of waiting around that can happen at this point in the process.

ADDITIONAL MATERIALS

In some settings, a search committee will meet to review initial applicants for a position and then will contact the applicants to ask for additional materials. Or, some of these materials may have been required in the initial process. Additional materials might include video or audio of performances, rehearsal videos for conductors, teaching videos or master classes, sample programs with program notes, and/or samples of writing or scholarship. Some institutions ask for evidence of teaching and this could include course evaluations as well as syllabi and other course materials.

PHONE INTERVIEWS

Phone interviews are often used by search committees as a way to choose three or four candidates to bring to campus from a "short list" of eight to ten. In some cases, the entire search committee will be on a conference call for a phone interview. Each of the eight to ten candidates will usually be asked the same questions. This allows the committee to compare responses and decide on the three or four most qualified for the position. In other instances, individual committee members will set up phone interviews with candidates and report back to the committee regarding the phone interview. Know that phone interviews are always a bit awkward. If there are certain questions that the search committee member must ask, then it is difficult for the interview to feel like a conversation and this can be frustrating. Prepare your answers to sample questions and do the best you can to sound interesting and energetic.

INTERVIEWING FOR A JOB AS A MUSIC PROFESSOR

First impressions are very important at a job interview. In some ways, the interview begins as soon as a search committee member picks you up from the airport. Search committees usually divide their time, so different members spend time with the candidate throughout the few days of the interview. Dress professionally. We suggest a suit for both men and women at the actual interview. Men should wear a tie. Even if you do not intend to dress conservatively in going to school every day, dress conservatively for the interview. Gather details about the music department at the school and information about the institution from the web. Then, try to incorporate what you have learned about department and institution in your interactions during the interview.

Most interviews center around core questions, so it is possible to prepare for the interview by practicing your answers to typical questions in advance. We would suggest writing out responses to common interview questions and then practicing articulating the response. In addition to practicing your interview answers, practice confident interview posture (standing and seated), hand gestures, handshake, confident smile, and eye contact. Videorecord a mock interview and watch for your level of confidence and engagement. Several sample questions are included here. It is recommended that applicants review discipline-specific questions (applied music, music theory, music history, ensembles, etc.) with faculty prior to the interview. Some discussion regarding responses to these questions follows after this list.

SAMPLE INTERVIEW QUESTIONS:

1. Tell us a little about your background and preparation as a teacher and performer.
2. Share some of your most powerful teaching experiences.
3. What interests you in a teaching position in music in higher education?
4. What interests you most about this particular position?
5. What do you want your students in (insert a music class) to know and be able to do at the end of a semester?
6. Talk with us about your syllabus for (insert music course here).
7. Share some of your strategies for teaching in an interactive way.
8. Share some of your strategies for good assessment of musical behaviors.
9. Discuss your strategies for establishing and maintaining good rapport with students in your course.
10. Discuss how you might approach a course differently depending on whether the students in the group are freshmen or seniors.
11. How will you balance your performing or presenting (academic areas) career with teaching?
12. Discuss some of your strategies for recruiting students into the program here.

DISCUSSION OF INTERVIEW RESPONSES

Although different search committee members will be looking for different characteristics in a candidate and there are no right answers to these questions, we have tried to outline issues to consider in relation to these questions. Of course, you want to represent yourself as honestly and accurately as possible and try to get a sense of the institution and the faculty as part of the interview process. It is best if the interview can feel like a spontaneous conversation. Work to weave content from these and other interview questions together to show the committee that you understand the types of issues they will want to discuss.

1. Tell us a little about your background and preparation as a teacher and performer. In answering this question, it will be important to consider the type of institution and the specific position. For many new professors, their preparation as a performer is

much more extensive than their preparation as a teacher and yet, for some positions, the committee will want to hear about the teaching preparation. Work to balance this in a way that fits the institution. Interviews often begin with this sort of "get to know you" question and it is important to consider what it is that you want the search committee to know about you first.

2. Share some of your most powerful teaching experiences. Work to include as many examples of you in a teacher's role in your interview responses. Try to avoid examples from your experience as a student as the committee needs to consider you in a professor's role and not a student's role. Answer this type of question with a "student-centered" response if possible so that the example is really an example of learning that was as a result of powerful teaching.

3. What interests you in a teaching position in music in higher education? Discuss your interest in student learning and your curiosity about the teaching and learning process. Discuss the balance between teaching and scholarship you aim for in your career.

4. What interests you most about this particular position? Work to make a connection between your background and the specific institution in your response to this question. If you attended a small liberal arts program as an undergraduate and this position is in a small liberal arts college, make that connection. Or, if you attended graduate school in a large urban center and this position is in a large urban center, make that connection.

5. What do you want your students in (insert a music class) to know and be able to do at the end of a semester? Work to provide a learner-centered response to this question. You might bring sample syllabi for courses you might teach to the interview so that you have them to refer to. Let the committee know that you have an understanding of the many issues facing teaching and learning in music classes today. Ask questions about the specifics of the institution or a course when you begin to talk at the specific level to be sure that you are not suggesting things that do not fit with the context.

6. Talk with us about your syllabus for (insert music course here). This type of question is an extension of "what do you want students to know and be able to do" above. Be prepared to discuss textbooks, sample assignments and ideas for specific units within a course you might teach. Be prepared to discuss this sort of information in what might be considered your "secondary" teaching area as well.

7. Share some of your strategies for teaching in an interactive way. Let the committee know that you have experience with a wide variety of teaching techniques including lectures, discussions, cooperative groups, cases, games, simulations, fieldwork, and so on. Focus on student learning and share specific examples of interactive moments in your teaching.

8. Share some of your strategies for good assessment of musical behaviors. Be ready to discuss documentation of student grades, clear grading policies, varied tools for assessment and the challenges in balancing grading and feedback in music courses.

9. Discuss your strategies for establishing and maintaining good rapport with students in your course. Focus on how you will create a culture for learning in your

classes. Share some of your understandings of learning styles, motivation, and self-regulation in music classes.

10. Discuss how you might approach a course differently depending on whether the students in the group are freshmen or seniors. Share your understanding of intellectual as well as musical development and present strategies for teaching to individual differences in applied lessons as well as larger class settings.

11. How will you balance your performing or presenting (academic areas) career with teaching? In most settings, there will be interest in you maintaining your career as a scholar or performer. Be prepared to discuss teaching, research, and service as defined in Chapter 12 as part of your interview interaction. The committee is trying to get a sense of whether you are on a trajectory to be successful in this setting. Be prepared to talk about your balance.

12. Discuss some of your strategies for recruiting students into the program here. Discussion of recruitment is a common interview topic. The committee wants to know that you will be active in the community, in the state, in the region, and in the nation in getting the word out about your program. Discussion of good follow-up and communication as well as outlining your strategies to be visible as a performer and/or scholar are important issues to address for this response.

CONCLUSION

We suggest practicing responses to these various questions with peers or mentors. Try to include specific musical examples for questions about music and try to include specific instructional examples that you have used in your responses regarding education. It is okay to say that you do not know or have no experience with something you are unfamiliar with. Be confident, but do not try to pretend that you know it all. As mentioned earlier, review content-specific questions with your faculty mentors. Know the controversial areas. For example, questions about solfege systems (fixed versus movable DO or Do-based versus La-based minor) for music theory classes can be hotbeds for controversy.

MUSIC TEACHING AT THE INTERVIEW

For most positions, you will be asked to teach a course or master class as part of the interview process. The goal of this type of activity is to get a sense of your rapport and interaction with students and to get a glimpse of your musicianship. Work to show both aspects in your teaching presentation. If possible, find a way to model musically either with your instrument or voice (even for academic area positions). Engage students and try to get to know them within the time that you are given. Work to model several different types of teaching including an organized lecture, some group discussion, and possibly some other group interaction. Your interaction with the students is more important than the content of your lesson. Unless you are asked to present on something specific, avoid controversial content areas at the job interview. For example, if interviewing for a position in instrumental music education, we would suggest avoiding a lesson on the advantages and disadvantages of festivals and competitions as this is controversial.

PERFORMANCE OR RESEARCH PRESENTATION

Applied music applicants will be asked to perform at the interview and academic applicants will usually be asked to provide a research presentation. This is usually the part of the interview that we feel most relaxed about as it is "what we do" so to speak. However, choose repertoire carefully and prepare the music or the presentation well. Search committees will not hire someone who did everything else well but "did not play well" or "did not have solid research." This presentation does "make or break" the interview.

HIRING AND NEGOTIATION PROCESS

For those who are new to higher education, the extended process of hiring and negotiation can be a mystery. In most institutions, a search committee will make a recommendation to a Dean or advisory committee at the completion of the interview process. Sometimes, the search committee must submit an "unranked" list of applicants who were interviewed and the administrator or other committee makes the final hiring choice based on the comments of the search committee. In some institutions, the Dean or music chair must then bring the applicant list to another administrator (or several others going up the administrative food chain) before an offer can be made. It is not uncommon in smaller colleges to meet with the college President as part of the interview process. This process can often take several weeks. If the institution is considering more than one of the applicants, the wait can be several months if the first choice candidate turns down the job and then the committee begins the paperwork process again with the next applicant.

It is difficult as a new professor to know how to "negotiate" the terms of employment. In some institutions, there is no negotiation. The salary for the line is set and the offer is made. If the faculty is unionized, you enter at a specific salary "step" based on your previous years of teaching experience. Some schools count part-time teaching in this calculation, others may not. It is appropriate to ask about money for travel and research, start-up funds for performance or research, recording equipment, computers and software, office furniture, as well as salary. The search committee chair will most likely be able to let you know the terms of negotiation if the Dean or Chair does not offer this information.

QUESTIONS FOR DISCUSSION

1. Explore the *Chronicle of Higher Education* and *College Music Society* websites and collect several postings for higher education that interest you.
2. Compare the terms used in the posting you find to the language discussed in the chapter.

3. Prepare a curriculum vitae and share with your peers for feedback.

4. Discuss additional materials that may be required for a job you are interested in. Get feedback from you peers on your audio or video recordings, teaching videos, and/or writing samples.

5. Hold a mock phone interview with several of your peers to get a sense of how a phone interview "feels."

6. Practice your answers to the sample interview questions listed in this chapter.

7. Generate additional interview questions that are more specific to your area of expertise.

8. What are some of the controversial topic areas within your field? How will you address them in an interview or teaching situation?

9. Plan a 25–30 minutes lesson for "teaching at the interview." Work to include multiple strategies in your demonstration.

CHAPTER 11

Learning from Student Feedback

One of the key tenants in a learner-centered classroom is for the professor to reflect on teaching and work to change approaches to best meet the needs of students. In *Becoming a Critically Reflective Teacher* (1995) Brookfield suggests that critical reflection on our teaching needs to accomplish two purposes:

> The first is to understand how considerations of power undergird, frame and distort educational processes and interactions. The second is to question assumptions and practice that seem to make our teaching lives easier but actually work against our own best long-term interests. (p. 8)

We begin this chapter with a discussion of reflection in college teaching in general (not critical reflection) and the development of reflection as a professor. The second section of the chapter focuses on strategies for collecting constructive feedback from students and considerations for applying student suggestions. We then turn to a discussion of critical reflection. We conclude with questions for discussion and suggested extension activities.

REFLECTION IN COLLEGE TEACHING

Reflective thinking is defined by Dewey (1933) as "active, persistent, and careful consideration of any belief or supposed knowledge in the light of the grounds that support it, and the further conclusions to which it tends" (p. 6). Sebren (1992) (based on L. S. Shulman, 1986, 1987; and Schon, 1983, 1987) adds to Dewey's definition regarding teachers:

Reflection is what a teacher does when he or she looks back at the teaching and learning that has occurred, reconstructs and recaptures what happened and the reasons underlying what happened, generates alternatives for change, and considers the moral, and perhaps political implications of those teaching events. What is learned through the reflection process is then incorporated into the teacher's knowledge base and repertoire to be drawn upon in future teaching and reflection episodes. (p. 33)

Reflection is a skill for the professor that can be learned and developed. The following strategies are provided as ways for the professor to learn to look back on teaching and learning in the effort to change and improve instruction.

TEACHING JOURNALS

One strategy for learning to reflect on your own teaching is to keep a teaching journal. We suggest writing a paragraph or two after each class as a way of documenting what you are thinking is going well or needs improvement. This journal works as a sort of diary for documenting class interactions. At the end of the semester, this allows you to go back and consider the semester with "up to the minute" data about the course. If you opt to collect video of your teaching, the journal will provide you more information as you consider the video. When you collect feedback from students, a journal will allow you to compare your perceptions of the course to theirs.

Dr. Herbert Marshall from Baldwin Wallace Conservatory suggests the following framework for starting a teaching journal:

- **What?**—Describe an interesting occurrence or situation.
- **So What?**—Tell why this was significant.
- **Now What?**—What course of action will you take, or what have you learned as a result of this event?

Dr. Louis Bergonzi from the University of Illinois developed a teaching observation form that may be used as a reflection tool by a new professor. The form asks the instructor to comment on the instructional techniques observed (see Figure 11–1).

VIDEORECORD

Another tool for use in learning to reflect on teaching is to videorecord your class. Teaching resource centers on campus (discussed in Chapter 13) will often come to your course and videorecord at your request. Barbara Davis (2001) suggests:

Watching a videotape of yourself is an extremely valuable experience. Videotaping allows you to view and listen to the class as your students do; you can also scrutinize your students' reactions and responses to you teaching. By analyzing a videotape of the dynamics in your classroom, you can check the accuracy of your perceptions of how well you teach and identify those techniques that work and those that need revamping. (p. 355)

I. Introduction to Lesson
   A. Did the instructor establish good initial contact with the class?
   B. Were the objectives clear?
   C. Was appropriate motivation toward learning evident?

II. Presentation
   A. Was the material well organized?
   B. Was the pace of instruction appropriate?
   C. Did the instruction have continuity between activities?
   D. Were illustrations and examples used to reinforce the material?
   E. Were media aids effectively used?

III. Teaching Procedures
   A. Were the activities appropriate for achieving the stated objectives?
   B. Were the explanations and demonstrations coordinated?
   C. Were the procedures appropriate for the students?
   D. Were students provided with supportive assessments?
   E. Was the instructor sensitive to individual student differences?
   F. Were the closing activities effective?

IV. Instructor Qualities and Verbal Fluency
   A. Did the instructor possess poise and confidence?
   B. Did he/she display a positive attitude?
   C. Was the instructor sensitive to the feelings, needs, and interests of the students?
   D. Did he/she maintain eye contact with the class?
   E. Were there any distracting mannerisms?
   F. Were instructions expressed clearly and fluently?
   G. Did the instructor's voice project to all parts of the room?
   H. Was the phraseology and usage of English appropriate?

V. Musical Skills
   A. Were the following skills effectively used:
      • Modeling skills?
      • Visual diagnostic skills?
      • Aural diagnostic skills?
      • Accompaniment skills?
      • Performance skills?
      • Conducting skills?
   B. Was the singing voice effectively used in instruction?
   C. Did the instructor demonstrate comprehensive musicianship?

VI. Classroom Management
   A. Were routine matters properly handled?
   B. Were any discipline problems apparent?
   C. Did the instructor maintain awareness of the entire class?
   D. Was rule enforcement consistent?
   E. Were students engaged in learning?
   F. Did the instructor properly plan for student participation?
   G. Were students' questions handled with skill?

VII. Student Education
   A. Did the class (or the students) achieve the instructional objectives?
   B. Were evaluative procedures effectively used?
   C. What was the level and quality of student responses?

Figure 11–1 Teaching Observation Form
(*Based on form developed by Louis Bergonzi, Associate Professor at the University of Illinois*)

Let students know in advance that you are intending to tape the class and try to capture both the students and the instructor, if possible. The reflection form (Figure 11–2) might provide a useful tool for self-observation as well.

PEER OBSERVATION

A final strategy to consider is that of having colleagues observe your class and provide feedback. Try to bring someone to the class who can provide objective feedback, someone who knows the content and the students, and someone who you know can be honest. It is also important that you have someone who you feel comfortable with. This will most likely be someone who is not involved in your evaluation process. Retired professors or other junior faculty members may be helpful.

Some higher education institutions have formalized faculty mentor programs and if you have an assigned faculty mentor, that person would be a good observer for your course. Although you may feel nervous to invite an experienced professor into your classroom, it is absolutely crucial that the mentor has a sense of the teaching context for the new professor. You might start the year by observing your mentor in his/her own course first. It is important for you to feel comfortable inviting the mentor in to help. When you invite the mentor into your classroom, let your students know that the mentor is coming and will be helping you in your work as a new professor. Introduce the mentor to your students when he/she comes. If possible, try to meet with your mentor in advance of the observation and have a discussion regarding what you would like for him/her to see and react to. You might also videorecord the observation so that you and the mentor can view your classroom together.

MEETING BEFORE AN OBSERVATION

- How do you want the mentor to help?
- What would you like the mentor to notice?
- What would you like the mentor to document? You might ask the mentor to just script every word that you say. Or, you might ask of the mentor to describe the entire room. Or, you might ask him/her to document the responses of a few students or a section.
- What do you expect will be the challenges on that day? Let the mentor know that in advance.
- Do you want the mentor's thoughts regarding improvement? Or do you want him/her just to describe what he/she sees?
- Discuss where the mentor will sit in the room. Will he/she participate in the musical activity? Sit at the back of the room? Sit at the front? You decide what you will be most comfortable with.

I. Describe what you notice about the following aspects of your teaching.

     A. Were the objectives clear?

     B. Was the class well organized?

     C. Did you properly set up the learning environment?

     D. Was there continuity between activities?

     E. How well did the students complete your objectives?

     F. Did you offer assessments after students performed?

     G. Did you display a good posture/sense of confidence?

     H. Did you maintain eye contact with the entire class?

     I. Did you display any distracting mannerisms?

     J. Were your instructions clear?

     K. Was your voice well projected and understandable?

     L. Were your musical models of good quality? Were your visual models of good quality?

     M. How well did you diagnose the problems (visually & aurally)?

     N. Did you offer remediation activities for poor student performances?

     O. How well did the students pay attention?

     P. Were you aware of the entire classroom?

II. Describe three aspects of your teaching that you consider as strengths, and give at least one specific example from this class.

III. Describe three aspects of your teaching that you think can be improved, give at least one example from this class, and how you would do it differently next time.

Figure 11–2 Reflection Form *(Based on form developed by Louis Bergonzi, Associate Professor at the University of Illinois)*

MEETING AFTER THE OBSERVATION

• Begin with a discussion of what you think went well in that class /rehearsal.

• Share with your mentor your concerns from that day.

• If you are comfortable, ask the mentor for his/her suggestions for improvement. Based on the suggestions, create your own strategies for meeting future goals.

STUDENT FEEDBACK ON YOUR COURSE

There are formal and informal ways to collect feedback from students regarding your course. Most institutions require a formal course evaluation at the end of the semester and we suggest a formal evaluation at midterm time in the course as well. In addition to these formal written or verbal strategies, there are several ways to gather student perceptions even as early as on the first day in the course. We suggest that you tell students about the mechanisms for feedback on the first day. Let them know that there will be a formal course evaluation on the last day of class and if you plan to do a formal midterm evaluation, let them know this as well. You might announce a midterm evaluation coming up in the next class so that students can prepare their responses.

Set up a culture in your classroom that invites student feedback. You might have students respond in writing on the very first day of class about their expectations for the course and what they think now that they have seen the syllabus and been to the first day of class. Or, you might ask students to write their anonymous responses to a particular activity. If a discussion or class activity does not go well in your estimation, you may begin the next class with a discussion of the poorly received activity and get some feedback from students regarding what may be wrong. Other informal means of collecting student feedback could include individual student meetings in the first few weeks of class to get a sense of the students' impressions of the class.

MIDTERM COURSE EVALUATIONS

We suggest that professors consider a formal evaluation at midterm time. This gives you the opportunity to change your approach or the culture of the course if you learn about something that could be changed. Final course evaluations often provide excellent feedback regarding things that could be changed in the course, but in a sense, it is too late. The course is already over. Midterm reports work best when done after midterm grade reports are out to students as they will be more ready to discuss the class when they have a sense of how they are doing. Not all institutions require midterm grade reports. However, we recommend that you provide students with a midterm grade report whether it is required or not. Campus resources like the University of Michigan's Center for Research on Teaching and Learning that will be discussed in Chapter 13 often provide a midterm course evaluation service. Staff from the center or office will come to your class and talk with students about the course. You will, of course, not be present in the the room. Then, you meet with the staff and they share what they have learned from talking with the students. This type of "outsider" midterm evaluation could also be done with a written evaluation form rather than by way of interviews.

It is also possible to collect yourself the written midterm feedback from students during class. You might develop a short survey about the course and have students complete it right after the midterm exam or on the day midterm grade reports are given. Or you might pass around a blank sheet of paper and ask for student comments about the course so far. Be sure that students understand that you are trying to collect information that you can use to alter the course this semester. You might have them reflect on the course so far and look at the syllabus to consider what is coming next. Curzan and Damour (2006, p. 170) provide the following suggestions for prompts in midterm evaluations:

- I would like to see more/less time spent on...
- In the second half of the term, I would like to talk about...
- Written comments on my paper would be more helpful if...

Instruct students to save comments for the final course evaluation if they are more general about the course design or the text for the course. The disadvantage to this approach is that student comments may vary and the very thing that some students hate about the course, other students will love. You may be left trying to figure out how to appear as if you are listening to student suggestions when the suggestions often contradict one another.

In smaller size courses (under 20 participants) you might try leaving the room and allowing students to have a group discussion about the course and their suggestions. Then, choose one student to report the conversation to you when you return to the room. The advantage to this approach is that students have to come to some consensus as a group regarding their suggestions. If one student is particularly unhappy about a certain aspect of the course and he is the only one, he may realize this as part of this approach and begin to reconsider his concern. The disadvantage to any midterm evaluation is that you must be willing to consider student feedback and suggestions and potentially alter the course or you should not bother asking for feedback. We have found that students rarely are irresponsible about their suggestions. Typical suggestions often include getting more information about assignments or changing interaction is some way (i.e., more group discussion and less lecture or more lecture and less small-group discussion). Discuss the feedback with the entire class and let them know what you can try to change and what you may not be able to change. Students will appreciate your honesty and concern. If you can let students in on the issues of the course (i.e., some important topics that got left out just because of lack of time), it will help them to appreciate your efforts.

STUDENT FINAL COURSE EVALUATIONS

Most institutions have carefully designed procedures for collecting final course evaluations. It is common for a staff member from the Dean's office to bring in course evaluations on the last day of class. The professor usually leaves the room while the students complete the forms and then the staff member takes the forms back to the Dean's office. At the University of Michigan, faculty choose their own questions and create a course evaluation from the form provided in Figure 11–3. However, this is fairly rare. It is more common for the department or college to have a form that is used for all courses. Regarding these generic course evaluations, McKeachie and Svinicki (2006) suggest:

> Student ratings are now administered in almost all colleges and universities in the United States and are becoming common in other countries. However, their primary purpose is often to collect data for personnel evaluation, and this complicates and sometimes conflicts with their usefulness for improving teaching. One problem is that those who use student ratings for personnel purposes often feel (unjustifiably) that they need to use a standard form that can be used to compare teachers, across disciplines, in a variety of types of classes, in required as well as elective courses, in large and small classes, and in a variety of contexts. The result is that the questions on the form, are so general that they may be irrelevant to a particular class and, even if relevant, are worded so generally that they offer little guidance for improvement. Moreover, they are typically given at the end of the semester, when it is too late to make much improvement for the class from which the feedback comes. (p. 351)

As will be discussed in Chapter 12, student final course evaluations do often provide important documentation for promotion and tenure reviews. However, they can also give you helpful information to consider for the next time that you teach the course. As mentioned above, one disadvantage to a final course evaluation is that the faculty member usually gets the results from these forms a few weeks, or even months, after the course has concluded. You might consider inviting students to write comments on a blank sheet of paper that will come back directly to you on the last day of class for additional feedback. However, some students will not feel comfortable providing feedback in this way since they would have to handwrite the comments, when you have not yet completed the final grades.

If you administer the final evaluation, it is suggested that you remind students of the value of these evaluations and let them know that the forms provide an opportunity for anonymity. Be sure to leave the room while students are completing the form. We suggest that you choose one student in the course to collect the evaluations and deliver them to the appropriate office. At the University of Michigan, although the forms go to the Office of Examinations and Evaluations to be tallied and reported, the originals of the course evaluation form itself are also returned to the faculty member. In many institutions, the comments from the originals are typed up for the faculty member and the originals are destroyed. It is important for students to know the process. Let them know how this works in your institution.

We are providing the final course evaluation development form from the University of Michigan Office of Examinations and Evaluations here to give examples of the types of questions that may appear on course evaluations (Figure 11–3). If you have the opportunity to design your own form, these questions will also be useful. Forms that are designed specifically for music might also include questions that evaluate the following:

- Level of musicianship modeled by the professor
- Use of teaching techniques to promote comprehensive musicianship (meaning connecting music theory and history with performance)
- Use of teaching techniques to foster independent musical thinking
- Choice of musical repertoire
- Quality of recordings or live musical examples
- Level of student practice, rehearsal or pre paration outside of class

---

SECTION 1: University-Wide Questions

These questions ask for an overall evaluation of a course and instructor. Students respond on a five-point scale of agreement–disagreement.

1. Overall, this was an excellent course.
2. Overall, the instructor was an excellent teacher.
3. I learned a great deal in this course.
4. I had a strong desire to take this course.

SECTION 2: Student Course-Guide Questions

Students respond on a five-point scale of agreement–disagreement unless otherwise prompted.

1. The workload for this course was (5 = LIGHT; 1 = HEAVY)
2. Students felt comfortable asking questions.

Figure 11–3 Cont.

3. Graded assignments reflected the material covered.

4. The grades in this course were fairly determined.

5. Students' difficulty with the material was recognized.

6. My expected grade in this course is (5 = A; 1 = E).

7. The course requirements were clearly defined.

8. The instructor presented material clearly in lectures/discussions.

SECTION 3: Teaching Improvement Questions

Student responses to these questions can help teachers find strengths and weaknesses in their teaching. Students respond on a five-point scale of agreement–disagreement.

STUDENT DEVELOPMENT

Knowledge

1. I learned a good deal of factual material in this course.

2. I gained a good understanding of concepts/principles in this field.

3. I learned to apply principles from this course to new situations.

4. I learned to identify main points and central issues in this field.

5. I learned to identify formal characteristics of works of art.

6. I developed the ability to solve real problems in this field.

7. I developed creative ability in this field.

8. I developed the ability to communicate clearly about this subject.

9. I developed ability to carry out original research in this area.

10. I developed an ability to evaluate new work in this field.

11. I learned to recognize the quality of works of art in this field.

12. I became more aware of multiple perspectives on issues of diversity.

13. I learned to think critically about difficult issues of diversity.

Interests and Values

14. I deepened my interest in the subject matter of this course.

15. I developed enthusiasm about the course material.

16. I was stimulated to do outside reading about the course material.

17. I was stimulated to discuss related topics outside of class.

18. I developed plans to take additional related courses.

19. I developed a set of overall values in this field.

Participation

20. I participated actively in class discussion.

21. I developed leadership skills in this class.

22. I developed new friendships in this class.

Social Awareness

23. I developed greater awareness of societal problems.

Figure 11–3 Cont.

24. I became interested in community projects related to the course.

25. I learned to value new viewpoints.

26. I reconsidered many of my former attitudes.

27. I increased my appreciation of other students in this class.

Self-concept

28. I gained a better understanding of myself through this course.

29. I gained an understanding of some of my personal problems.

30. I developed a greater sense of personal responsibility.

31. I increased my awareness of my own interests and talents.

32. I developed more confidence in myself

Vocational Skills and Attitudes

33. I developed skills needed by professionals in this field.

34. I learned about career opportunities.

35. I developed a clearer sense of professional identity.

INSTRUCTOR EFFECTIVENESS

Instructor Skill

36. I was very satisfied with the educational experience this instructor provided.

37. The instructor explained material clearly and understandably.

38. The instructor handled questions well.

39. The instructor gave clear explanations.

40. The instructor made good use of examples and illustrations.

41. The instructor stressed important points in lectures/discussions.

42. The instructor was enthusiastic.

43. The instructor put material across in an interesting way.

44. The instructor seemed to enjoy teaching.

45. The instructor appeared to have a thorough knowledge of the subject.

46. The instructor seemed knowledgeable in many areas.

47. The instructor was not confused by unexpected questions.

48. The instructor was skillful in observing student reactions.

49. The instructor was sensitive to student difficulty with course work.

50. The instructor taught near the class level.

51. The instructor used examples that had relevance for me.

52. The instructor taught in a manner that served my needs as a student.

53. The instructor was sensitive to multicultural issues in the classroom.

54. The instructor was effective in handling multicultural issues and content.

55. The instructor promoted meaningful discussions of issues of diversity.

56. The instructor handled controversy in the classroom productively.

Figure 11–3 Cont.

57. The instructor challenged stereotypic assumptions in discussions.

58. The instructor accommodated students with various learning needs.

59. The instructor accommodated the needs of students with disabilities.

60. The instructor tried to accommodate individual rates of learning.

61. The instructor tried to accommodate individual styles of learning.

62. The instructor responded to the different language needs of students.

Instructional Climate

63. The instructor was friendly.

64. The instructor was permissive and flexible.

65. The instructor maintained an atmosphere of good feeling in class.

66. The instructor acknowledged all questions insofar as possible.

67. The instructor treated students with respect.

68. The instructor encouraged constructive criticism.

69. The instructor was willing to meet and help students outside class.

70. The instructor gave individual attention to students in the class.

71. The instructor treated all students fairly.

72. The instructor encouraged student participation in an equitable way.

73. The instructor valued the diversity of life experiences among students.

74. The instructor tried to learn the names of all students.

75. The instructor made me feel known as an individual in this class.

76. The classroom's physical environment was conducive to learning.

77. The instructor appeared open to viewpoints besides her or his own.

78. The instructor was open to contributions from all class members.

79. The instructor saw cultural and personal differences as assets.

Interaction

80. Students frequently volunteered their own opinions.

81. One real strength of this course was the classroom discussion.

82. Students in this course were free to disagree and ask questions.

83. The instructor made me feel valued in this class.

84. I felt included and valued when working with other students.

85. Group activities in this class contributed to my learning.

86. Collaborative group activities helped me learn the material.

87. Working with other students helped me learn more effectively.

Feedback

88. The instructor suggested specific ways students could improve.

89. The instructor told students when they had done especially well.

90. The instructor kept students informed of their progress.

Organization

91. The instructor had everything going according to schedule.

Figure 11–3 Cont.

92. The instructor followed an outline closely.

93. The instructor used class time well.

94. The instructor seemed well prepared for each class.

95. The objectives of the course were clearly explained.

96. Work requirements and grading system were clear from the beginning.

Difficulty

97. The amount of work required was appropriate for the credit received.

98. The amount of material covered in the course was reasonable.

99. The instructor set high standards for students.

100. The instructor made the course difficult enough to be stimulating.

WRITING ASSIGNMENTS

101. Writing assignments seemed carefully chosen.

102. Writing assignments were interesting and stimulating.

103. Writing assignments made students think.

104. Directions for writing assignments were clear and specific.

105. Writing assignments required a reasonable amount of time and effort.

106. Writing assignments were relevant to what was presented in class.

107. Writing assignments were graded fairly.

108. Writing assignments were returned promptly.

109. Writing assignments encouraged the inclusion of diverse perspectives.

READING ASSIGNMENTS

110. Reading assignments seemed carefully chosen.

111. Reading assignments were interesting and stimulating.

112. Reading assignments made students think.

113. Reading assignments required a reasonable amount of time and effort.

114. Reading assignments were relevant to what was presented in class.

115. Reading assignments covered material from diverse perspectives.

116. The course pack covered material from diverse perspectives.

LABORATORY ASSIGNMENTS

117. The laboratory was a valuable part of this course.

118. Laboratory assignments seemed carefully chosen.

119. Laboratory assignments were interesting and stimulating.

120. Laboratory assignments made students think.

121. Directions for laboratory assignments were clear and specific.

122. Laboratory assignments required a reasonable amount of time and effort.

123. Laboratory assignments were relevant to what was presented in class.

124. Laboratory reports were graded fairly.

125. Laboratory reports were returned promptly.

Figure 11–3 Cont.

OTHER ASSIGNMENTS

126. Group assignments helped me to learn the material.

127. The term project was very useful in learning the material.

TEXTBOOK

128. The textbook made a valuable contribution to the course.

129. The textbook was easy to read and understand.

130. The textbook presented various sides of issues.

131. A textbook would be a useful addition to this course.

AUDIOVISUAL MATERIALS

132. Films were a valuable part of this course.

133. Audio materials were a valuable part of this course.

134. Films used in this course were a great help to learning.

135. Multimedia materials were a valuable part of this course.

136. Audiovisual materials were a valuable part of this course.

137. Videotapes used in this course were a great help to learning.

138. Slides/overheads were a valuable part of this course.

INSTRUCTIONAL COMPUTING

139. Electronic presentations were a valuable part of this course.

140. E-mail discussions were a valuable part of this course.

141. Use of the World Wide Web was a valuable part of this course.

142. Computer labs were a valuable part of this course.

143. Computer tutorials were a valuable part of this course.

EXAMS

144. Examinations covered the important aspects of the course.

145. The exams covered the reading assignments well.

146. The exams covered the lecture material well.

147. Exams were creative and required original thought.

148. Exams were reasonable in length and difficulty.

149. Examination items were clearly worded.

150. The exams were returned in a reasonable amount of time.

151. The examinations were graded very carefully and fairly.

152. The test items were adequately explained after a test was given.

GRADING

153. Grades were assigned fairly and impartially.

154. The grading system was clearly explained.

155. The instructor had a realistic definition of good performance.

STUDENT RESPONSIBILITY

156. I tried to relate what I learned in this course to my own experience.

157. I attended class regularly.

Figure 11–3 Cont.

158. I utilized all the learning opportunities provided in this course.

159. I created my own learning experiences in connection with the course.

160. I helped classmates learn.

SECTION 4: Open-ended Questions
These questions ask students to write short answers.

1. Comment on the quality of instruction in this course.

2. How can the instructor improve the teaching of this course?

3. Which aspects of this course did you like best?

4. Which aspects of this course did you like least?

5. What changes would you make in the lectures?

6. What changes would you make in the readings?

7. What changes would you make in the examinations?

8. How would you change this course?

9. Which aspects of this course were most valuable?

10. Which aspects of this course were least valuable?

11. How might the class climate be made more inclusive of diverse students?

12. How might the course content be more inclusive of diverse groups?

13. How might the course materials be more inclusive of diverse groups?

14. How might the teaching methods used be more sensitive to diverse needs?

15. How might working in groups be made more inclusive for diverse students?

Figure 11–3 University of Michigan Office of Examinations and Evaluations Course Evaluation Form

APPLYING STUDENT SUGGESTIONS

Student evaluations can be helpful, powerful and painful at the same time. Remember that you can never please everyone all the time. If your course is a required course that is out of the comfort zone of the students (i.e., aural skills), some of what you see on a course evaluation will be an evaluation of the very concept of the course and not necessarily a reflection of your instruction. We have found over the years that there is often a connection between student grades and course evaluations in that if, for example, two students fail the course, you can usually count on two course evaluations that say you were a bad instructor. Failing students often need someone to blame for their failure. However, even with all the issues, research suggests that student ratings do provide a valid measure of the course. McKeachie and Svinicki (2006) report that there have been over 2000 studies on student ratings in higher education and that this research supports student ratings as one reasonable way to assess the effectiveness of an instructor. Davis (2001, p. 398) reviews much of this research and suggests the following:

- Students tend to rate courses in their major fields and elective courses higher than required courses outside their major. Within music, the major might really be considered performance or music education and any music courses outside of lessons, ensembles, and methods courses might be considered by students as "outside" their major field.
- Faculty tend to receive more positive ratings than graduate students.
- The gender of a student has little effect on ratings. The gender of an instructor, however, may have an impact.
- Ratings can be influenced by class size (very small classes tend to receive higher ratings), by discipline (humanities instructors tend to received higher ratings than instructors in the physical sciences), and by type (discussion courses tend to receive higher ratings than lecture courses)
- Students' expectations affect their ratings: students who expect a course or teacher to be good generally find their expectations confirmed.

We suggest reviewing the course evaluations with a department chair or more experienced colleague so that you can consider what might be helpful and useful and what is not. Although course evaluations can be "high stakes" in terms of tenure and promotion, most committees looking at faculty dossiers understand the issues regarding the accuracy of student course evaluations.

STRATEGIES FOR CRITICAL REFLECTION

To be critically reflective is more than just looking back on the teaching and examining the experience from your own perspective. Brookfield (1995) suggests that critical reflection is a process that occurs when a professor considers his/her own teaching in relation to four distinct but interconnected views. The first view or lens is that of autobiography. This text has encouraged readers to consider their personal experiences in relation to teaching and learning and regularly reflect on how their own experiences relate to their identity as a music professor. The second lens in the reflection process is that of students. Brookfield suggests that we learn about our teaching from talking with students and listening to their feedback and concerns. We have provided suggestions for the process of collecting student feedback earlier in this chapter but provide additional information regarding, as Brookfield says, "seeing ourselves through our students eyes" in the next section. The third lens that Brookfield discusses is that view that can be provided by our colleagues and we have discussed bringing colleagues into our classrooms earlier in this chapter as well. The final lens in the Brookfield model is to view teaching practice through the lens of literature. In other words, professors should continue to read and study teaching and learning within their field. Chapter 13 provides additional information on the scholarship of teaching and studying our teaching through action research. Not all reflection is critical reflection. It is important for the professor to learn to reflect on teaching as well as to critically reflect. We continue next with suggestions on critical reflection more specifically.

Brookfield (1995) discusses the problematic nature of formal student evaluations and suggests that these measures provide only a limited understanding of student learning:

> Gathering information about the effects of our teaching on students is probably something that most of us feel we do already. After all, many colleges require faculty to hand out to

students some kind of standardized evaluation form at the last meeting of a course. . . . Yet, this approach suffers from two drawbacks. First, it is summative, after the fact. . . Second, these forms are frequently satisfaction indexes—measures of how much people liked us. . . . There is also the danger that students may give the highest satisfaction ratings to the teachers who challenge them the least. . . . One could almost predict that those teachers who most emphasize critical thinking will get the worst ratings from students. (pp. 92–93)

So, what can we do to really view our teaching from the perspective of our students? Brookfield discusses action research (presented in Chapter 13 of this book) as one strategy for stepping away and trying to examine issues of power, culture, and learning. He also discusses learning journals (discussed previously in Chapter 6) where students are asked to write about their learning and their learning experience. Another strategy is to devote a few minutes of every class to what Brookfield calls "Troubleshooting" about the course. I (Conway) reserve the first 5–8 minutes of every class for what I call "Course Check-up." This is a time that students know they can bring up concerns about the process of the course and not just the content. If there are questions about assignments or "hard feelings" from a debate in the class before, we use the "check-up" or "troubleshooting" time to clear the air, answer the questions, etc. It is sometimes very surprising to hear student comments regarding an assignment, a reading, or a discussion that I thought has gone well. They do not always agree.

As a way to collect more in-depth information than a generic final course evaluation may provide, Brookfield (1995, p. 107) describes what he calls a "letter to successors" activity. He asks students on the last day of class to write letters to students who will take the class the next time. They are to provide helpful suggestions for completing the class successfully. He then has students get in to groups and compare letters. The groups compile a composite letter and then share with the entire class. In this way, students can remain anonymous to the professor and still report in-depth information.

A final strategy for collecting detailed information from students provided by Brookfield is what he calls the "critical incident questionnaire" (p. 114). This is designed to get weekly feedback from students regarding what the students consider the most significant events of the course that week. He uses this tool at the end of the week (for classes that meet several times in the week) and has students handwrite a response on a form with carbon paper so that the instructor and the student both keep a copy. It might also be possible to use these questions in a weekly e-mail, web-based communication, or text message. We provide the questions below (based on Brookfield, 1995, p. 115) with consideration for music classes specifically.

- At what moment in the class this week did you feel most engaged with what was happening in general?
- At what moment in the class this week did you feel most engaged with what was happening musically?
- At what moment in the class this week did you feel most distanced from what was happening in general?
- At what moment in the class this week did you feel most distanced from what was happening musically?
- What action that anyone (professor or student) took in class this week did you find most puzzling or confusing?
- What about the class this week surprised you the most?

Although it takes some time for this sort of student feedback, the answers to these questions can help you to redesign instruction. Brookfield (1995) shares that he has a panel of students from past years come to class on the first day and discuss the value of this process. A new professor does not have the advantage of a "tradition" of critical reflection being a part of a course, but a new professor does have the advantage of being "new" and sometimes students are willing to consider "new" strategies with a "new" professor. The degree to which this strategy or any of the others suggested in this chapter may work in any setting relates back to the culture of the institution as discussed way back in Chapter 1. No strategy will work in every setting. However, students in every setting deserve a professor who works to critically examine teaching and learning in the effort to improve.

QUESTIONS FOR DISCUSSION AND SUGGESTED ACTIVITIES

1. Discuss the definitions of reflection provided at the beginning of the chapter and consider reflecting in and on action for your teaching context.
2. Share your strategies for keeping a teaching journal.
3. Think about who might be a useful observer for your classroom. What issues of teaching and learning might you ask an observer to consider?
4. Videorecord your classroom and bring the videorecord to class and examine it with your peers.
5. Discuss informal ways of collecting feedback from students that might work for your course.
6. Share your own memories of midterm and final course evaluations in classes you have taken.
7. Examine the Office of Examination and Evaluation form provided and choose questions for a final course evaluation form in a class you might teach.
8. Discuss the challenges in interpreting course evaluations from students.

CHAPTER 12

Navigating a Music Career
in Higher Education

Musicians perform, teach, and work in diverse educational settings. Some teach in departments or colleges that are primarily focused on undergraduate teaching. Other faculty is employed by institutions that are primarily teaching institutions but where there is some expectation for scholarship and service. Still others work in institutions where there is a balance between a focus on teaching (both undergraduate and graduate), research and service. Size of the institution does not always dictate the focus on teaching versus research as some small schools may be research-focused while some larger schools may focus on undergraduate teaching. Some musicians will spend their careers working exclusively with music majors while others will work primarily with nonmajors.

We begin this chapter with a presentation of the Tenure and Promotion policy document from the School of Music, Theater and Dance University of Michigan and use that to frame our consideration of teaching, research, and service. The University of Michigan document begins with an overview of procedures for promotion and tenure and includes appropriate documentation of teaching, scholarship and service, checklists for tenure and promotion document preparation, and suggestions for the creation of a teaching portfolio. Although the process of tenure and promotion will be slightly different in every school, it is hoped that the University of Michigan document will be helpful. The University of Michigan document is likely to be more detailed than what one might find within a liberal arts college or in a music department that is part of a college of arts and humanities. However, the music detail provided in the University of Michigan document may be helpful to those seeking tenure and promotion in other settings.

UNIVERSITY OF MICHIGAN
SCHOOL OF MUSIC, THEATRE & DANCE
PROMOTION AND TENURE REVIEW POLICY

Approval by the Governing Faculty: December 14, 2006

These criteria and procedures shall serve as guidelines for the dean and the Executive Committee of the School of Music, Theatre & Dance in making recommendations for appointment to the faculty, for promotion, and for tenure. It is the policy of the School that the faculty shall consist of the most highly qualified persons obtainable. Nothing in these guidelines shall be construed to prevent the dean and the Executive Committee from acting, within the Regents' Bylaws and University policies, in pursuit of this objective.

This document is based in part on the regulations and policies stated in The University of Michigan Faculty Handbook, the Standard Practice Guide, the Regents' Bylaws, and policy directives of the Provost and Executive Vice President for Academic Affairs. These sources should be consulted for additional pertinent regulations and for more complete information concerning the policies discussed here.

The instructional-track appointment must be "full-time" within the University, which means an academic year or academic term appointment fraction of 80% or more as recorded in the official notice of appointment. The appointment may be split between two or more instructional-track appointments as long as the total effort is at least 80%.

An explanation of the academic ranks and conferral of tenure follows.

A. **Assistant Professor:**

Review for promotion from instructor to assistant professor will normally occur during the third year of service and must occur not later than the fourth year. Review prior to the third year of service can be undertaken only with the approval of the department chair, dean, and Executive Committee. No review shall be conducted for a person on terminal notice. An instructor not recommended for promotion, following review, shall not be reappointed.

B. **Associate Professor:**

Review for promotion from assistant professor to associate professor will normally occur during the sixth year of combined service as an instructor and an assistant professor at the University of Michigan. Time on leave will count unless exempted in writing before the leave. Review prior to the sixth year of combined service can be undertaken only with the approval of the department chair, dean, and Executive Committee. No review shall be conducted for a person on terminal service. An assistant professor not recommended for promotion following review will not be reappointed.

C. **Professor:**

Review for promotion from associate professor to full professor is not automatic. Review prior to the sixth year of service as an associate professor can be undertaken only with the approval of the department chair, dean, and Executive

Committee and in concurrence with the associate professor. The Executive Committee shall identify associate professors in their eighth year of service who have not been reviewed for promotion to professor. Their professional profiles will be discussed with department chairs during the annual review for merit.

D. <u>Conferral of Tenure:</u>

The future distinction of the School and the University depends in large part upon the quality of the judgment exercised in making tenure decisions. For this reason, and because the awarding of tenure represents a commitment of substantial resources on the part of the University, each such recommendation will be made with the greatest possible care and will be the result of thorough and rigorous scrutiny of all relevant information. Each review for appointment or promotion to the rank of associate professor or professor with tenure shall be conducted with the same care and thoroughness, and shall be based on the same criteria as a review for tenure. Each untenured member of the faculty must be reviewed for tenure not later than his or her sixth year of service at the University of Michigan excluding service as a lecturer, adjunct faculty member, or visiting faculty member.

The objectives and needs of the School are subject to change from time-to-time, and an excessively high proportion of tenured faculty members impede significantly the ability of the School to respond to necessary changes in curriculum or emphasis. Financial constraints and a wide variety of other factors also affect tenure decisions. It is quite possible, and in some instances likely, that persons with excellent records of teaching, research, and professional activity may not, for reasons unrelated to their own adequacy or inadequacy, be recommended for tenure.

Appointment or promotion to untenured ranks may be based largely upon the potential of the individual for future achievement. However, the extended commitment implied by the granting of tenure requires not only the potential for future achievement but also a firm record of past achievement. It is expected that each person awarded tenure, whether through promotion or appointment from outside the University, will be the most highly qualified person available for the position in terms of teaching ability, professional activity or research, professional stature, and service. It is further expected that each such person will show clear evidence of the ability to achieve the rank of professor.

On an annual basis, the provost and senior vice president for academic affairs, in conjunction with the president and board of regents, provides all units at the University of Michigan with **Promotion Guidelines and Procedures.** Faculty will be notified annually when it is received and where it may be located on the University's webpage. Upon request, candidates, chairs, and directors will be provided with a copy of the document. Although a small portion of the contents may change from year-to-year, recommendations for promotion and for tenure will generally be based on the record of the faculty member in the following categories.

[Provost's Annual Promotion Guidelines—Teaching. Essential qualifications for appointment or promotion are character and the ability to teach, whether at the undergraduate or the graduate level. Some of the elements to be evaluated are experience, knowledge of subject matter, skill in presentation, interest in students, ability to stimulate youthful minds, capacity for cooperation, and enthusiastic devotion to teaching. The responsibility of the teacher as a guide and friend properly extends beyond the walls of the classroom into other phases of the life of the student as a member of the University community. It also involves the duty of initiating and improving educational methods both within and outside the departments.] (**University Faculty Handbook regarding Promotion, 5.1, Adopted by the Board of Regents**)

Teaching represents the most important single function of the School. It is expected that each member of the faculty will excel in teaching. Enthusiasm for teaching and the ability to stimulate students to achieve at the highest level possible are important attributes of the faculty member.

A. **Teaching**—Evidence to be considered in the evaluation of teaching may include:

1. demonstrated excellence in instruction in the classroom, studio, or rehearsal hall;
2. demonstrated ability to attract talented students to the School;
3. demonstrated success of former students;
4. written statements by colleagues, including the department chair;
5. unsolicited letters from former students;
6. teaching evaluation forms completed anonymously by students (and, when necessary to protect the student's anonymity, administered and collected by a third party), provided that the forms for an entire class are submitted and not a selected sampling;
7. the extent to which students elect the faculty member's courses (with due regard for such matters as the level of difficulty of a course, its role in the curriculum, and whether or not it is required);
8. knowledge of the subject matter taught, including range, depth, and currency and use of diverse repertoire and teaching techniques when appropriate (including, for example, modern technology, improvisation, contemporary music, American music, and historically informed performance practices); and
9. development of new courses, programs, teaching materials, or teaching techniques.

[**Provost's Annual Promotion Guidelines—Research.** All members of the faculties must be persons of scholarly ability and attainments. Their qualifications are to be evaluated on the quality of their published and other creative work, the range and variety of their intellectual interests, their success in training graduate and professional students in scholarly methods, and their participation and leadership in professional associations and in the editing of professional journals. Attainment may be in the realm of scientific investigation, in the realm of constructive contributions, or in the realm of the creative arts.] (**University Faculty Handbook regarding Promotion, 5.1, Adopted by the Board of Regents**)

Creative and professional activity and research may include any of a wide variety of activities, depending upon the field of specialization and the interests of the faculty member. It is expected that each member of the faculty will pursue research or professional activities appropriate to his or her field of specialization and will achieve recognition among his or her peers in one or more *such fields of activity*.

B. **Creative and Professional Activity and Research**—Evidence to be considered in the evaluation of creative and professional activity and research may include (work in progress and commitments accepted should be so indicated):

1. publication as the author, coauthor, editor, or translator of books, chapters in books, articles, reviews, monographs, and nonprint materials, and reviews of these publications (publications subjected to substantial peer review prior to publication shall be more highly regarded than publications not subjected to such review);

2. the conduct of research contributing significantly to the state of knowledge in the faculty member's field of specialization, and publication of the results;

3. commissions for musical compositions;

4. publication of musical compositions or arrangements;

5. obtaining funds, either internal or external, for research or development or for instructional or program improvement;

6. appearances off-campus as a speaker, conductor, soloist, actor, director, designer, ensemble member, panelist, or clinician, or as a director of a workshop or institute;

7. presenting papers, speaking, participating on panels, presiding at sessions, adjudicating, performing as soloist, actor, director, designer, ensemble member, or conductor, or otherwise participating in the meetings or activities of professional associations;

8. appearances off-campus as recitalist, actor, director, designer, guest soloist, or conductor with paid professional groups or in professional (paid) settings;

9. participation in symposiums and other selective gatherings of distinguished colleagues;

10. performances by off-campus groups or individuals of compositions by the faculty member;

11. performances on commercial recordings by the faculty member or performances on commercial recordings of compositions by the faculty member;

12. service as a consultant to or on behalf of educational institutions, professional associations, or government agencies when it is clearly an honor to have been selected;

13. service as an adjudicator in major competitions when it is clearly an honor to have been selected; and

14. winning of prizes, awards, fellowships, or other recognition.
    (Note: Activities for which the faculty member receives compensation will be recognized provided that when possible he or she is identified as a member of the faculty of The University of Michigan and provided that the activity serves to enhance the prestige of the School or that the activity is likely to attract talented music students to the University. See also related policies concerning outside employment, including Regents' Bylaw 5.12.).

[**Provost's Annual Promotion Guidelines—Service.** The scope of the University's activities makes it appropriate for members of the staff to engage in many activities outside of the fields of teaching and research. These may include participation in com-mittee work and other administrative tasks, counseling, clinical duties, and special training programs. The University also expects many of its staff to render extramural services to schools, to industry, to local, state, and national agencies, and to the public at large.] **(University Faculty Handbook regarding Promotion, 5.1, Adopted by the Board of Regents)**

Service refers to activities that utilize the professional expertise of the faculty member. Each member of the faculty is expected to render a reasonable amount of service to the School, to the University, to the profession or to professional organizations, and to the public at large. Service is subordinate to the other two categories of activity, however, and no amount of service can compensate for a lack of skill in teaching or for a lack of professional activity or research.

C. **Service**—Evidence to be considered in the evaluation of service may include:

1. effective service as an advisor to students;
2. effective service as a department chair;
3. performance of other administrative duties for the School;
4. effective service on committees of the School and the University and participation in meetings and other official activities of the School and its departments;
5. effective contributions to recruiting, fund-raising, or public relations efforts on behalf of the School or the University;
6. service in elective or appointive leadership roles in professional associations at the national, international, regional, state, or local levels;
7. appearances on-campus, beyond the normal responsibilities of the faculty member, as a speaker, conductor, soloist, actor, director, designer, ensemble member, panelist, or clinician, or as a director of a workshop or institute; and
8. utilization of the professional abilities and expertise of the faculty member without compensation or with nominal compensation on behalf of continuing education in music or in the service of government agencies, citizens' groups, educational or religious institutions, or charitable organizations at the local, state, national, or international levels.

   It is not expected that a faculty member will engage in all of the activities listed under any category. Neither is it expected that a faculty member will be equally active in each of the three categories. The question of what constitutes an appropriate balance of activities for a given faculty member should be discussed with the department chair and the dean. Each individual case will be considered on its own merits. The quality of the contributions is of greater importance than the quantity.

   Each candidate and chair/director is expected to work together to provide the Executive Committee with all requested documentation. The chair is also expected to confer and work with all tenured members of the department in (a) compiling the list of external reviewers; and (b) contacting those external reviewers. **Important:** Packets are sent via U.S. mail during the first two weeks of June. Correct summer addresses for each reviewer is vital. Due date for return of external assessment letters is September 1. All letters must be on letterhead stationery and signed.

For a review involving promotion and/or tenure, the dean will seek, in accordance with established University policies, confidential written statements concerning the work of the faculty member from all of the persons in the appropriate rank whose names are submitted by the faculty member and by the departmental chair. This procedure is also to be used for the review of a candidate being hired from outside the School into a tenured faculty position in the School.

In addition, the dean will seek confidential written statements concerning the work of the faculty member from each tenured member of all departments in which the candidate teaches or holds an appointment, and, at the option of the Dean, from any other persons qualified to contribute relevant information. A copy of each candidate's promotion dossier will be maintained in the Dean's Office and, upon request, may be reviewed by relevant individuals. Note: Promotion dossiers include all documentation provided by the candidate but will not include copies of external or internal letters of assessment.

If the case warrants it, and if the dean, department chair, and candidate agree, a special committee may be appointed to take responsibility for reading and discussing fully and carefully the major publications, the artistic endeavors of the candidate, his/her teaching and research statements, and the record of his/her work as indicated by the curriculum vitae. This committee shall then forward to the Executive Committee a written, objective analysis of the candidate's application.

At the discretion of the Executive Committee, a faculty member familiar with the candidate's field may be invited to address the Executive Committee in order to answer questions that may arise. Selection of the representative will be by agreement between the department and the dean. This representative will be asked to leave the room before the vote of the Executive Committee.

Promotion dossiers include all documentation provided by the candidate but will not include copies of external or internal letters of assessment.

Executive Committee Procedures for Deliberating and Voting on Promotions/Conferral of Tenure

First available agenda after **September 15**: Elected and *ex officio* members of EC begin reviews of promotional files.

A review of a promotional case will follow a motion made and seconded. After discussion, and as a procedure *pro forma*, an elected member may make an incidental motion (with second) to commit the matter to an executive session of the Committee. It is understood that this executive session, which will be scheduled toward the end of the fall term, will involve only elected members and the Dean. At that time, all promotional cases may be discussed and final votes taken. Prior to the executive session, the Dean may discuss concerns raised during the reviews with individual candidates, their department chairs, and/or other interested faculty, such as mentors previously appointed by the Committee.

Review for Promotion or Tenure

Review for promotion to any rank or for tenure may be undertaken at the initiative of the dean, the department chair, or the faculty member. However, tenure-track assistant professors are generally reviewed in the sixth year of their appointment, and associate professors, without tenure, are generally reviewed one year before their contract expires.

A. The deadline for requesting/recommending a review for promotion and/or tenure shall be no later than **September 1** of the **preceding** academic year.

B. The faculty member seeking review should submit a **written request** to the department chair, with a copy to the dean.

C. The department chair will meet with the faculty member to review the promotion and/or tenure guidelines. If the chair and faculty member agree on moving forward, the chair will submit a **written recommendation** to the Dean.

D. The dean will submit the request to the School Executive Committee for review and action. The Executive Committee will provide its decision in writing to both the candidate and chair.

A. **Information from the Chair/Director**

   1. **Summary Cover Memorandum** *(NOTE: This paragraph pertains only to the Departments of Theatre and Drama and Dance).* This assessment should be written from an evaluative, not an advocacy, perspective and should present a balanced summary of the case. The information that should be addressed includes:

     (a) years in rank for the current appointment

     (b) any special circumstances concerning the candidate

     (c) nontraditional forms of scholarly production as well as the more traditional/disciplinary work—ensuring that individuals receive full credit for their contributions to interdisciplinary and/or collaborative scholarly projects

     (d) strengths and weaknesses of the candidate as a teacher of undergraduate and graduate students, including a statement of how the candidate has enriched the curriculum of the department and other programs

     (e) a description of the outcome of the promotion review at each stage of evaluation in the unit

     (f) an explanation of the reasons for recommending promotion and tenure (if appropriate), and

     (g) teaching effectiveness, research, and service.

SUBMIT the memorandum electronically AND provide one hard copy no later than May 31.

2. **External Reviewers**

    (a) An **external reviewer** is "external" to the University of Michigan. Letters from faculty in other departments or colleges at the University can in no case be used as "external" evaluations. External reviewers must be at "ARM'S LENGTH" and ABOVE the rank of the candidate being considered. If circumstances necessitate letters from out-of-rank reviewers, those should be explained.

    (b) After consultation with and oversight by the tenured members of the department, chairs or a tenured designee must contact all reviewers in advance (including those recommended by the candidate) asking for permission to submit their names on behalf of the candidate.

(c) A summary page listing **at least FIVE ARM'S LENGTH** recommended reviewers must be submitted for each candidate. More than five names may be submitted if desired, but they must be different from those submitted by the candidate. The listing MUST contain the following information for each in the format indicated in **Sample 1**.

    (1) Full Name

    (2) Complete address including zip code

    (3) Phone number with area code

    (4) E-mail address

    (5) A short summary paragraph (copied bios for the short paragraph will not be accepted). It should identify the reviewers by institution or organization, field of expertise, title, and stature, if applicable.

    (6) Designate each external reviewer as either arm's length" or "not arm's length."

    (7) Designate each external reviewer as being "suggested by the chair" or "suggested by the candidate.

    (8) If any reviewer has an especially close personal or professional relationship with the candidate (e.g., classmate, personal friend, graduate instructor, dissertation advisor or member of dissertation committee, postdoctoral mentor, coauthor or coinvestigator), indicate the nature of the relationship.

(d) When the summary of external reviewers is submitted to the Dean's Office, it is expected that the chair or his tenured designee has contacted all reviewers, including those submitted by the candidate, and all have agreed to serve.

(e) Packets are sent via U.S. mail by June 15. Correct summer address information for each reviewer is vital. Due date for return of assessment letters is **September 1**. All assessment letters must be returned on letterhead stationery and signed. Chairs are requested to share this information with the reviewer.

The Dean's Office will be responsible for sending letters and support documentation to all external reviewers. Support documentation will include all material submitted by the candidate, e.g., curriculum vitae, teaching statement and/or portfolio, course summaries, course descriptions, research statement, books, manuscripts, CDs, videos, service activities statement, etc.

3. **Internal Reviewers.** The department may recommend internal reviewers if there are those having special knowledge of the candidate's work. The listing must contain the following:

    (a) full name

    (b) complete SUMMER address, including zip code, and

    (c) e-mail address.

All tenured members of the respective department(s) will be asked by the Dean to submit assessment letters, also due no later than September 15.

SUBMIT the list electronically AND provide one hard copy no later than May 31.

The Dean's Office will be responsible for providing letters and curriculum vitae to internal reviewers. Internal reviewers will be notified that a copy of each candidate's promotion dossier will be maintained in the Dean's Office and may be reviewed upon request.

4. **Summaries of Student Evaluations.** The Provost's Office does not accept individual student feedback forms. Summaries of the individual student feedback forms, compiled by the chair or tenured designate, will be accepted as well as summaries from the Office of Evaluations and Examinations. Candidates may not compile summaries of student feedback forms for the obvious reasons.

SUBMIT the summaries electronically AND provide one hard copy no later than May 31.

5. <u>**Mandatory Checklist for Promotion/Tenure File Submitted to the School**</u> **(See Appendix 1) SUBMIT 1 hard copy only no later than May 31.**

B. <u>**Information from the Candidate**</u>
Each candidate should submit the dossier in its entirety to the Dean's Office no later than May 31 (please note that items 1–6 will be made available to all external and internal reviewers). Each document must be separate from the others, titled as stated, and in *WORD* format (do not send *PDF* files). Do not place any part of the dossier in a notebook or encase in any like item.

1. **Curriculum Vitae.** There is no set format for creating curriculum vitae, but examples of items not to include are dates of birth, ages, names of spouse and children, wedding date, etc. Even though most vitae contain part of the information noted below, separate documents are still required for each section.

SUBMIT CV electronically AND provide one hard copy no later than May 31.

2. **Documentation of Teaching Effectiveness.** Because of the central role of teaching among the objectives of the School, documentation of teaching effectiveness is an important element in the promotion dossier of the faculty member. This documentation may take any of a variety of forms but must include the following.

   (a) **Summaries of Student Evaluations**. The Provost will no longer accept individual student feedback forms. Summaries of the individual student feedback forms, compiled by the chair or tenured designee, will be accepted as well as summaries from the Office of Evaluations and Examinations. Candidates may not compile summaries of student feedback forms for the obvious reasons.

   (b) Dissertation Committee(s) List.

   (c) Teaching Statement or Teaching Portfolio. (See Sample) The teaching statement may not be longer than five pages in length.

   Other documentation may include copies of examinations administered; outlines, courses of study, prospectuses, reading lists, or statements of objectives, course requirements, or grading standards; or information concerning steps taken by the faculty member to evaluate and to improve the quality of teaching.

3. <u>**Creative and Professional Activity Statement.**</u> The statement should include a written narrative and a listing of all publications, funded and unfunded research,

professional appearances and contributions, memberships and offices held in professional associations, commissions, prizes and awards, and other evidence of creative or professional activity, research, and scholarship, including activities in progress. Do not include individual programs or playbills.

SUBMIT statement electronically AND provide one hard copy no later than May 31.

4. **Research Statement** (optional). If the candidate conducts research, he/she is encouraged to provide a narrative because it may prove to be valuable in the review process.

SUBMIT statement electronically AND provide one hard copy no later than May 31.

5. **Service Statement**. A narrative and list with dates of activities involving service to the School, the University, and to the profession or to professional organizations during the preceding five years or since the most recent promotion, together with activities involving service to government agencies, educational or religious institutions, or charitable organizations.

SUBMIT statement electronically AND provide one hard copy no later than May 31.

6. **Publications, Books, Manuscripts, Articles, Portfolios, Selected Book Chapters, Videos, CDs, etc.** If it is the intention of the candidate to provide each external reviewer with copies of all or some of the above, the candidate should submit 15 of each. In the past, candidates have chosen to submit selected chapters on a disc or 15 hard copies of each. If the choice is to submit 15 hard copies of selected chapters, they should be stapled or clipped in the upper left-hand corner. DO NOT encase or place in notebooks. Most performers have chosen to submit 15 copies of CDs and videos.

SUBMIT no later than May 31.

7. **Student Information**.
   (a) Provide a list with the names and e-mail addresses of all students the candidate taught during this academic year, which may include students not graduated and still at the University; and
   (b) Provide a list of names and e-mail addresses of at least ten (10) former, graduated students.

SUBMIT lists electronically AND provide one hard no later than May 31.

The Dean's Office will be responsible for contacting only those students listed by the candidate.

8. **External Reviewers.**
   (a) An **external reviewer** is "external" to the University of Michigan. Letters from faculty in other departments or colleges at the University can in no case be used as "external" evaluations. External reviewers must be at "ARM'S LENGTH" and ABOVE the rank of the candidate being considered. If circumstances necessitate letters from out-of-rank reviewers, those should be explained.
   (b) A summary page listing **at least FIVE ARM'S LENGTH** recommended reviewers must be submitted. More than five names may be submitted if

desired, but they must be different from those submitted by the chair. The listing MUST contain the following information for each in the format indicated in **Sample 1**.

(1) Full Name

(2) Complete address including zip code

(3) Phone number with area code

(4) E-mail address

(5) A short summary paragraph (copied bios for the short paragraph will not be accepted). It should identify the reviewers by institution or organization, field of expertise, title, and stature, if applicable.

(6) Designate each external reviewer as either "arm's length" or "not arm's length."

(7) Designate each external reviewer as being "suggested by the chair" or "suggested by the candidate."

(8) If any reviewer has an especially close personal or professional relationship with the candidate (e.g., classmate, personal friend, graduate instructor, dissertation advisor or member of dissertation committee, postdoctoral mentor, coauthor or coinvestigator), indicate the nature of the relationship.

(c) Packets are sent via U.S. mail by June 15. Correct summer address information for each reviewer is vital. Due date for return of assessment letters is **September 1**. All assessment letters must be returned on letterhead stationery and signed. Chairs are requested to share this information with the reviewer.

(d) When the summary of external reviewers is submitted to the Dean's Office, it is expected that all reviewers have been contacted by the Chair or tenured designate and all have agreed to serve. The candidate should consult with the chair before submitting the summary to ensure that this mandate has been completed.

(e) Candidates will have an opportunity to review lists of recommended external reviewers before packets are distributed. If the candidate objects to anyone listed, the candidate must contact the Dean immediately. Tenured members of relevant departments will be requested to write assessment letters.

SUBMIT summary electronically AND provide one hard copy no later than May 31. The Dean's Office will be responsible for sending letters and support documentation to external reviewers. Support documentation will include all material submitted by the candidate, e.g., curriculum vitae, teaching statement and/or portfolio, course evaluations, course descriptions, research statement, books, manuscripts, CDs, videos, service activities statement, etc.

9. **Internal Reviewers.** Candidates may recommend internal reviewers if there are those having special knowledge of the candidate's work. The listing must contain the

(a) full name

(b) complete SUMMER address, including zip code, and

(c) e-mail address.

All tenured members of the respective department(s) will be asked by the Dean to submit assessment letters, also due no later than September 15.

SUBMIT list electronically AND provide one hard copy no later than May 31.

The Dean's Office will be responsible for sending letters and curriculum vitae to internal reviewers. Internal reviewers will be notified that a copy of each candidate's promotion dossier will be maintained in the Dean's Office and may be reviewed upon request.

10. **Mandatory Checklist for Promotion/Tenure File Submitted to the School (See Appendix 2) Submit 1 hard copy only no later than May 31.**

C. **Promotion and Tenure Timeline**

1. **May 31 (On or Before)**—Candidates for promotion and/or tenure in the School submit their promotional dossiers (curriculum vitae; teaching, research, service statements; materials relating to creative and/or scholarly work; etc.) to Dean's Office.

2. **First Week in June**—Via e-mail, a list of external reviewers will be sent to candidates for review. Candidates are urged to check e-mail for the list and must, upon receipt, reply *"I have no objections to the list"* or *"I have an objection and will contact your office."* The Dean will be notified and arrangements made to meet with the candidate or to discuss objections via telephone. No letter will be sent without authorization.

3. **June 15 (On or Before)**—The Dean's Office will begin mailing completed dossiers to all approved reviewers.

4. **September 1 (On or Before)**—Final revisions of pending projects may be added to candidates' dossiers. The Dean's Office will inform *internal* reviewers of the updated materials and make them available; *external* reviewers will not be so notified. Candidates may inform the Dean's Office for Executive Committee consideration of awards and accomplishments unanticipated on the CV until **December 1**.

5. **September 1**—Due date for receipt of assessment letters from external reviewers.

6. **September 15**—Due date for receipt of assessment letters from internal reviewers. The Executive Committee begins its review of promotion/tenure files after that date.

7. **October–December**—Promotion dossiers reviewed and processed by the School Executive Committee.

   (a) If additional information is requested, the candidate/chair will be contacted by the dean.

   (b) If the Executive Committee's decision is not favorable, the dean will contact the candidate and chair immediately.

8. **Third Week in December**—Candidates will be notified in writing that the School Executive Committee recommended that their promotion dossiers be advanced to the Provost for the next step in the review process.

9. **December and January**—Dean's Office staff will compile electronic promotion dossiers for Regental review.

10. **Mid-February**—Promotion dossiers electronically delivered to the Office of Academic Human Resources and Affirmative Action for the first review, which will be conducted under the guidance of the Provost's Office. If additional information and/or documents are requested, the dean will contact the candidate/chair.

11. **Late March–Early April**—The Office of Academic Human Resources and Affirmative Action submits the electronic promotion dossiers to the Office of the Provost, where the Provost and several advisors conduct further reviews. If additional information and/or documents are requested, the Dean will be contacted.

12. **Mid-April**—The Provost meets with the President to review and discuss bids for promotion and/or tenure. Promotion dossiers advanced electronically to the Board of Regents.

13. **Second/Third Week in May**

    (a) Promotions are presented to the Board of Regents for action.

    (b) Each candidate receives written notification from the Provost that the Board of Regents approved his or her bid for promotion and/or tenure.

    Effective date of new appointment: September 1.

THE TEACHING PORTFOLIO

By
Matthew Kaplan, Instructional Consultant
Center for Research on Learning and Teaching

At institutions across the country, faculty are creating opportunities to exchange ideas on teaching and, in the process, becoming more reflective about their teaching. In part, this is a response to national discussions about the false dichotomy that is often drawn between teaching and research. To move beyond this debate, there have been calls for expanding the idea of scholarship to include certain teaching products, as well as research products (Boyer, 1990).

Three strategies for taking a scholarly approach to reviews of teaching are ones that are common to discussions of research as well (Shulman, 1993). First, scholarship is firmly grounded in the disciplines, and a scholarly approach to the review of teaching would focus on the teaching of a specific discipline. Second, just as research becomes scholarship when it is shared, faculty would need to begin making teaching community property. And finally, scholarship often involves making judgments about faculty work, which, for teaching, would mean that faculty would become more involved in reviewing each others' accomplishments in teaching and learning.

The teaching portfolio is one of the tools faculty can use to document their scholarly work in teaching. This Occasional Paper contains a discussion of the nature and purpose of the teaching portfolio (and its offshoot, the course portfolio) and suggestions for how individuals and units can use portfolios most effectively.

What Is a Teaching Portfolio?

A record of accomplishments in teaching: Based on the model of the portfolio kept by artists and architects, the teaching portfolio contains evidence of a faculty member's achievements in teaching:

What is a teaching portfolio? It includes documents and materials, which collectively suggest the scope and quality of a professor's teaching performance.... The portfolio is not an

exhaustive compilation of all of the documents and materials that bear on teaching performance. Instead, it presents *selected information* on teaching activities and *solid evidence* of
their effectiveness. (Seldin, 1997, p. 2)

Documentation in Context

The portfolio should be more than a simple collection of documents. It also should
contain reflective statements on the material included and on the faculty member's
approach to teaching and student learning. The reflective portions of the portfolio
help set the documents in context for the reader; the materials provide evidence to
back up the assertions made in the reflective statement.

What Might Go into a Portfolio?

When considering the contents of a portfolio, faculty must distinguish clearly between
being *representative* and being *exhaustive*. Attempts to create an exhaustive com-
pendium of an instructor's work in teaching run the risk of becoming exhausting,
both for the person collecting the materials and for any readers who might choose
(or need) to respond to the portfolio.

Furthermore, the attempt to be completely comprehensive can turn the project
of developing a portfolio into a paper chase. Such a large collection of documents
makes it difficult to maintain the reflective aspect of the portfolio, which is one of its
chief purposes and advantages.

The portfolio should, instead, be representative of the various aspects of a
faculty member's teaching. This means looking beyond the most obvious part of
teaching—what goes on in the classroom. While the activities and interactions with
students in class are important, they do not fully reflect faculty work with teaching. Other items might include planning courses, assessing student learning, advising students (in office hours or in larger projects such as theses and dissertations),
curriculum development and assessment, supervising student research, working to
improve one's teaching, and publishing articles on teaching and learning.

One way to categorize items that a faculty member might include is to divide them
into three categories based on the source of the item: materials from oneself (e.g., reflective statements, descriptions of course responsibilities, syllabi, assignments), materials
from others (e.g., statements from colleagues who have observed or reviewed teaching
materials, student ratings, letters from students or alumni, honors or recognition); and
products of good teaching (student essays or creative work, a record of students who
have succeeded in the field, evidence of supervision of theses). Some of these sources
may be more appropriate for certain aspects of teaching than for others. See Appendix A
for a more comprehensive list.

Purposes of Portfolios

Self-reflection and improvement

Assembling a portfolio involves reflection. Most portfolios include a reflective statement that can cover topics such as the instructor's approach to teaching and learning,

his or her assumptions about the roles of students and teachers, and goals the instructor expects students to achieve (Chism, 1997/1998). In addition, faculty need to collect documents that support their reflective statement, a process that also involves reflection (selecting some items over others, reviewing past work, etc.). As a result, the portfolio is well suited to helping faculty examine their goals for teaching and student learning, and compare those goals to the reality of their praxis.

The comparison between the ideal and the real is the first step in the process of improving teaching. Instructors can gain a sense of how effective their teaching is and how they could improve from a variety of sources: student ratings of instruction, mid-semester feedback, self-perception, discussions with colleagues, etc. By constructing a portfolio, faculty will look systematically at the various sources of data about their teaching; therefore, they can make more informed decisions about teaching strengths on which they wish to build and problems in their teaching they wish to address. The reflection and improvement process can be further enhanced when faculty work together (in pairs or small groups) as they develop their portfolios.

Colleagues can offer support and advice, exchange new ideas and solutions to problems, and broaden each other's views of the teaching and learning process. Moreover, such exchanges help create a community of scholarship around teaching that is based on a concrete, discipline31 specific context.

Decision-making

Accomplishments in teaching are becoming a more important factor in administrative decisions such as tenure, promotion, reappointment, and merit increases. The teaching portfolio enables faculty and departments to insure that an instructor's work in teaching is judged using multiple forms of evaluation, seen by multiple eyes. This is important, since no one perspective can accurately represent faculty teaching. For instance, students can evaluate certain aspects of teaching that focus on classroom interactions, such as organization, rapport, and ability to stimulate discussion. On the other hand, faculty colleagues are in a position to judge items that are beyond the expertise of students, such as how up-to-date material is, how well a course is integrated into the curriculum, etc.

Self-evaluation and reflection are also important, especially for providing a context for understanding data about teaching effectiveness. The portfolio as a whole gives individual faculty a sense of control over the evaluation process. In addition, departments that encourage faculty to submit portfolios will need to have discussions about what, if any, documents will be required and what will be left up to the individual faculty; how long the document can (or should) be; and how much reflection is required. Such discussions provide a useful venue for creating a shared sense of what constitutes good teaching in a department.

Graduate student portfolios

Graduate students who apply for faculty positions commonly use portfolios because many colleges and universities now require job applicants to provide some proof of teaching experience. Graduate students are turning to the portfolio as a way of organizing their work in this area. Currently, the requirements vary widely among schools. Some require just a list of courses taught or a reflective statement on teaching, and some ask for specific items (such as proposed syllabi for certain types of courses, student ratings, demonstrations of commitment to undergraduate research, etc.). The earlier in their teaching careers that graduate students begin to think about their portfolios, the more chance they will have to retrieve the documents they find most representative of their accomplishments. Aside from its value for the job market, the portfolio often represents the first time graduate students have had the opportunity to reflect on their teaching, which they often find both challenging and rewarding.

An Alternative to the Teaching Portfolio: Course Portfolios

A variation on the teaching portfolio is a course portfolio. As the name implies, these documents focus on a specific course, with a special emphasis on student learning. A course portfolio, therefore, is analogous to a scholarly project. It includes sections on goals (intended student learning outcomes), methods (teaching approaches used to achieve outcomes), and results (evidence of student learning) for a specific course.

Moreover, it is the relationship or congruence among these elements that makes for effectiveness. We expect a research project to shed light on the questions and issues that shape it; we expect the methods used in carrying out the project to be congruent with the outcomes sought. And the same can be said of teaching. By encompassing and connecting all three elements – planning, implementation, and results—the course portfolio has the distinctive advantage of representing the intellectual integrity of teaching (Cerbin, 1993, p. 51).

Course portfolios offer advantages for the person developing them as well as for the curriculum. For the faculty member developing the portfolio, the advantages are similar to those of assembling a teaching portfolio (e.g., self-reflection and a chance to compare intentions with outcomes), but with more in-depth insight into the impact of teaching on students. For departments, course portfolios can provide continuity and reveal gaps in the curriculum. For example, a course portfolio becomes a record of the purpose and results of a course that can be passed on to the next person in charge of that course or to the faculty member who teaches the next course in a sequence. By examining a set of course portfolios, a curriculum committee can gain an overview of what students are learning and what is missing, which could help with the process of curriculum revision.

How Are Portfolios Evaluated?

Just as there is no one model for a teaching portfolio, there is no one method for evaluation. Again, this is a strength of the portfolio, since it means that individual units will need to develop criteria for evaluation and make them relevant to faculty in that unit. The process of deciding on criteria can also help to clarify what faculty in that unit value with respect to teaching. For one example of an evaluation scheme, see Appendix B.

As units develop criteria for evaluating portfolios, they should first consider the ways they plan to use the portfolio. Will portfolios be limited to faculty being considered for tenure or promotion or for instructors nominated for teaching awards, or will all faculty prepare a course portfolio in preparation for a department-wide curriculum review? These purposes differ and so should the requirements for the portfolios involved.

Once the purpose is clear, faculty will probably want to create guidelines for assembling portfolios. While it is important to maintain the flexibility of the portfolio, it is also necessary to insure some degree of consistency in order to make evaluation fairer and more reliable. Faculty might establish consensus on required items, such as a page limit for the overall size of the portfolio, the focus (a single course, an overview of teaching, or a combination), opportunities for reflection, or a template (so that faculty do not need to worry about format and can concentrate instead on the content). Ideally, such guidelines will be established with input from potential reviewers in the unit as well as those faculty who will be under review.

Advantages of Portfolios

In the AAHE monograph *The Teaching Portfolio: Capturing the Scholarship of Teaching*, the authors describe four main benefits of the teaching portfolio (Edgerton et al., 1991, pp. 4–6). Course portfolios have similar attributes.

1. *Capturing the complexity of teaching*
   - Portfolios contain evidence and reflection in the context of what is being taught to whom under what conditions.
   - The portfolio can present a view of a teacher's development over time.
   - Entries in the portfolio can be annotated to explain their significance for the faculty member's teaching.

2. *Placing responsibility for evaluation in the hands of faculty*
   - Faculty are actively involved in presenting their own teaching accomplishments so that evaluation is not something done "to" them.
   - Portfolios extend evaluation beyond student ratings and encourage peer review and collaboration.
   - The need to evaluate portfolios can lead to discussions on standards for effective teaching.

3. *Encouraging improvement and reflection*
   - Assembling a portfolio involves reflection.
   - Because they involve reflection, portfolios allow faculty to compare their ideals with their actions, a first step in efforts to improve.
   - A faculty member's portfolio reveals both products (evidence) and processes (reflection) of teaching to colleagues who read it.

4. *Fostering a culture of teaching*
   - Portfolios can provide a rich and contextualized source of evidence about teaching achievements that can be used for a variety of purposes, including evaluation, improvement, summary of faculty careers, and defining "good teaching" in a department.

How Can Faculty Get Started?

Faculty can begin at any time to collect materials for their portfolios. At first, this process might entail simply saving relevant materials related to teaching so that they are readily accessible for review. At some point, the faculty member will need to sort through the materials and decide which ones best represent his or her teaching accomplishments. Often this process is enhanced when faculty collaborate with each other as they build their portfolios.

CRLT offers campus-wide workshops on teaching and course portfolios, and we can bring a customized workshop to departments. The focus of the workshop is to help faculty develop a clear idea of what a portfolio is and what items it might include and to give faculty an opportunity to begin a reflective statement on teaching. When workshops are conducted in a department, faculty can begin to answer the question, "What is good teaching in our department?" CRLT also provides one-on-one consultations for individual faculty who are working on their portfolios and for units as they develop a systematic approach to portfolios.

REFERENCES

Boyer, E. 1990. *Scholarship reconsidered: Priorities of the professoriate*. Princeton, NJ: Carnegie Foundation for the Advancement of Teaching.
Cerbin, W. 1993. Inventing a new genre: The course portfolio at the University of Wisconsin-La Crosse. In P. Hutchings (Ed.), *Making teaching community property: A menu for peer collaboration and peer review* (pp. 49–56). Washington, DC: American Association for Higher Education.
Chism, N. V. 1997/1998. Developing a philosophy of teaching statement. *Essays on Teaching Excellence: Toward the Best in the Academy*, 9(3).
Edgerton, R., Hutchings, P., and Quinlan, K. 1991. *The teaching portfolio: Capturing the scholarship of teaching*. Washington, DC: American Association for Higher Education.
Seldin, P. (1997). *The teaching portfolio* (2nd ed.). Bolton, MA: Anker.

Possible Items for Inclusion

Faculty members should recognize which of the items that might be included in a teaching dossier would most effectively give a favorable impression of teaching competence and which might better be used for self-evaluation and improvement. The dossier should be compiled to make the best possible case for teaching effectiveness.

The Products of Good Teaching

1. Students' scores on teacher-made or standardized tests, possibly before and after a course, has been taken as evidence of learning.
2. Student laboratory workbooks and other kinds of workbooks or logs.
3. Student essays, creative work, and project or fieldwork reports.
4. Publications by students on course-related work.
5. A record of students who select and succeed in advanced courses of study in the field.
6. A record of students who elect another course with the same professor.

7. Evidence of effective supervision of Honors, Master's or Ph.D. theses.
8. Setting up or running a successful internship program.
9. Documentary evidence of the effect of courses on student career choice.
10. Documentary evidence of help given by the professor to students in securing employment.
11. Evidence of help given to colleagues on teaching improvement.

Material from Oneself—Descriptive Material on Current and Recent Teaching Responsibilities and Practices

1. List of Course Titles and numbers, unit values or credits, enrollments with brief elaboration.
2. List of course materials prepared for students.
3. Information on professor's availability to students.
4. Report on identification of student difficulties and encouragement of student participation in courses or programs.
5. Description of how films, computers or other nonprint materials were used in teaching.
6. Steps taken to emphasize the interrelatedness and relevance of different kinds of learning.

Description of Steps Taken to Evaluate and Improve One's Teaching

1. Maintaining a Record of the Changes resulting from self-evaluation.
2. Reading journals on improving teaching and attempting to implement acquired ideas.
3. Reviewing new teaching materials for possible application.
4. Exchanging course materials with a colleague from another institution.
5. Conducting research on one's own teaching or course.
6. Becoming involved in an association or society concerned with the improvement of teaching and learning.
7. Attempting instructional innovations and evaluating their effectiveness.
8. Using general support services such as the Education Resources Information Centre (ERIC) in improving one's teaching.
9. Participating in seminars, workshops and professional meetings intended to improve teaching.
10. Participating in course or curriculum development.
11. Pursuing a line of research that contributes directly to teaching.

12. Preparing a textbook or other instructional material.
13. Editing or contributing to a professional journal on teaching one's subject.

Information from Others

Students

1. Student course and teaching evaluation data, which suggest improvements or produce an overall rating of effectiveness or satisfaction.
2. Written comments from a student committee to evaluate courses and provide feedback.
3. Unstructured (and possibly unsolicited) written evaluations by students, including written comments on exams and letters received after a course has been completed.
4. Documented reports of satisfaction with out-of-class contacts.
5. Interview data collected from students after completion of a course.
6. Honors received from students, such as being elected "teacher of the year".

Colleagues

1. Statements from colleagues who have observed teaching either as members of a teaching team or as independent observers of a particular course, or who teach other sections of the same course.
2. Written comments from those who teach courses for which a particular course is a prerequisite.
3. Evaluation of contributions to course development and improvement.
4. Statements from colleagues from other institutions on such matters as how well students have been prepared for graduate studies.
5. Honors or recognition such as a distinguished teacher award or election to a committee on teaching.
6. Requests for advice or acknowledgement of advice received by a committee on teaching or similar body.

Other sources

1. Statements about teaching achievements from administrators at one's own institution or from other institutions.
2. Alumni ratings or other graduate feedback.
3. Comments from parents of students.
4. Reports from employers of students (e.g., in a work-study or "cooperative" program).
5. Invitations to teach for outside agencies.
6. Invitations to contribute to the teaching literature.
7. Other kinds of invitations based on one's reputation as a teacher (for example, a media interview on a successful teaching innovation).

TEACHING

It is important to consider what constitutes evidence of excellence of instruction for the music professor. Course evaluations from students are certainly one measure of instructor excellence. However, as was discussed in Chapter 11, course evaluations cannot be relied on as the only evidence of teaching. The issues surrounding required courses and the relationship between grades and course evaluations make course evaluations a somewhat unreliable measure of instructor success. The music professor must keep track of student honors and awards as these can be a measure of success. If students are winning concerto competitions and getting hired into orchestras and schools, this is a measure of good teaching. As discussed in Chapter 11, it is important to invite colleagues and peers in to your classroom so that they have first-hand knowledge of your teaching.

The University of Michigan policy includes "recruitment of students" to the campus under teaching. Some schools may place that under service. Another discrepancy is that the University of Michigan places all publications under "Scholarship," while some institutions would consider the publication of textbooks or other materials for teaching as part of the "teaching" category. It is important to ask about the various categories and expectations as they are slightly different in every school.

RESEARCH AND SCHOLARSHIP

The area of research and scholarship is defined broadly across institutions. McKeachie and Svinicki (2006) state that "In many universities, for example, formal definitions of the criteria for promotion give research and teaching equal weight, but it is not uncommon to find that research is "more equal" (p. 4). It is extremely important for the new professor to speak with a chair or dean to get specific information regarding what is expected for tenure and promotion. In large research institutions, we have found that McKeachie and Svinicki's comment above can hold true for music professors as well. Although teaching is supposedly considered "equal" to research, the research piece may be "more equal." For music, research and scholarship are very broad. Performance faculty are expected to perform and academic faculty are expected to write and present. However, beyond that loose definition, expectations change greatly from institution to institution.

QUESTIONS FOR THE APPLIED FACULTY MEMBER TO ASK

1. Is there a minimum number of solo performances required in a year?
2. What is considered a local, versus a regional, versus a national performance venue?
3. How does ensemble performance "count" in the research/scholarship consideration?
4. Is there an expectation for publication specifically? If so, in what publication venues?
5. Are there specific professional organizations considered important for research/ scholarship/presentation? Is there a hierarchy? For example, does it "count" more to present at The Midwest Clinic in Chicago than at the state music teacher conference?
6. How does choice of repertoire for performance fit into the research/scholarship consideration?

QUESTIONS FOR THE ACADEMIC FACULTY MEMBER TO ASK

1. Are there a minimum number of publications required in a year?
2. Which are the specific journals that will "count" in relation to tenure and promotion?
3. Do textbooks and other teaching materials "count" as Research or Teaching?
4. Does editorial review board work "count" as Research/Scholarship or Service?
5. How will performance "count" for the academic faculty member (including adjudication, guest conducting, vocal or instrumental performance)?
6. How are coauthored publications considered? What are the issues of authorship (first author, second author) that need to be considered?

SERVICE

Student academic advising is often considered a part of service (as it is on the University of Michigan paperwork) although some institutions may consider advising a part of teaching. Undergraduate student advising looks very different across institutions. Some schools still require advisor signatures in order for students to register while other schools have moved to a completely on-line process that requires no interaction with an academic advisor. Some institutions have a director of undergraduate studies who does all of the advising for all music students and faculty do no advising at all. Advising can be a very time-consuming process for the music professor. We suggest meeting with more experienced colleagues as soon as you find out about advising expectations so that they can help you to learn the degree programs and understand the issues. Do not be shy about questioning your advising load. Junior faculty (those untenured) should be protected from excessive service work, yet this is often not the case.

The lines between teaching, research, and service become even more blurred when we consider graduate advising. In some institutions, if you are chair for a thesis or dissertation, this work "counts" toward your teaching load. In other places, this sort of advising is "service." In some ways, graduate advising can also fall under "research" as we have found that working with graduate students on research papers is a helpful and stimulating research activity. Some institutions will not allow junior faculty to chair dissertations, but many do allow it. The challenge for the new professor is to learn how to manage the many types of "service" activities that you may be asked to be a part of. In addition to advising of students in your department, you may be asked to be a committee member for students outside of your department. This is very common for academic faculty as many graduate schools require a minimum number of PhDs on a graduate committee and music performance faculty do not always have the degrees needed for the graduate school rules.

As can be seen in the University of Michigan policy, you will be asked to comment on your service work at the national, regional, local, institution, college or unit, and department level. Most institutions consider service as an officer in a professional organization (i.e., The Double Reed Society or the International Horn Society) as important National or Regional service. Consult with a chair or dean before agreeing to any service work. Many faculty find they get bogged down in local service or university/college committees and then they do not have time to attend to teaching and research/scholarship. Again, junior faculty should be protected from too much committee work but this is not always the case. There is a delicate balance needed in service. It is important to get to know other faculty and members of the university and college community. So, some service work is recommended, but too much is a problem.

A final area to consider in relation to service is community outreach or what some institutions may call the "town and gown" focus. Depending on where you will be working, there may be a high expectation to share your musical expertise with members of the local community through local recitals, master classes, clinics and institutes. There are often strong traditions associated with these organizations and events and the new professor must take care in understanding the history of the university and community collaborations.

SECURING REVIEWERS

In the University of Michigan tenure process outlined in this chapter, the professor is asked to share the names of potential external and internal reviewers for a tenure file. External reviewers refer to members of the profession who are outside the institution. In most cases, these reviewers need to be full-time music faculty in other higher education institutions and they usually need to have a rank higher than the rank of the candidate they are reviewing. The term "arm's length reviewer" that is used in the Michigan document refers to the need to secure reviewers who have not had direct, regular interaction with the professor who is going up for promotion. So, you may not list your dissertation advisor or a coauthor as an "external reviewer." Internal reviewers refer to other faculty in the school or department. As you might imagine, securing reviewers can be a bit uncomfortable but the spirit of the process is that the committee wants to get a sense of how you are perceived beyond the department and beyond the institution at a regional or national level. These reviewers are usually contacted in confidence and you will not know for sure who has been contacted to write on your behalf.

LEVELS OF DOCUMENTATION

One of the challenges for the professor is to keep track of teaching, research and scholarship activities for an annual report. In addition to the extended information submitted for tenure and promotion, most institutions require an annual report of faculty activity. Many schools require that course evaluations be submitted each year as well. The University of Michigan requires that professors submit the following information every year.

FACULTY ACTIVITIES REPORT

THE UNIVERSITY OF MICHIGAN
School of Music, Theatre & Dance
Ann Arbor, Michigan 48109–2085

Instructions

Each member of the faculty, *including Department Chairs*, of the School of Music, Theatre & Dance are asked to submit this report each year. *Faculty who are being considered for Promotion & Tenure will be exempt from completing a FAR in the year of review. In addition, it is at the Chairs' discretion whether or not to have LEO faculty in their department complete this report.* The information provided will be used by the Executive Committee in its annual merit evaluation of faculty and will serve as the basis for determining your salary increase for next year. Please be certain that the information is as complete as possible.

Include activities projected for that portion of the calendar year following submission of the report. Attach additional sheets as needed. In section B include activities in progress and describe specifically the progress that was made during the current year. Note that no faculty member is expected to engage in all of the activities listed under any category. Include also any relevant information not specifically requested.

In reviewing and summarizing the contributions of each faculty member the various activities are normally weighted by the Executive Committee as follows: teaching 50%, professional activities 40%, and service 10%. The weightings may be adjusted within the following limits when it is advantageous to the faculty member: teaching 40% to 60%, professional activities 30% to 50%, service 0% to 20%. Any faculty member may submit a written request to the dean that his or her teaching be weighted still more heavily. The quantity and quality of the students recruited to the School by the faculty member, when identifiable, will be given special consideration under the category of teaching. The Executive Committee would especially welcome any documentation of teaching success deemed relevant by colleagues completing this form.

Because the contributions of our faculty are so extensive and so varied, it is sometimes difficult to know how to classify certain activities. For example, off-campus activities falling under item B.5 are often useful in recruiting students and could be listed under item A.6. The choice of where to list an activity should be made on the basis of what you consider to be its major purpose or effect. There is no "right" answer. No activity should be listed more than once. The difference between items A.6 and C.5 with respect to recruiting is that the former refers to activities to recruit to your own studio or program while the latter refers to activities to assist the School as a whole. In item C.2 you need not list activities that can be inferred from your position or title, though particularly important activities may be pointed out.

A. Teaching

1. List the courses taught by course number or name of ensemble (except applied music courses); indicate the credit hours of each course and the number of students enrolled.

2. List the number of hours of private studio instruction per week, by term, and the number of studio classes per term.

3. List student recitals and performances supervised; give the names of the students.

4. List doctoral examinations participated in by name of the student; specify the type of exam.

5. List theses and dissertations supervised by name of enrolled student (indicate if you are/were the chair).

6. List activities undertaken to recruit talented in-state students at the undergraduate level or to recruit talented in-state or out-of-state students at the graduate level.

7. List positions held by recent former students and awards and honors achieved by former students not previously reported, insofar as you have knowledge of them.

B. **Creative and Professional Activities and Research**

1. List the one or two professional achievements or activities during the year that you consider most significant (these need not be cited again elsewhere).

2. List publications (indicate by * items that were subject to substantial peer review prior to publication).

3. List prizes, awards, fellowships, grants, commissions, or other recognition received.

4. List research projects; list grants from University or non-University sources for research or development or for instructional or program improvement.

5. List appearances or activities off-campus or on-campus as a speaker, conductor, soloist, ensemble member, adjudicator, actor, director, designer, panelist, clinician, consultant, director of a workshop or institute, or chair of a session at a professional meeting; list performances of your compositions or arrangements; list recordings you have made or recordings of your works; list other forms of recognition unique to your field of specialization.

C. **Service**

1. Indicate the number of students advised.

2. List by name any School of Music, Theatre & Dance faculty members for whom you are serving as official mentor, and describe the extent of the assistance you have provided.

3. Indicate service as department chair or division head; list other administrative duties or leadership initiatives on behalf of the School including participation in examinations for students outside your department.

4. List service on committees of the School, your department, or the University (indicate if chair) and participation in meetings and other official activities of the School and its departments beyond routine department and School faculty meetings.

5. List service in elective or appointive leadership roles in professional associations at the national, international, regional, state, or local levels.

6. List nonroutine contributions to recruiting, fund-raising, or public relations efforts on behalf of the School or the University not listed elsewhere.

7. List instances of your contributing your professional abilities and expertise without compensation or with nominal compensation on behalf of continuing education in music or in the service of government agencies, citizens' groups, educational or religious institutions, or charitable organizations at the local, state, national, or international levels.

INSTITUTIONAL SUPPORT FOR TEACHING/CHALLENGES TO GOOD TEACHING

Fink (2003) devotes a complete chapter of his book *Creating Significant Learning Experiences* to a discussion of the need for better organizational support for faculty in institutions of higher education. He states that the audience for this discussion is both faculty who want to be leaders and administrators who are already in decision-making positions. Although that is not the audience for our book, we share some of the information from Fink as a way of helping the new professor to be aware of institutional challenges to good teaching. Based on Fink and with additional consideration for teaching music, we outline the following challenges to good music teaching in higher education:

- Music professors are often so busy that they do not take the time (or do not have the time) to closely examine the quality of their teaching.
- Music professors are often unaware of the research on teaching and learning and professional development is not often provided in this arena.
- Music faculty members do not spend meeting time in healthy dialogue about music teaching and learning. Most faculty meetings are spent on the minutia of keeping the status quo.
- The classic view of faculty work in "teaching, research, and service" does not provide time for professional development in teaching.
- New ideas and teaching approaches are not always welcomed by colleagues or students. Music departments and schools are quite traditional in their thinking about teaching and learning.

For the new professor, it is important to have an awareness of this culture and realize that some institutions in higher education do want to encourage faculty to focus on teaching. However, time and other resources are not always provided for this focus. Fink (2003) states that "Faculty need access to consulting services, support groups, reading material, and workshops and conferences that give them the intellectual and emotional resources necessary for change" (p. 198). As discussed in Chapter 11, many institutions have centers for teaching and learning but not all faculty are even aware of these resources. We suggest that the new professor work to keep a focus on teaching and make this personal focus known to administrators and colleagues so that all can work together to keep higher education focused on teaching.

QUESTIONS FOR DISCUSSION AND SUGGESTED ACTIVITIES

1. Consider issues of balance between teaching, research, and service in relation to the job postings you may have collected in Chapter 10.
2. Think about the issues of teaching in relation to applied music specifically and then in relation to academic courses specifically. How are the issues the same or different?
3. Discuss the issues associated with evaluating music professors within a college of fine arts or a college of arts and sciences. Think about how you will work to educate those in your institution about your particular area of scholarship.
4. Discuss your understanding of your potential role as an advisor to undergraduate students.
5. Discuss your understanding of your potential role as an advisor/mentor to graduate students.
6. Share your ideas regarding recruitment of students to campus. Relate this to teaching and service.
7. Using the teaching statement provided in the University of Michigan tenure and promotion paperwork, write a sample teaching statement and share it with your peers.
8. Discuss your strategies for community outreach and connections.
9. Create a file on your computer and organize it by the categories provided in the University of Michigan Faculty Activity Report. Share your strategies for this level of documentation.

CHAPTER 13

Professional Development and Improvement of Teaching

We hope that the focus throughout the book on reflection on teaching has led the reader to understand that "Good teachers are made, not born." In *What the Best College Teachers Do*, Bain (2004) suggests:

> Perhaps the biggest obstacle we face is the notion that teaching ability is somehow implanted at birth and that there is little we can do to change whether we have it or not. Our subjects struggled to learn how to create the best learning environments. When they failed to reach students, they used those failures to gain additional insights. Most important, because they subscribed to the learning rather than the transmission model of teaching, they realized that they had to think about ways to understand students' learning. (p. 173)

It takes time to learn to teach. All good professors work at teaching and have good classes and bad classes, good semesters and bad semester, good years and bad years. This chapter provides suggestions for professional development of the college professor and a focus on the career-long improvement of teaching. It includes sections on campus teaching improvement initiatives, a focus on the study of teaching, and a section exploring the question "Why teach?" We conclude with an overall summary of the book and questions for discussion and review.

FACULTY RESOURCES FOR THE IMPROVEMENT OF TEACHING

Most institutions have a center or an office dedicated to helping professors to improve teaching and learning. Details regarding the mission of the center at the University of Michigan are provided here as an example of this kind of resource:

Center for Research on Learning
and Teaching (CRLT)

University of Michigan

Mission Statement

The Center for Research on Learning and Teaching (CRLT) is dedicated to the support and advancement of learning and teaching at the University of Michigan. Staff at the Center work collaboratively with faculty, Graduate Student Instructors (GSIs), and the academic administration to develop a University culture that values and rewards teaching, respects and supports individual differences among learners, and encourages the creation of learning environments in which diverse students can learn and excel.

CRLT focuses on:

Faculty and GSI Development

- Providing grant support for faculty, departmental, and college projects that advance effective innovative learning and teaching
- Consulting on curricular development and evaluation
- Assisting with the infusion of multiculturalism into the curriculum
- Providing programs that emphasize the teaching and learning of diverse students
- Consulting with individual faculty members and GSIs regarding teaching
- Providing campus-wide seminars and orientations for faculty and GSIs
- Assisting with departmental and college seminars and retreats
- Assisting with the advocacy for effective settings for learning and teaching

Evaluation and Assessment

- Assisting with program evaluation: for example, the evaluation of teaching, instructional technology, and curriculum
- Assisting with the assessment of student learning
- Assisting with faculty grants that include educational components

Instructional Technology

- Disseminating technologies that enhance teaching and learning
- Providing information about useful applications and facilitating information exchange among units

Research and Dissemination

- Generating research knowledge that advances learning and teaching at the University of Michigan
- Disseminating research knowledge and information about learning and teaching to University faculty, academic administrators, and the national higher educational community

Staff Development and Collaboration

- Collaborating with other University offices and programs involved in learning and teaching initiatives
- Providing a challenging, stimulating, varied, collaborative, and supportive environment for CRLT staff members.

We have found the university resources mentioned above to be valuable in all of the institutions that we have worked in. Attending workshops on teaching, meeting with other professors to discuss teaching and learning, and inviting team members from campus centers to observe your class and talk with students are all helpful for the improvement of teaching.

OTHER STRATEGIES FOR THE IMPROVEMENT OF TEACHING

McKeachie and Svinicki (2006) suggest that professors in general education who are "looking for new ideas, new methods, and alternative strategies for handling problems" have three possibilities including reading, hearing, and seeing (p. 347). We would agree that these same three possibilities are reasonable strategies for the music professor as well.

Reading

We have worked throughout this text to provide additional resources for all of the topics addressed in the book. Specifically, the "Suggestions for Further Reading" for each of the three parts of this book can provide more research-based information regarding the teaching and learning of music. An extensive list of references can be found at the end of the book and we encourage readers to expand their knowledge through reading.

Hearing (and Discussing)

One of the key sources of professional development in teaching comes from listening and discussing issues of teaching and learning with colleagues. Many music organizations include a focus on teaching and learning at their annual events, most notably the *College Music Society*. Informal interactions with colleagues may very well represent the most powerful professional learning experiences for you in your career. However, even informal interactions do not usually happen by accident. You must be proactive in meeting with colleagues and engaging in these important discussions.

Seeing

Make arrangements to observe other music professors in your department or school. You can learn about your students by watching them interact with a different professor. And, you can learn about teaching from watching it in action. It is also valuable to observe music professors in other colleges or universities so as to examine the effect of the culture of a school on teaching and learning. The possibilities for growth through reading, hearing, and seeing are really endless. We encourage you to bring the same curiosity that you most likely bring to your field of expertise to your thinking about teaching and learning. The next section encourages the professor to take this sort of curiosity about music teaching and learning to the next level through the study of teaching.

THE STUDY OF TEACHING

Scholars in higher education in recent years have begun to examine what they call the "Scholarship of Teaching" (Shulman, 2008). One of the specific ways to study teaching and improve teaching and learning is through what is called action research, teacher research, or practitioner research. I have written about the use of action research or teacher research in music education publications (Conway & Borst, 2001; Conway and Jeffers, 2004) in the past and we are providing an overview of this information as we believe it is relevant for music educators in higher education as well.

In defining teacher research or action research, Burnaford et al. (1996) suggest that "Research can be seen as the search for practical possibilities—teachers and students searching themselves, their classrooms, and their worlds for educational meaning" (p. xii). In relating this concept of action research to music classrooms specifically, Bresler (1995) states: "Action research aims at the direct improvement of teaching and curriculum within a particular classroom, gaining a more critical perspective from which the teacher/researcher can reflect and change" (p. 15). Action research refers to inquiry that is designed by teachers to make change and affect teaching. We encourage music professors to learn about action research as a strategy for personal growth, professional development and scholarship. As was discussed in the tenure and promotion section in Chapter 12, professors are asked by university committees to provide evidence of teaching improvement and a focus on teaching. The implementation of a classroom action research project can often provide this evidence.

WHAT TO STUDY

The first step for professors interested in doing action research is to identify a problem or formulate a question regarding music teaching or learning. Since the goal of action research is to affect change, the most important aspect to consider is the usefulness of the inquiry in terms of one's own teaching. Action researchers are not concerned with generalizations to populations outside of their own context. However, in many cases, results documented in one study may be transferable to other contexts. It is important that the action researcher carefully describes the setting of the research and the participants involved in the study so that other music professors may consider how findings may relate to other contexts.

A professor might opt to study student reactions to various types of classroom activities. Or, a professor might collect data on the effects of instruction on attitudes toward a topic. I co-authored an action research study with Allison Reynolds (Allison Reynolds and Colleen Conway. 2003. Service-learning in music education methods: Perceptions of participants. *Bulletin of the Council for Research in Music Education*, 155: 1–10). In that investigation we gathered data from undergraduate music education students regarding their experiences in a service-learning partnership where they were teaching elementary music to children. Interested readers are encouraged to read this and other studies of college professors doing research in their own classrooms.

DATA AND ANALYSIS

Once a problem has been identified for action research, the action researcher must begin to gather information and create documentation of the issues relating to the problem. Many action researchers find it valuable to keep a diary or a teaching journal so that they may keep track of daily incidents that may relate to the research. In some cases, one may want to videorecord one's classroom and use the video transcript as a form of observation data. Interviews with students and colleagues may also be appropriate data depending on the study. Existing documents such as student grade reports, student compositions, portfolios, practice records, concert programs, audiotapes of performances, and so on may also be used as data in the inquiry. In studies done in collaboration with colleagues, observations of a classroom performed by the collaborative partner may provide valuable insight for the study.

The teacher–researcher must reflect throughout the research process to determine when enough data has been gathered. The data collection and analysis phases of an action research project meld together so that thoughts regarding the meaning of the data begin to emerge during the process of the project. The action researcher must search for meaning in the data collected by coding the data and developing categories that help to describe and organize the themes presented in the observations, diary notes, interviews, and so on. In collaborative action research projects, colleagues may analyze the data together. This discussion adds another important dimension of reflection to the research process.

DISSEMINATION IN MUSIC

The final steps for the action researcher include making decisions regarding teaching and learning based on the results of the study. In a less systematic way, good professors make these kinds of decisions every day. What action research does is provide a model for teachers to use in reflecting on their work. The documentation of these decisions and reflections contribute to the knowledge base of teaching. Nieto (2003) suggests:

> All good teachers, whether they consciously carry out research or not, are researchers in
> the broadest sense of the word. This is because good teachers are also learners, and they

recognize that they need to keep learning throughout their careers if they are to improve. They probe their subject matter, constantly searching for material that will excite and motivate their students; they explore pedagogy to create a learning environment that is both rigorous and supportive; they talk with their colleagues about difficult situations. Above all, they value the intellectual work that is at the core of teaching. (pp. 76–77)

WHY TEACH?

As this text has relied heavily on several excellent nonmusic texts of teaching in higher education (Bain, 2004; Curzan and Damour, 2006; Davis, 2001; Fink, 2003; McKeachie and Svinicki, 2006; Weimer, 2002), we answer "Why Teach" in the words of some of these authors drawn from the concluding chapters of these books. All seem to agree that through reflective teaching we can assume a life of continued learning and intellectual growth. Bain (2004) situates teaching as ever-evolving, creative and intellectually stimulating work:

> Part of being a good teacher (not all) is knowing that you always have something new to learn—not so much about teaching techniques but about these particular students at this particular time and their particular set of aspirations, confusion, misconceptions, and ignorance...The best teaching is often both an intellectual creation and a performing art. It is both Rembrandt's brush strokes and the genius of insight, perspective, originality, comprehension, and empathy that makes a Dutch master. (p. 174)

Fink (2003) discusses teaching through the metaphor of whitewater rafting. She makes reference to the popular metaphor "Be a 'guide on the side' rather than a 'sage on the stage'" and suggests that although this metaphor creates awareness of the concern for too much lecturing in college classes that the "guide on the side" may be a role that is too passive. In her whitewater rafting metaphor she tries to present the professor as both proactive and reactive as well as teaching as a collaborative effort:

> Hence I would like to offer a new metaphor for teaching: the teacher as helmsman for the learning experience....Negotiating white water, several people work together in a raft to maneuver it down a challenging river and stay away from rocks so they can reach a destination somewhere downstream. Most of the people work as "oarsmen" who paddle on one side of the raft or the other. Another person, usually the most experienced, serves as "helmsman." The job of the helmsman is to steer and to coordinate the efforts of the oarsmen.
>
> The metaphor of the teacher–helmsman captures many of the important characteristics of the whole teaching situation as well as the interactions among the various actors. The whole group must see that they have an important and challenge job to do (significant learning); the helmsman (teacher) is a leader and plays an important role in coordinating the actions of everyone else. But the oarsmen (students) also have to understand both their individual role (to student and learn) and how to work together with others. That is, everyone has to support one another in the learning process. It is a coordinated team effort with the teacher playing an active leadership role. (pp. 243–244)

McKeachie and Svinicki (2006) state:

> The great thing about teaching is that there is always more to learn.... There are moments of frustration and despair, but there are enough good times to help us through those that are not so good.... In Robert Bolt's *A Man for All Seasons*, Sir Thomas More assures his protégé that, if he becomes a teacher, he will be an outstanding teacher. "But if I were," demurs the ambitious young man, "who would know it?" More replies, "You, your friends, your students, God. Not a bad audience that." Not a bad audience indeed! (pp. 357–358)

Weimer (2002) quotes Flachmann (1994, p. 1) and states:

> Good teaching is a journey rather than a destination. It's not like a subway stop where, once you are there, you can cease moving forward.... Inertia is an insidiously powerful negative force in teaching—the urge to keep doing things the way we've done them for years. It's a bit like belonging to the pedagogical equivalent of Alcoholics Anonymous: there's always a poor teacher in us waiting to emerge. We have to resist the temptation to stay as we are, to rest at the bus stop.

SUMMARY AND CONCLUSIONS

We conclude this chapter and the text with a review of key elements in the journey towards becoming an excellent teacher of music in higher education. The reader is reminded that the process of teaching is a powerful and challenging endeavor and most professors feel like they work for their entire career and are still challenged by the demands (both musical and intellectual) of teaching music in higher education. If you view teaching as a process of lifelong learning, you will learn from your students and strengthen your own knowledge of music through teaching music to others. Key elements in the journey are presented below followed by questions for discussion.

Reflect on Your Own Undergraduate Experiences

Begin your journey with a careful consideration of your own experiences as a learner in undergraduate courses. Try to highlight the characteristics of the teachers who have affected you the most. Think about how your own learning style affects how you choose to teach.

Develop Your Pedagogical Content Knowledge

Reflect on the differences between content knowledge and pedagogical content knowledge. Begin to document and collect teaching strategies that build your arsenal of pedagogical content knowledge approaches. Talk to your students about teaching strategies that are helpful to them and talk with knowledgeable colleagues about pedagogy, sequence, curriculum, and assessment.

Experiment with Course Planning and Assessment

Try something new every time you teach a class. Vary the texts and readings as well as the instructional strategies and class activities. Even strategies that work can be set aside for an experiment with some new element.

Understand Learning Styles and Stages of Intellectual Development

Continue to study the literature on learning styles and intellectual development. Every group of students offers a new challenge. The culture of a school can change throughout the years as can the students themselves. Researchers in the learning sciences uncover new information about learning and brain development every year and it is important to stay current with trends regarding learning.

Avoid the Transmission Model of Teaching

Part Two of this text has provided a variety of instructional strategies for use in the music classroom. Work to balance the instructional approach so as to use time wisely and create a learner-centered course and classroom. A focus on learner-centered pedagogy is not easy. It requires a shift in thinking about content coverage, power relationships, and the very purpose of music in higher education.

Build and Maintain Rapport with Students

Music teaching and learning centers around the individual relationships created between faculty and students. Providing for the individual learning needs of students as well as building and maintaining a healthy rapport with individual students and groups of students is also a challenging task. The learner-centered professor puts the needs of students at the forefront of all decisions, which is also somewhat difficult. Instructional decisions in institutions of higher education are often led by fiscal concerns or other nonstudent related issues. Keeping the focus on the students is the goal.

Stay Current in the Field and Reflect on Teaching

As was just discussed in this last chapter, teaching can be an extremely gratifying career. However, it is common for music professors to experience "burnout" later in the career. Staying current with educational as well as musical trends can help fight off this phenomena. Continued reflection on teaching and learning and the study of teaching and learning can help the professor to stay excited about and engaged in stimulating thought about the profession.

Teaching music in higher education is an important link in the preservation of the art of music in the country and the world today. Whether you are working with majors or nonmajors in large or small schools, the work that you do in sharing your music and your knowledge of music is important.

QUESTIONS FOR DISCUSSION AND SUGGESTED ACTIVITIES

1. Check online for the Center for Teaching and Learning resources at your institution. Discuss the various services provided.
2. Think about topics for action research in your classroom. What are your teaching and learning questions? What are you curious about?
3. Discuss various ways of collecting and analyzing data for your action research idea.
4. Reflect once again on the best teachers you have worked with in your own undergraduate experience. As you think of the various issues of teaching and learning addressed throughout this book can you highlight the teaching characteristics that made these teachers great?
5. Now that you have completed the text and focused on various strategies for teaching and elements of teaching, return to some of your original notions about pedagogical content knowledge. Discuss your emerging thoughts regarding the relationships between content knowledge for a music course and pedagogical content knowledge for that same course.
6. Go back to some of the materials you developed during your work with Part One of the text with regard to course planning and assessment. Think about how the teaching and learning strategies presented in Part Two intersect with the decisions regarding planning and assessment in Part One.
7. Discuss your personal professional development plan for staying current within your musical field as well as within the field of teaching in higher education.

FURTHER READING: PART THREE

Growth in Teaching Practice

Ernst Boyer, E. 1990. *Scholarship reconsidered: Priorities of the professoriate.* Princeton, NJ: Carnegie Foundation for the Advancement of Teaching.

Kolstoe, Oliver P. 1974. *College professoring.* Carbondale, IL: Southern Illinois University Press.
Reynolds, Allison and Colleen Conway. 2003. Service-learning in music education methods: Perceptions of participants. *Bulletin of the Council for Research in Music Education,* 155: 1–10.

Sawyer, R. McLaran, Keith W. Prichard, and Karl D. Hostetler. 2001. *The art and politics of college teaching: A practical guide for the beginning professor* (2nd Ed.) New York: Peter Lang Publishing.

Shulman, Lee 2004. *Teaching as community property: Essays on higher education.* Carnegie Foundation for the Advancement of Teaching: San Francisco, CA: Jossey-Bass.

References

Abrahams, Frank and Paul Head. 2005. *Case studies in music education* (Rev. Ed.). Chicago, IL: GIA Publications.

Atterbury, Betty and Carol P. Richardson. 1995. *The experience of teaching general music.* New York: McGraw-Hill.

Bandura, Albert. 1986. *Social foundations of thought and action: A social cognitive theory.* Englewood Cliffs, NJ: Prentice-Hall.

Bain, Ken. 2004. *What the best college teachers do.* Cambridge, MA: Harvard University Press.

Barnes, Louis B., C. Roland Christensen, and Abby J. Hansen. 1994. *Teaching and the case method* (3rd Ed.). Boston, MA: Harvard Business School Press.

Barr, Robert B. and John Tagg. 1995. From teaching to learning: A new paradigm for undergraduate education. *Change,* 27 (6): 13–25.

Belenky, Mary Field, Blythe M. Clinchy, Nancy R. Goldeberger, and Jill M. Tarule. 1997. *Women's ways of knowing: The development of self, voice and mind.* New York: Basic Books Inc.

Bloom, Benjamin. 1985. *Developing talent in young people.* New York: Balantine Books.

Bresler, Liora. 1995. Ethnography, phenomenology and action research in music education. *Quarterly Journal of Music Teaching and Learning,* VI (3): 4–16.

Brinson, Barbara. 1996. *Choral music: Methods and materials.* Belmont, CA: Wadsworth Group.

Brookfield, Stephen. 1995. *Becoming a critically reflective teacher.* San Francisco: Jossey-Bass.

Brophy, Jere. 2004. *Motivating students to learn.* Mahwah, NJ: Erlbaum.

Brown, George and Madeleine Atkins 1988. *Effective teaching in higher education.* London: Methuen.

Bruffee, Kenneth A. 1999. *Collaborative learning: Higher education, interdependence, and the authority of knowledge* (2nd Ed.). Baltimore, MD: Johns Hopkins University Press.

Burnaford, Gail, Joseph Fischer, and David Hobson. 1996. *Teachers doing research: Practical possibilities.* Mahwah, NJ: Lawrence Erlbaum Publishers.

Campbell, William and Karl Smith. 1997. *New paradigms for college teaching.* Edina, MN: Interaction Book Company.

Caron, Mark D., Susan K. Whitbourne, and Richard P. Halgin. 1992. Fraudulent excuse making among college students. *Teaching of Psychology,* 19 (2): 90–93.

Claxton, C. S. and P. H. Murrell. 1987. *Learning styles: Implications for improving educational practices.* ASHE-ERIC Higher Education Report No. 4. Washington, DC: Association for the Study of Higher Education.

Colwell, Richard and Carol P. Richardson (Eds.). 2002. *The new handbook of research on music teaching and learning.* New York: Oxford University Press.

Conway, Colleen M. 1997a. *The development of a casebook for use in instrumental music education methods classes.* Unpublished doctoral dissertation. Teachers College, Columbia University.

Conway, Colleen M. 1997b. Authentic assessment in brass methods class. *Journal of Music Teacher Education,* 7 (1), 6–15.Conway, Colleen M. 1999a. The case method in music teacher education. *Update: Applications of Research in Music Education,* 17 (2): 20–26.

Conway, Colleen M. 1999b. The development of teaching cases for instrumental music methods courses. *Journal of Research in Music Education,* 47 (4): 343–354.

Conway, Colleen M. and James Borst. 2001. Action research in music education. *Update: Applications of Research in Music Education,* 19 (2): 3–8.

Conway, Colleen M. and Thomas Jeffers. 2004. The teacher as researcher in instrumental music. *Update: Applications of Research in Music Education*, 22 (2), 35–45.

Conway, Colleen M. and Thomas M. Hodgman. 2003. *Handbook for the beginning music teacher.* Chicago, IL: GIA Publications.

Curzan, Anne and Lisa Damour. 2006. *First day to final grade* (2nd Ed.). Ann Arbor, MI: University of Michigan Press.

Daniel, J. W. 1988. Survival cards in math. *College Teaching*, 36 (3): 110.

Dewey, John. 1933. *How we think*. Buffalo, NY: Prometheus Books.

Davis, Barbara G. 2001. *Tools for teaching*. San Francisco, CA: Jossey-Bass.

Elbow, Peter and Mary Deane Sorcinelli. 2006. How to enhance learning by using high-stakes and low-stakes writing. In Wilbert J. McKeachie and Marilla Svinicki (Eds.) *Teaching tips* (12th Ed., pp. 192–212). Boston, MA: Houghton Mifflin.

Feldman, Kenneth A. and Theodore M. Newcomb. 1969. *The impact of college on students* (Vol. 2). San Francisco, CA: Jossey-Bass.

Fink, Dee L. 2003. *Creating significant learning experiences: An integrated approach to designing college courses*. San Francisco, CA: Jossey-Bass.

Gardner, Howard. 1993a. *Frames of mind: The theory of multiple intelligences*. New York: Basic Books, Harper Collins.

Gardner, Howard. 1993b. *Multiple intelligences: The theory in practice*. New York: Basic Books, Harper Collins.

Gardner, Howard. 2004. *Changing minds: The art and science of changing our own and other people's minds*. Cambridge, MA: Harvard University Press.

Gilligan, Carol. 1982. *In a different voice: Psychological theory and women's development*. Cambridge: Harvard University Press.

Gordon, Edwin E. 1989. *Advanced measures of music audiation*. Chicago, IL: GIA Publications.

Gordon, Edwin E. 1997. *Learning sequences in music*. Chicago, IL: GIA Publications.

Green, Lucy. 1997. *Music, gender, education*. Cambridge, UK: Cambridge University Press.

Hofer, Barbara. 2006. Motivation in the college classroom. In Wilbert McKeachie and Marilla Svinicki (Eds.) *Teaching tips* (12th ed., pp. 140–150). Boston, MA: Houghton Mifflan.

Hoffman, J. A. 1991. Computer-aided collaborative music instruction. *Harvard Educational Review*, 61 (3): 270–278.

Hourigan, Ryan. 2006. The use of the case method to promote reflective thinking in music teacher education. *Update: Applications of Research in Music Education*, 24 (2): 33–44.

Kassell, Cathy. 1998. Music and the theory of multiple intelligences. *Music Educators Journal*, 84 (5): 29–32, 60.

Kennell, Richard. 2002. Systematic research in studio instruction in music. In Richard Colwell and Carol P. Richardson (Eds.) *The new handbook of music teaching and learning* (pp. 243–256). New York: Oxford University Press.

Kilpatrick, Willian H. 1918. The project method. *Teachers College Record*, 19: 319–335.

Kingsbury, Henry H. 1988. *Music, talent, and performance: A conservatory cultural system*. Philadelphia, PA: Temple University Press.

Kohn, Alfie. 1999. *Punished by rewards*. Boston, MA: Houghton Mifflan.

Kurfiss, J. G. 1988. *Critical thinking*. ASHE-ERIC Higher Education Report No. 2. Washington, DC: Association for the Study of Higher Education.

Lehmann, Andreas C. and Jane W. Davidson. 2002. Taking an acquired skills perspective on music performance. In Richard Colwell and Carol P. Richardson (Eds.) *The new handbook of research on music teaching and learning* (pp. 542–560). New York: Oxford University Press.

Levine, Arthur and Jeanette S. Cureton. 1998. *When hope and fear collide: A portrait of today's college student*. San Francisco, CA: Jossey-Bass.

Luce, David. 2001. Collaborative learning in music education: A review of the literature. *Update: Applications of Research in Music Education,* 19(2): 20–25.

McKeachie, Wilbert J. and Marilla Svinicki. 2006. *McKeachie's teaching tips: Strategies, research, and theory for college and university teachers* (12th Ed.). Boston, MA: Houghton Mifflin.

McPherson, Gary E. 2006. *The child as musician: A handbook of musical development.* New York: Oxford University Press.

McPherson, Gary E. and Barry J. Zimmerman. 2002. Self-regulation of music learning. In Richard Colwell and Carol P. Richardson (Eds.) *The new handbook of music teaching and learning* (pp. 327–347). New York: Oxford University Press.

Nettl, B. 1995. *Heartland excursions: Ethnomusicological reflections on schools of music.* Urbana, IL: University of Illinois Press.

Nieto, Sonia. 2003. *What keeps teachers going?* New York: Teachers College Press.

Penner, Jon G. 1984. *Why many college teachers cannot lecture.* Springfield, IL: Thomas.

Perry, William G. 1970. *Forms of intellectual and ethical development in the college years.* New York: Holt, Rinehart & Winston.

Perry, William G. 1999. *Forms of ethical and intellectual development in the college years.* San Francisco, CA: Jossey-Bass.

Roschelle, J. and Stephanie D. Teasley. 1995. The construction of shared knowledge in collaborative problem solving. In C. E. O'Malley (Ed.) *Computer-supported collaborative learning* (pp. 69–197). Berlin: Springer-Verlag.

Schon, Donald. 1983. *The reflective practitioner.* New York: Basic Books.

Schon, Donald. 1987. *Educating the reflective practitioner: Toward a new design for teaching and learning in the professions.* San Francisco, CA: Jossey-Bass.

Sebren, Anne. 1992. *An interpretive inquiry or preservice teachers' reflections and development during a field-based elementary physical education methods course.* Unpublished doctoral dissertation, University of North Carolina, Greensboro.

Shulman, Lee S. 1986. Those who understand: Knowledge growth in teaching. *Educational Researcher,* 15(2): 4–14.

Shulman, Lee S. 1987. Knowledge and teaching: Foundations of the new reform. *Harvard Educational Review,* 57 (1): 1–22.

Shulman, Lee. 1992. Toward a pedagogy of cases. In Judith Shulman (Ed.) *Case methods in teacher education* (pp. 1–32). New York: Teachers College Press.

Shulman, Lee. 1993. Teaching as community property. *Change,* Nov/Dec: 6–7.

Shulman, Lee. 2008. http://www.carnegiefoundation.org/about/index.asp

Stanton, Henry. 1992. The University Teacher, 31 (1).

Tyler, Ralph. 1949. *Basic principles of curriculum and instruction.* Chicago, IL: University of Chicago Press.

Walker, Decker and Jonas Soltis. 2004. *Curriculum and aims* (4th Ed.). New York: Teachers College Press.

Weimer, Maryellen (2002). *Learner-centered teaching: Five key changes to practice.* San Francisco, CA: Jossey-Bass.

Weinstein, Claire Ellen, Debra K. Meyer, Jenefer Husman, Gretchen Van MaterStone, and Wilbert J. McKeachie. 2006. Teaching students how to become more strategic and self-regulated learners. In Wilbert McKeachie (Ed.) *Teaching tips: Strategies, research, and theory for college and university teachers* (pp. 300–317). New York: Houghton Mifflan.

"When They Don't Do the Reading." 1989. *Teaching professor,* 3 (10): 3–4.

Wiggins, Grant. 1998. *Educative assessment: Designing assessments to inform and improve student performance.* San Francisco, CA: Jossey-Bass.

Zimmermann, Barry J. 1986. Becoming a self-regulated learner: Which are the key subprocesses? *Contemporary Educational Psychology,* 11: 307–339.

Author Index

Subject Index

CPSIA information can be obtained at www.ICGtesting.com
Printed in the USA
BVOW06s0956130916

461527BV00021B/6/P